STAR WARS®
CLONE WARS
VOLUME 2

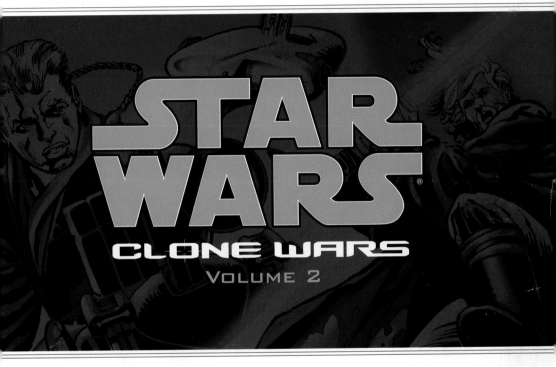

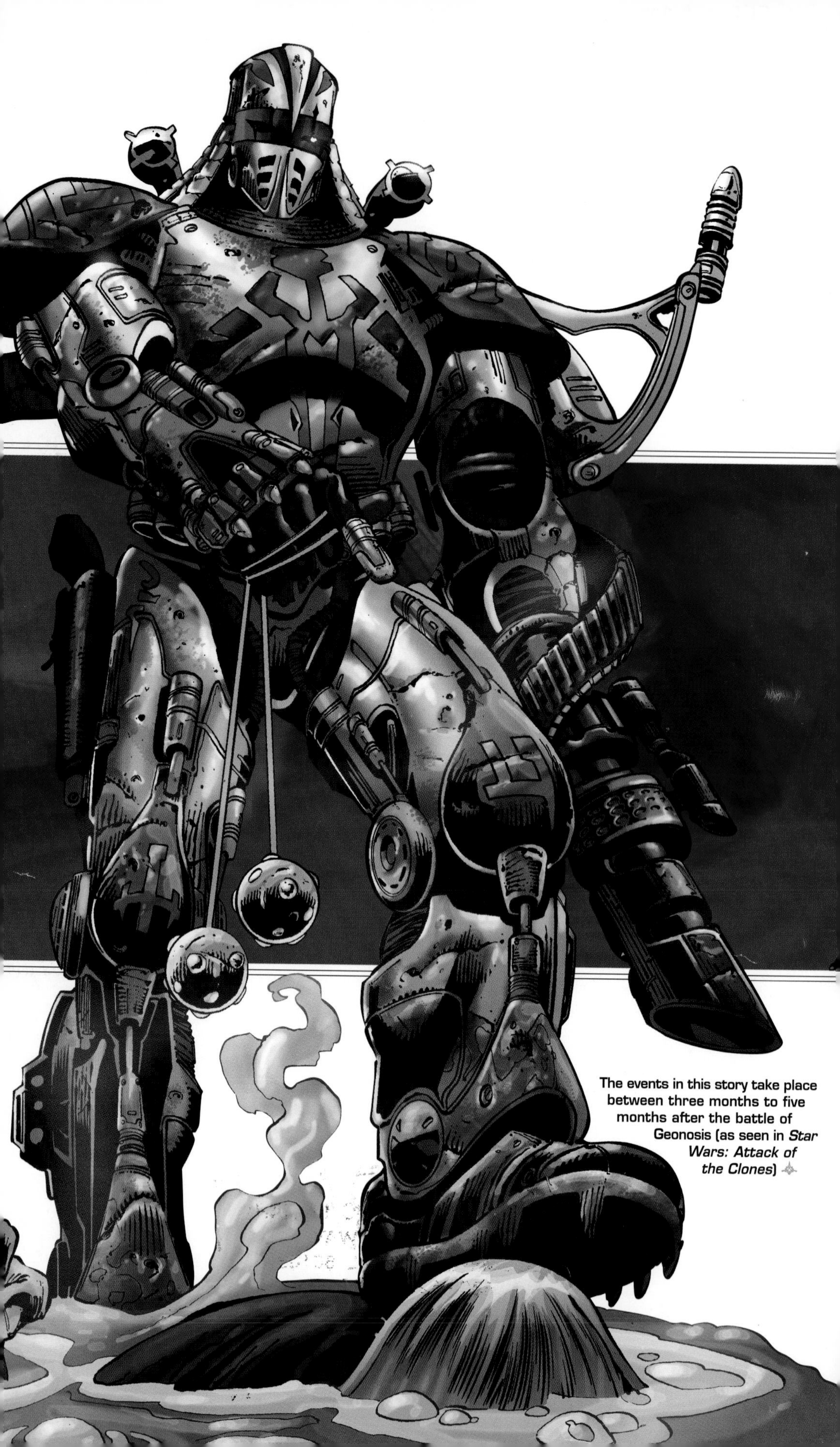

The events in this story take place between three months to five months after the battle of Geonosis (as seen in *Star Wars: Attack of the Clones*)

STAR WARS
CLONE WARS
VOLUME 2

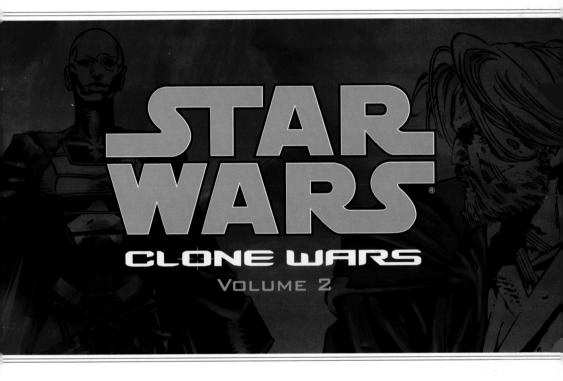

Victories and Sacrifices

Dark Horse Books™

colors by **Joe Wayne**

lettering by **Digital Chameleon**

cover illustration by **Carlo Arellano**

publisher **Mike Richardson**

collection designers **Darin Fabrick & Amy Arendts**

art director **Mark Cox**

assistant editor **Jeremy Barlow**

editor **Randy Stradley**

special thanks to **Sue Rostoni** and
Lucy Autrey Wilson at Lucas Licensing

STAR WARS®:CLONE WARS VOLUME 2

THIS VOLUME COLLECTS #51-53 OF *STAR WARS: REPUBLIC* **AND** *JEDI: SHAAK TI.*

PUBLISHED BY DARK HORSE BOOKS, A DIVISION OF DARK HORSE COMICS, INC.
10956 SE MAIN STREET · MILWAUKIE, OR 97222
WWW.DARKHORSE.COM   WWW.STARWARS.COM
To find a comics shop in your area, call the Comic Shop Locator Service
toll-free at 1-888-266-4226

FIRST EDITION: ISBN: 1-56971-969-1
1 3 5 7 9 10 8 6 4 2
PRINTED IN CHINA

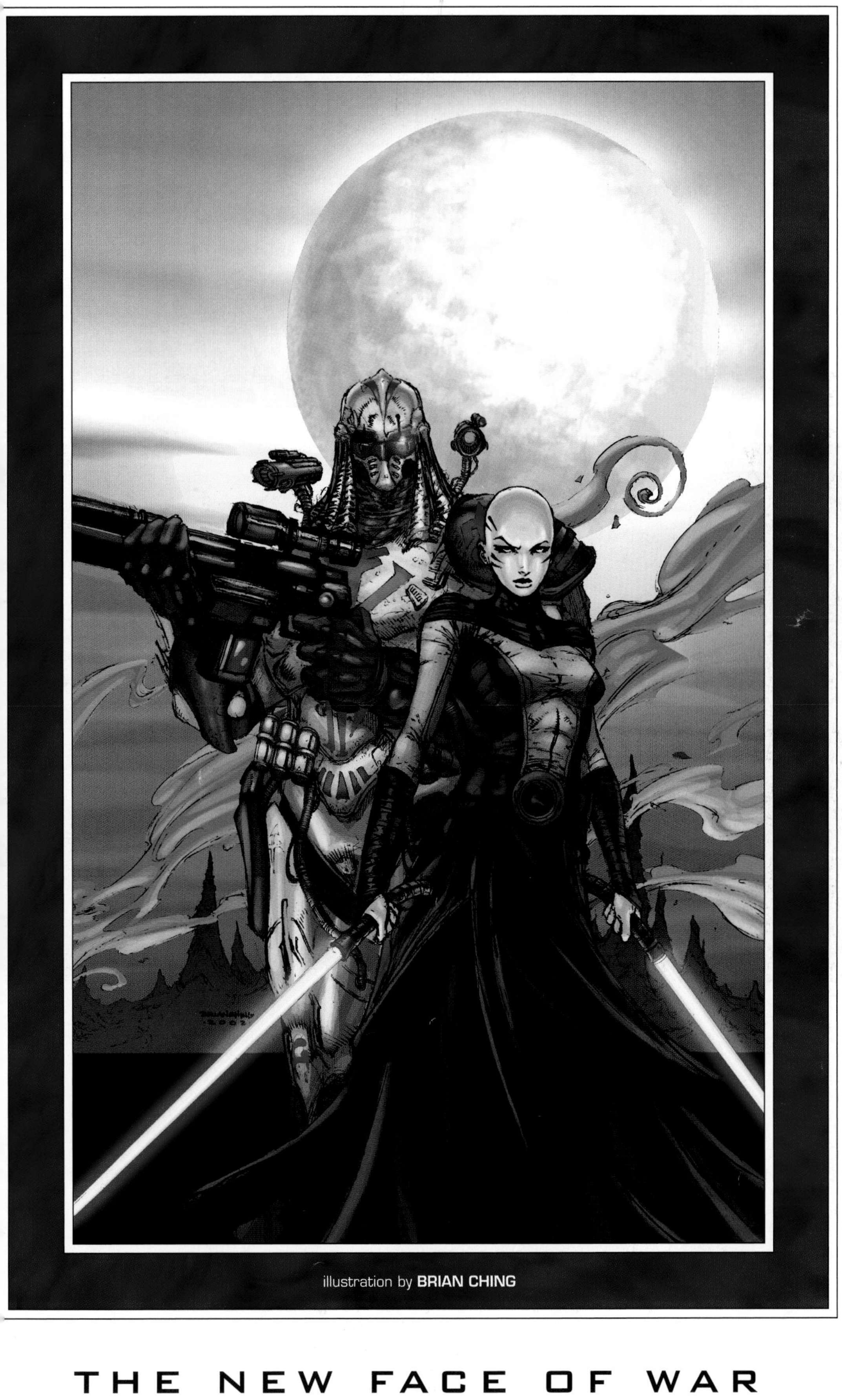

illustration by **BRIAN CHING**

THE NEW FACE OF WAR

APPROXIMATELY TEN WEEKS
AFTER THE BATTLE OF GEONOSIS...

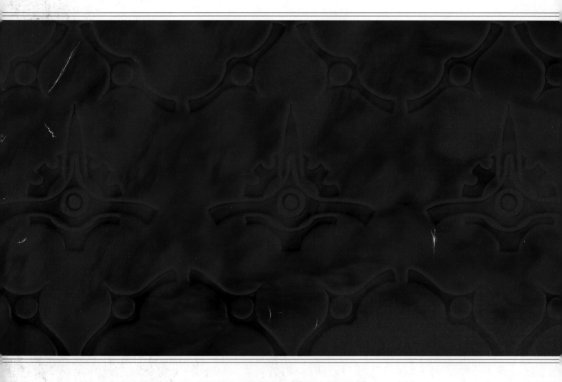

"The New Face of War"
written by **Haden Blackman**
pencilled by **Tomás Giorello**
inks by **Curtis Arnold**

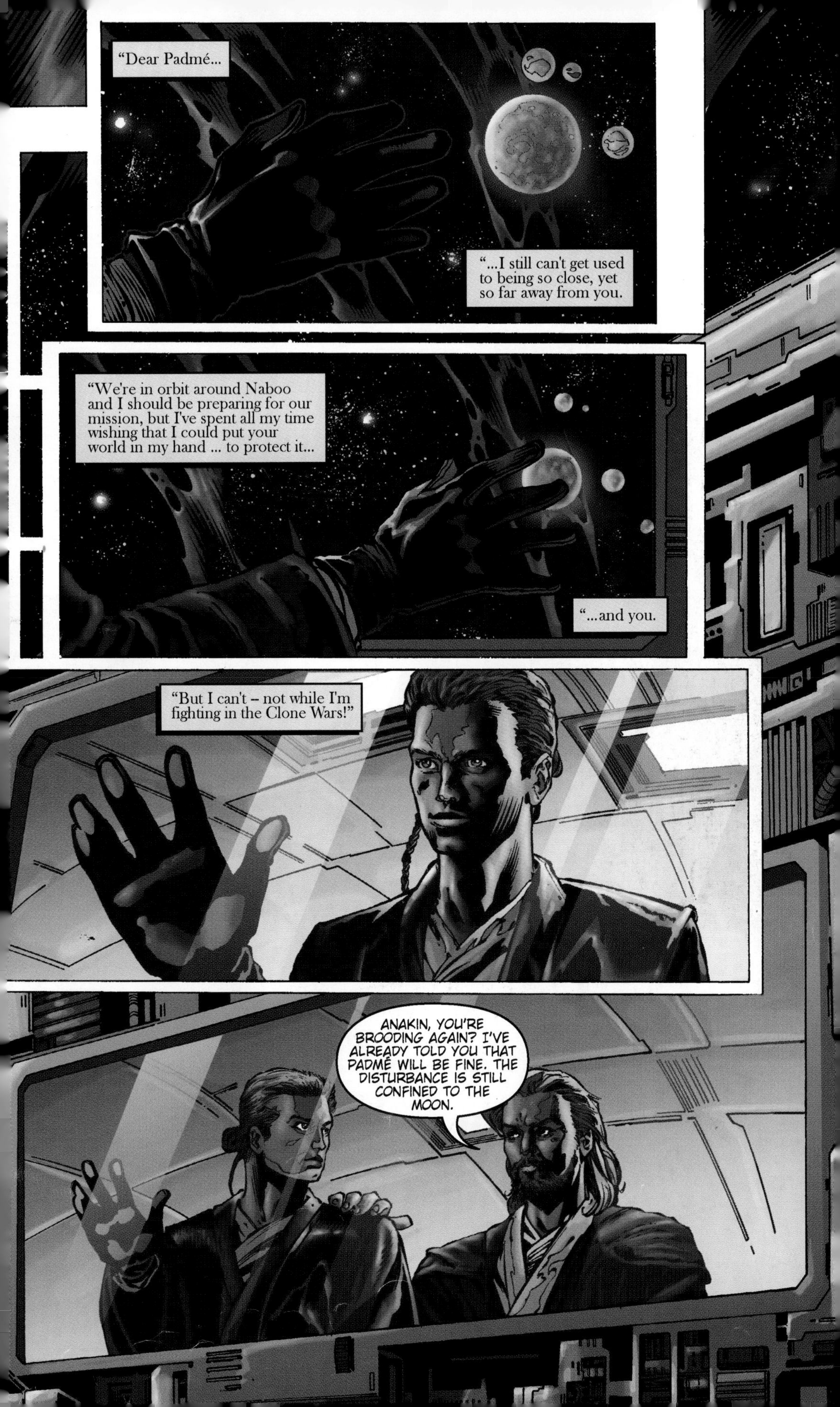
"Dear Padmé...
"...I still can't get used to being so close, yet so far away from you.
"We're in orbit around Naboo and I should be preparing for our mission, but I've spent all my time wishing that I could put your world in my hand ... to protect it...
"...and you.
"But I can't – not while I'm fighting in the Clone Wars!"
ANAKIN, YOU'RE BROODING AGAIN? I'VE ALREADY TOLD YOU THAT PADMÉ WILL BE FINE. THE DISTURBANCE IS STILL CONFINED TO THE MOON.

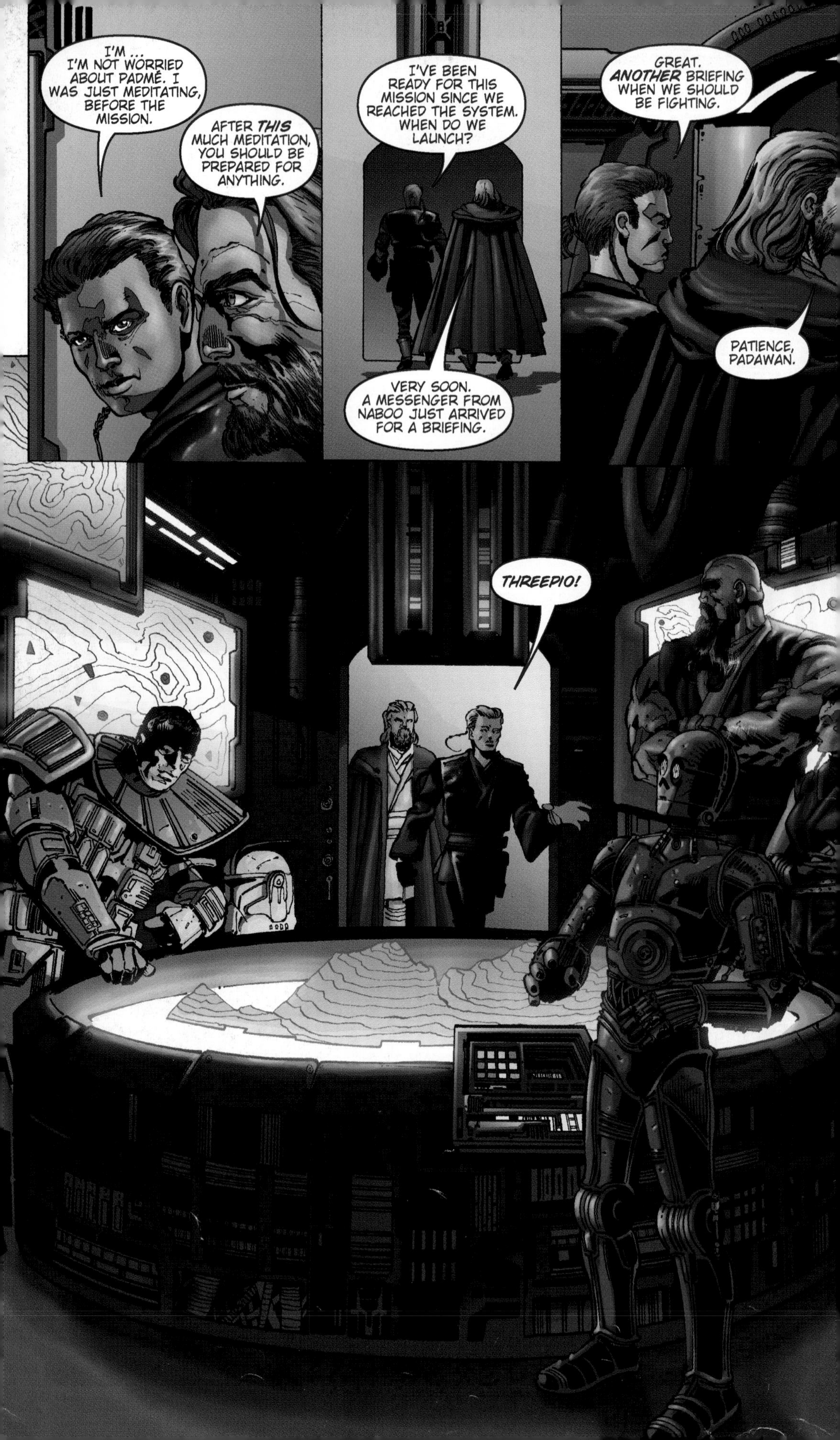
I'M ... I'M NOT WORRIED ABOUT PADMÉ. I WAS JUST MEDITATING, BEFORE THE MISSION.
AFTER THIS MUCH MEDITATION, YOU SHOULD BE PREPARED FOR ANYTHING.
I'VE BEEN READY FOR THIS MISSION SINCE WE REACHED THE SYSTEM. WHEN DO WE LAUNCH?
VERY SOON. A MESSENGER FROM NABOO JUST ARRIVED FOR A BRIEFING.
GREAT. ANOTHER BRIEFING WHEN WE SHOULD BE FIGHTING.
PATIENCE, PADAWAN.
THREEPIO!

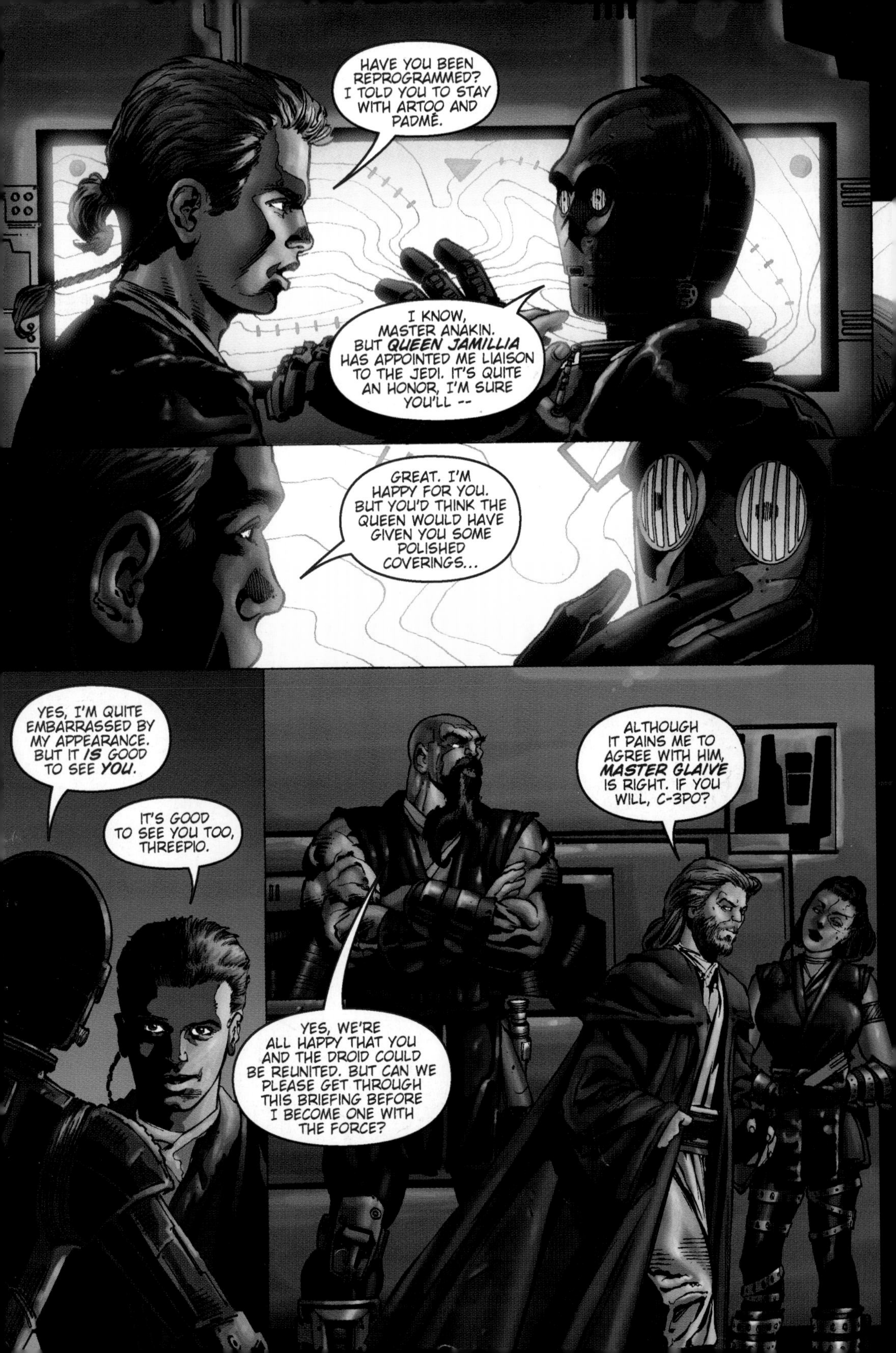
HAVE YOU BEEN REPROGRAMMED? I TOLD YOU TO STAY WITH ARTOO AND PADMÉ.
I KNOW, MASTER ANAKIN. BUT QUEEN JAMILLIA HAS APPOINTED ME LIAISON TO THE JEDI. IT'S QUITE AN HONOR, I'M SURE YOU'LL --
GREAT. I'M HAPPY FOR YOU. BUT YOU'D THINK THE QUEEN WOULD HAVE GIVEN YOU SOME POLISHED COVERINGS...
YES, I'M QUITE EMBARRASSED BY MY APPEARANCE. BUT IT IS GOOD TO SEE YOU.
IT'S GOOD TO SEE YOU TOO, THREEPIO.
YES, WE'RE ALL HAPPY THAT YOU AND THE DROID COULD BE REUNITED. BUT CAN WE PLEASE GET THROUGH THIS BRIEFING BEFORE I BECOME ONE WITH THE FORCE?
ALTHOUGH IT PAINS ME TO AGREE WITH HIM, MASTER GLAIVE IS RIGHT. IF YOU WILL, C-3PO?

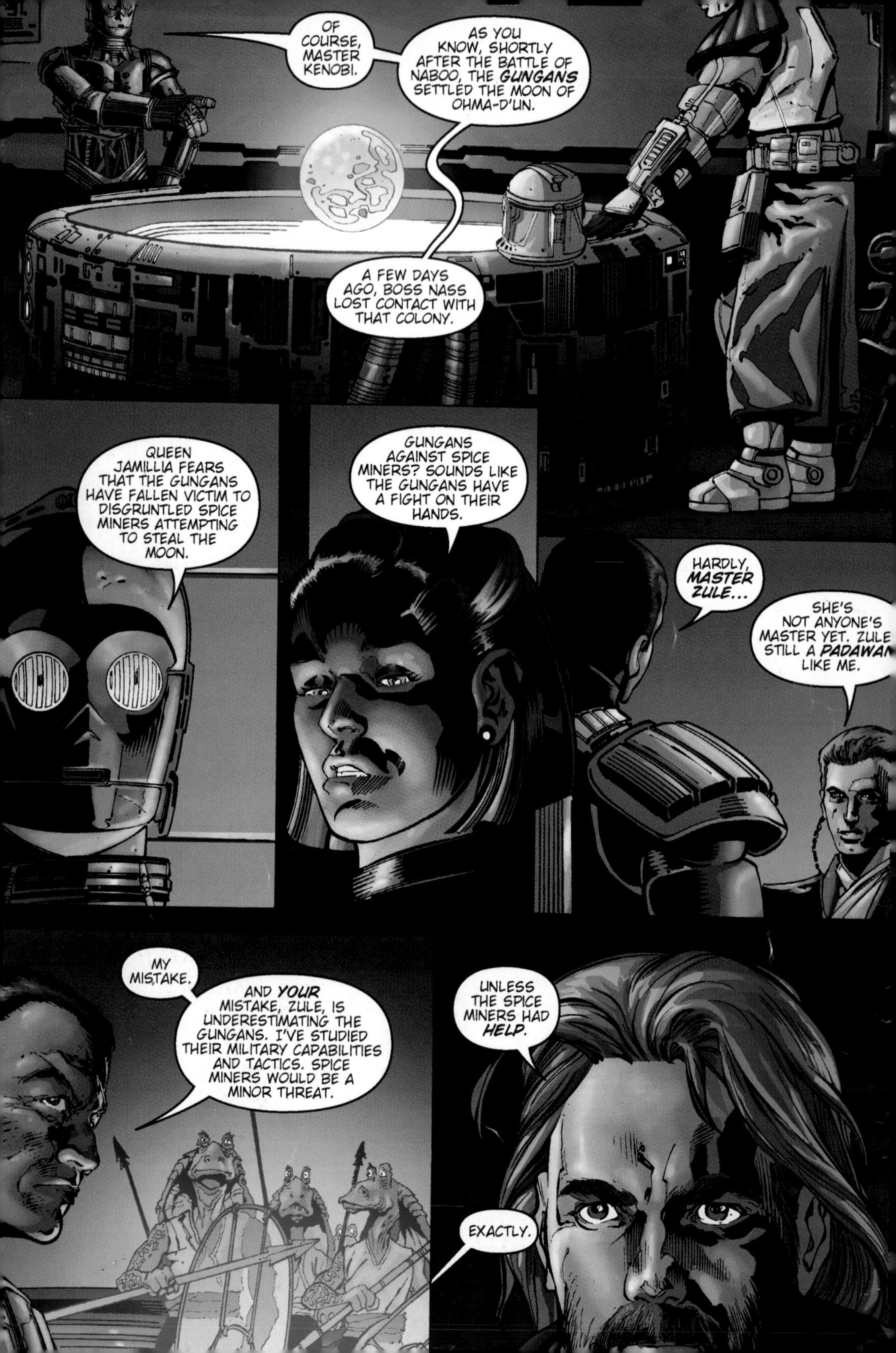
OF COURSE, MASTER KENOBI.
AS YOU KNOW, SHORTLY AFTER THE BATTLE OF NABOO, THE GUNGANS SETTLED THE MOON OF OHMA-D'UN.
A FEW DAYS AGO, BOSS NASS LOST CONTACT WITH THAT COLONY.
QUEEN JAMILLIA FEARS THAT THE GUNGANS HAVE FALLEN VICTIM TO DISGRUNTLED SPICE MINERS ATTEMPTING TO STEAL THE MOON.
GUNGANS AGAINST SPICE MINERS? SOUNDS LIKE THE GUNGANS HAVE A FIGHT ON THEIR HANDS.
HARDLY, MASTER ZULE...
SHE'S NOT ANYONE'S MASTER YET. ZULE STILL A PADAWAN LIKE ME.
MY MISTAKE.
AND YOUR MISTAKE, ZULE, IS UNDERESTIMATING THE GUNGANS. I'VE STUDIED THEIR MILITARY CAPABILITIES AND TACTICS. SPICE MINERS WOULD BE A MINOR THREAT.
UNLESS THE SPICE MINERS HAD HELP.
EXACTLY.

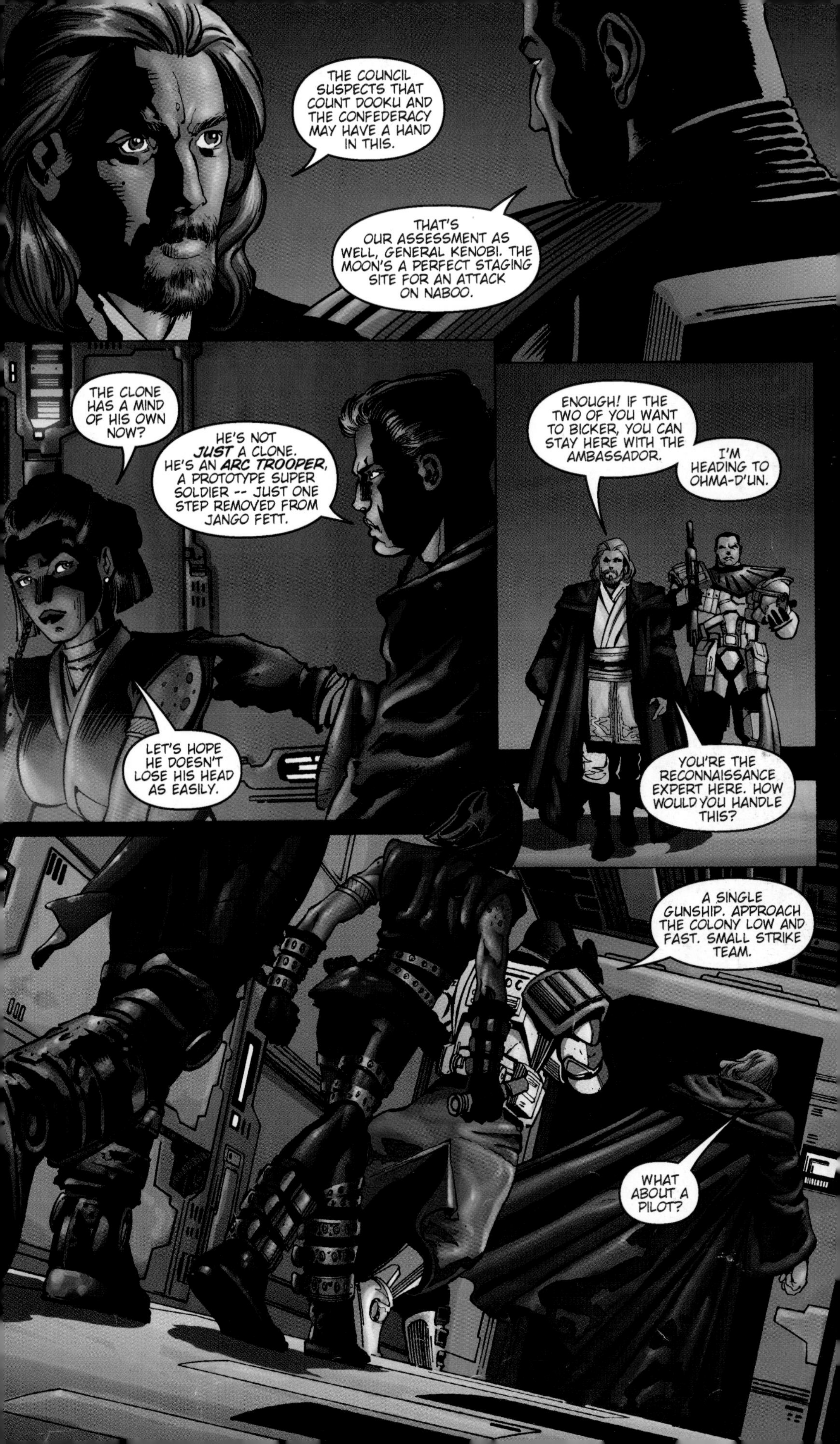
THE COUNCIL SUSPECTS THAT COUNT DOOKU AND THE CONFEDERACY MAY HAVE A HAND IN THIS.
THAT'S OUR ASSESSMENT AS WELL, GENERAL KENOBI. THE MOON'S A PERFECT STAGING SITE FOR AN ATTACK ON NABOO.
THE CLONE HAS A MIND OF HIS OWN NOW?
HE'S NOT ***JUST*** A CLONE. HE'S AN ***ARC TROOPER***, A PROTOTYPE SUPER SOLDIER -- JUST ONE STEP REMOVED FROM JANGO FETT.
LET'S HOPE HE DOESN'T LOSE HIS HEAD AS EASILY.
ENOUGH! IF THE TWO OF YOU WANT TO BICKER, YOU CAN STAY HERE WITH THE AMBASSADOR.
I'M HEADING TO OHMA-D'UN.
YOU'RE THE RECONNAISSANCE EXPERT HERE. HOW WOULD YOU HANDLE THIS?
A SINGLE GUNSHIP. APPROACH THE COLONY LOW AND FAST. SMALL STRIKE TEAM.
WHAT ABOUT A PILOT?

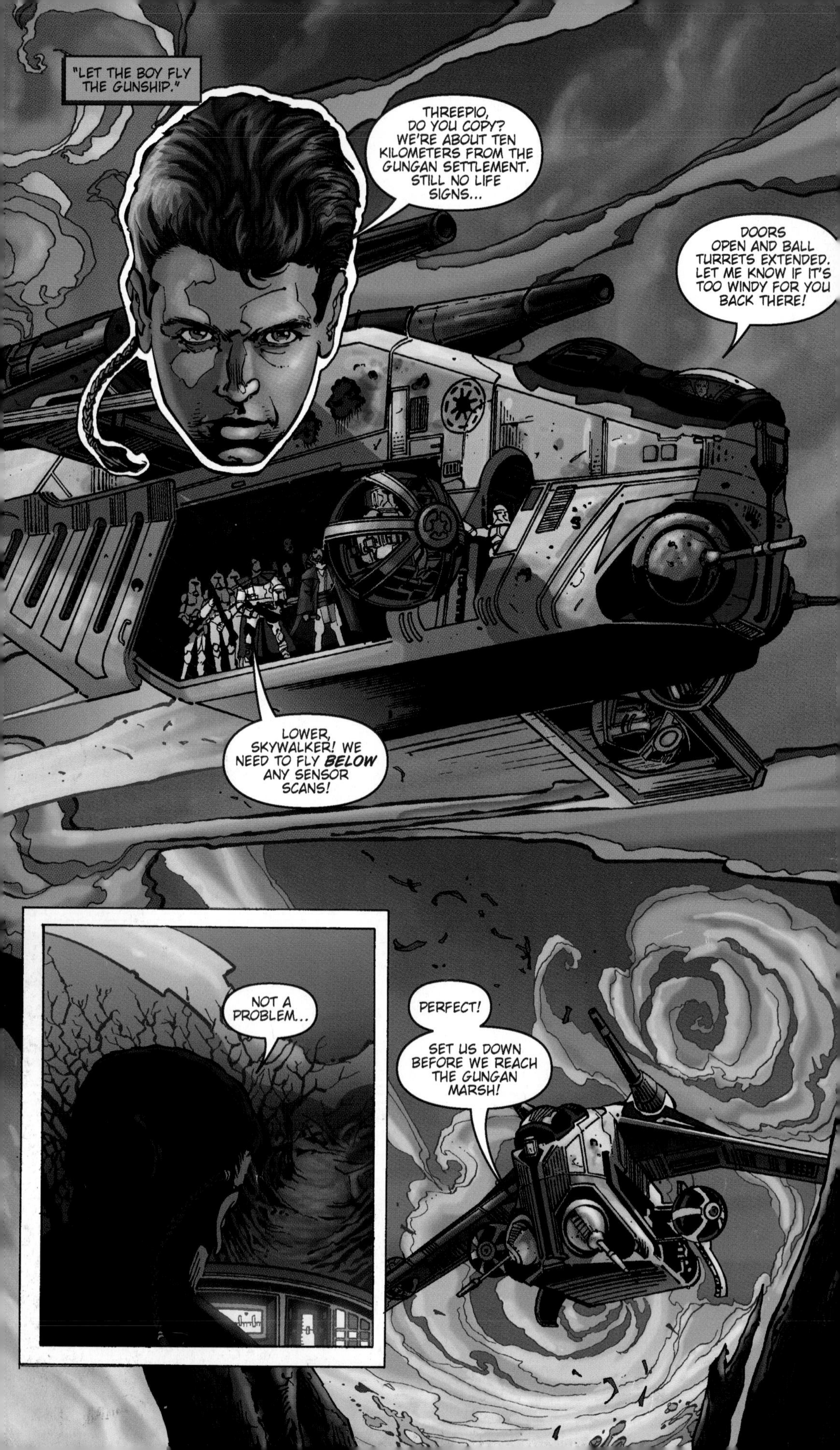
"LET THE BOY FLY THE GUNSHIP."
THREEPIO, DO YOU COPY? WE'RE ABOUT TEN KILOMETERS FROM THE GUNGAN SETTLEMENT. STILL NO LIFE SIGNS...
DOORS OPEN AND BALL TURRETS EXTENDED. LET ME KNOW IF IT'S TOO WINDY FOR YOU BACK THERE!
LOWER, SKYWALKER! WE NEED TO FLY **BELOW** ANY SENSOR SCANS!
NOT A PROBLEM...
PERFECT!
SET US DOWN BEFORE WE REACH THE GUNGAN MARSH!

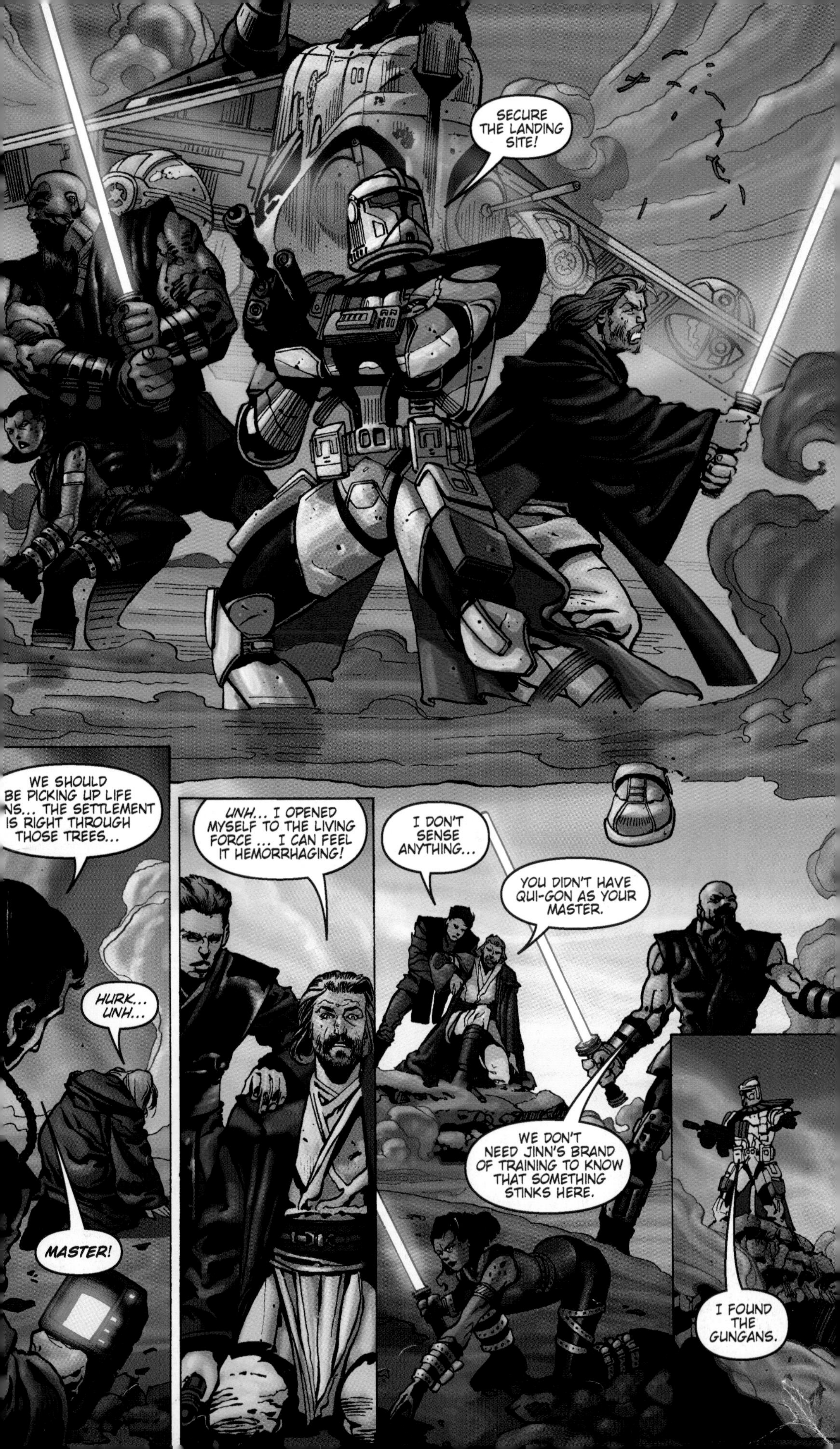
SECURE THE LANDING SITE!
WE SHOULD BE PICKING UP LIFE ...NS... THE SETTLEMENT IS RIGHT THROUGH THOSE TREES...
HURK... UNH...
MASTER!
UNH... I OPENED MYSELF TO THE LIVING FORCE ... I CAN FEEL IT HEMORRHAGING!
I DON'T SENSE ANYTHING...
YOU DIDN'T HAVE QUI-GON AS YOUR MASTER.
WE DON'T NEED JINN'S BRAND OF TRAINING TO KNOW THAT SOMETHING STINKS HERE.
I FOUND THE GUNGANS.

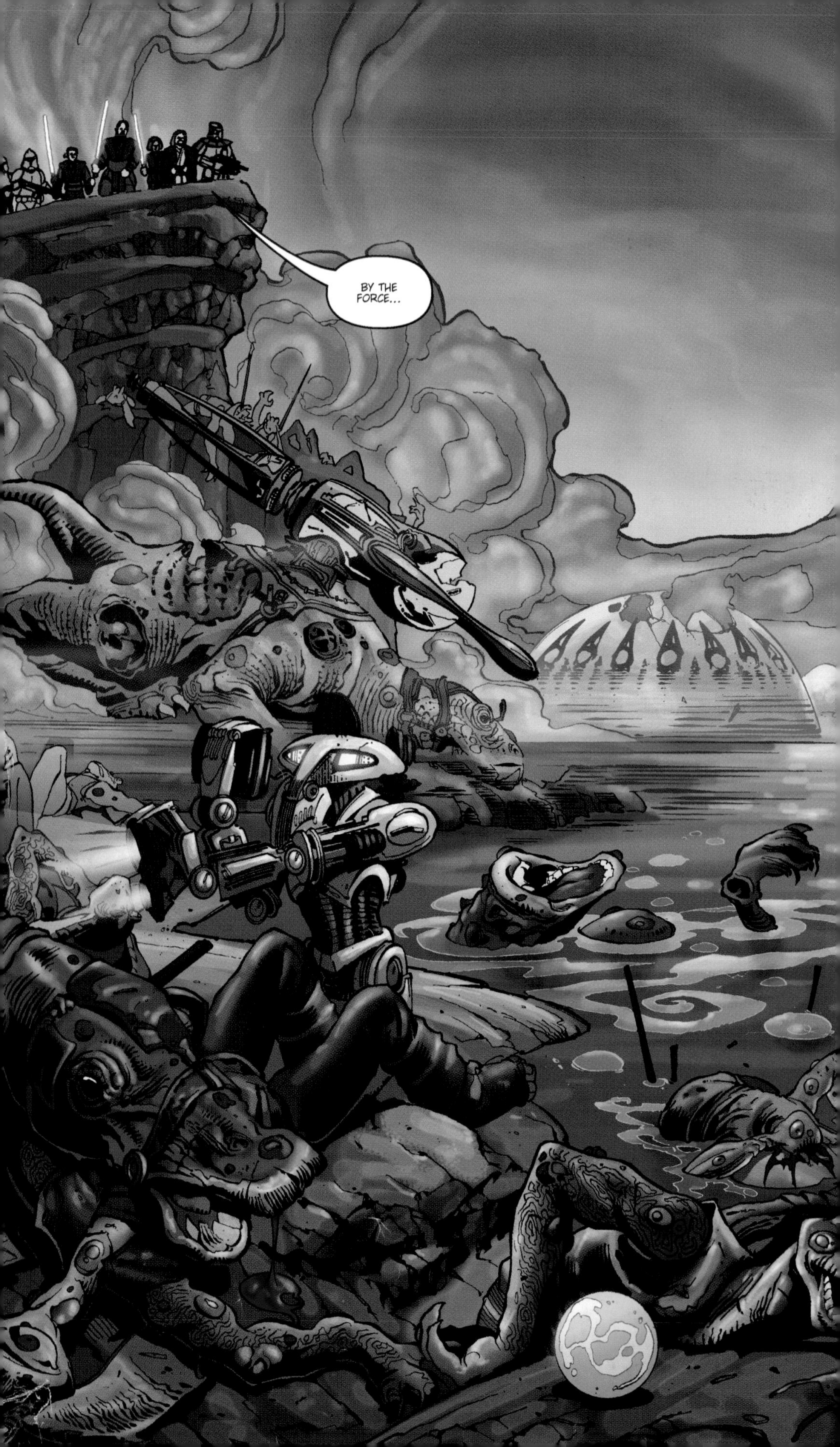
BY THE FORCE...

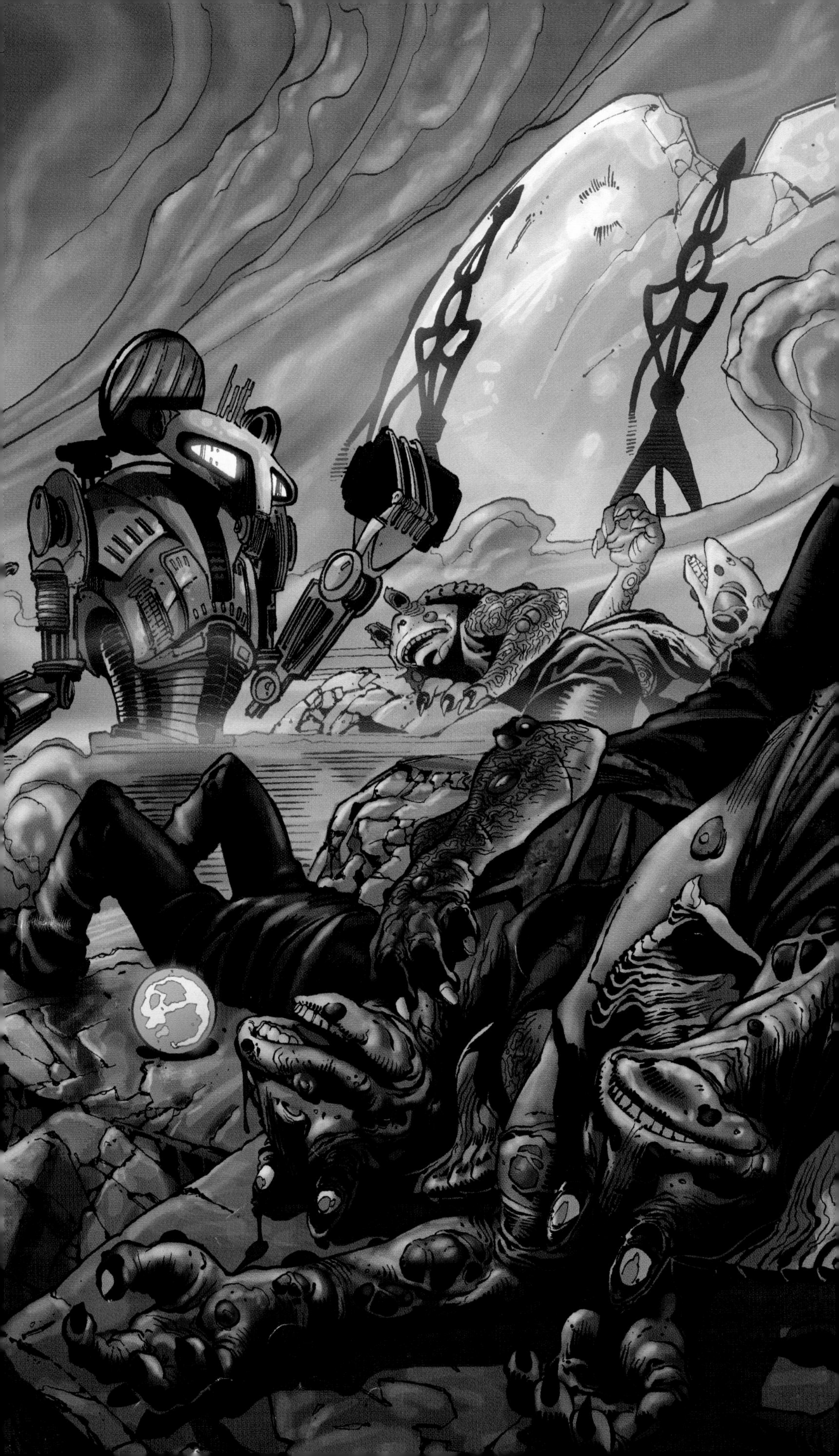

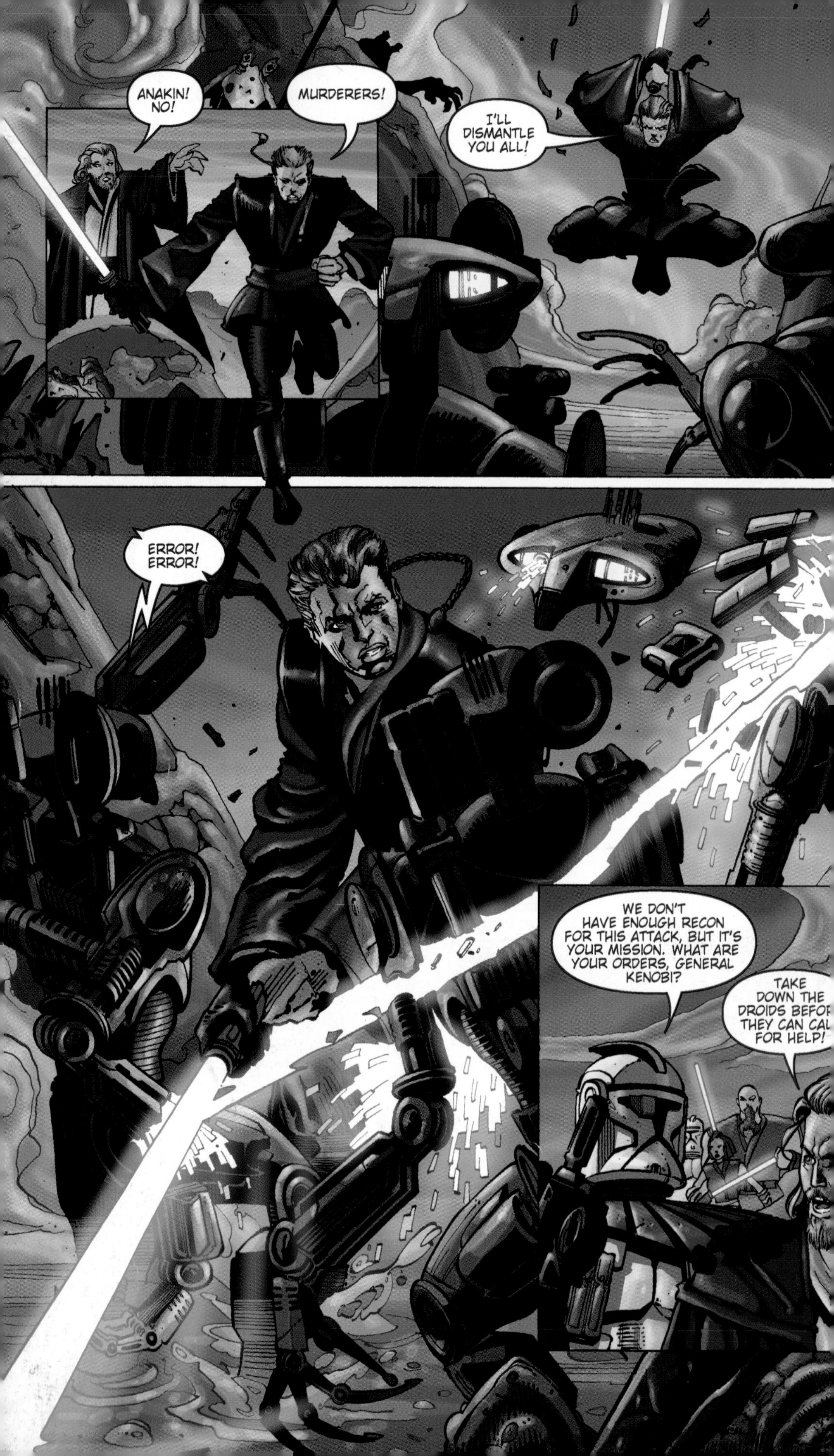
ANAKIN! NO!
MURDERERS!
I'LL DISMANTLE YOU ALL!
ERROR! ERROR!
WE DON'T HAVE ENOUGH RECON FOR THIS ATTACK, BUT IT'S YOUR MISSION. WHAT ARE YOUR ORDERS, GENERAL KENOBI?
TAKE DOWN THE DROIDS BEFOR THEY CAN CAL FOR HELP!

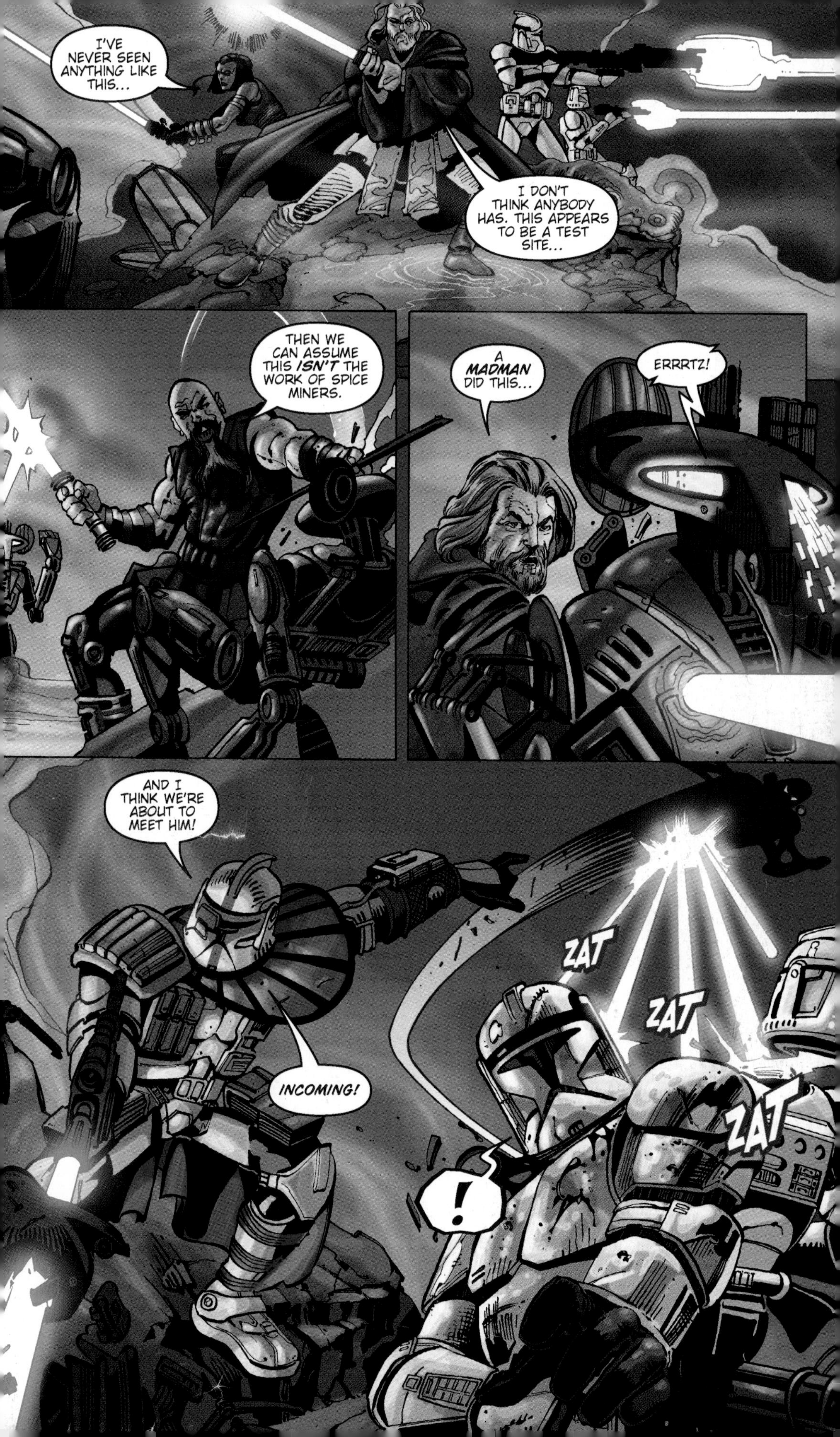
I'VE NEVER SEEN ANYTHING LIKE THIS...
I DON'T THINK ANYBODY HAS. THIS APPEARS TO BE A TEST SITE...
THEN WE CAN ASSUME THIS *ISN'T* THE WORK OF SPICE MINERS.
A *MADMAN* DID THIS...
ERRRTZ!
AND I THINK WE'RE ABOUT TO MEET HIM!
INCOMING!
ZAT
ZAT
ZAT
!

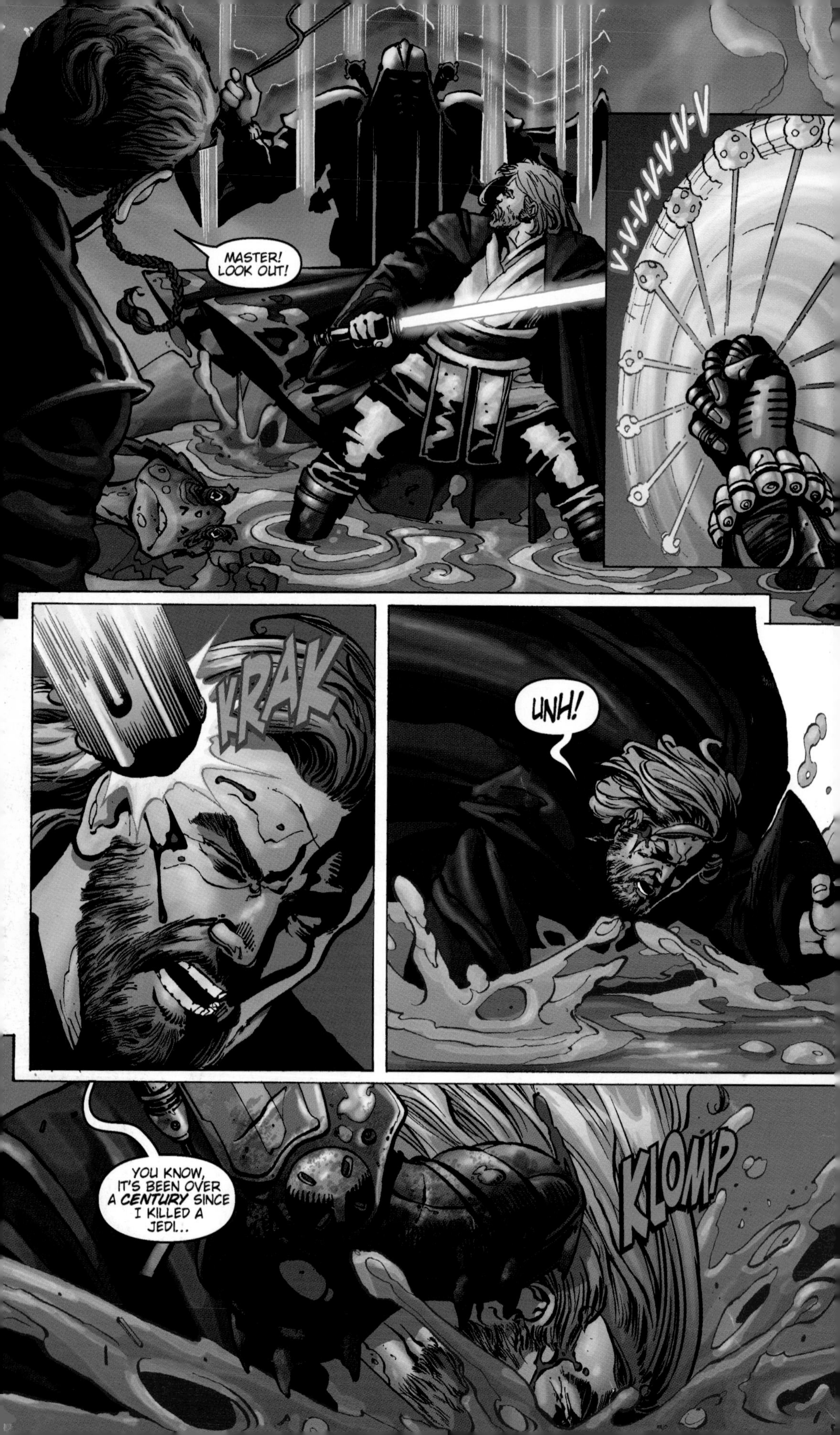
MASTER! LOOK OUT!
V-V-V-V-V-V-V-V
KRAK
UNH!
YOU KNOW, IT'S BEEN OVER A CENTURY SINCE I KILLED A JEDI..
KLOMP

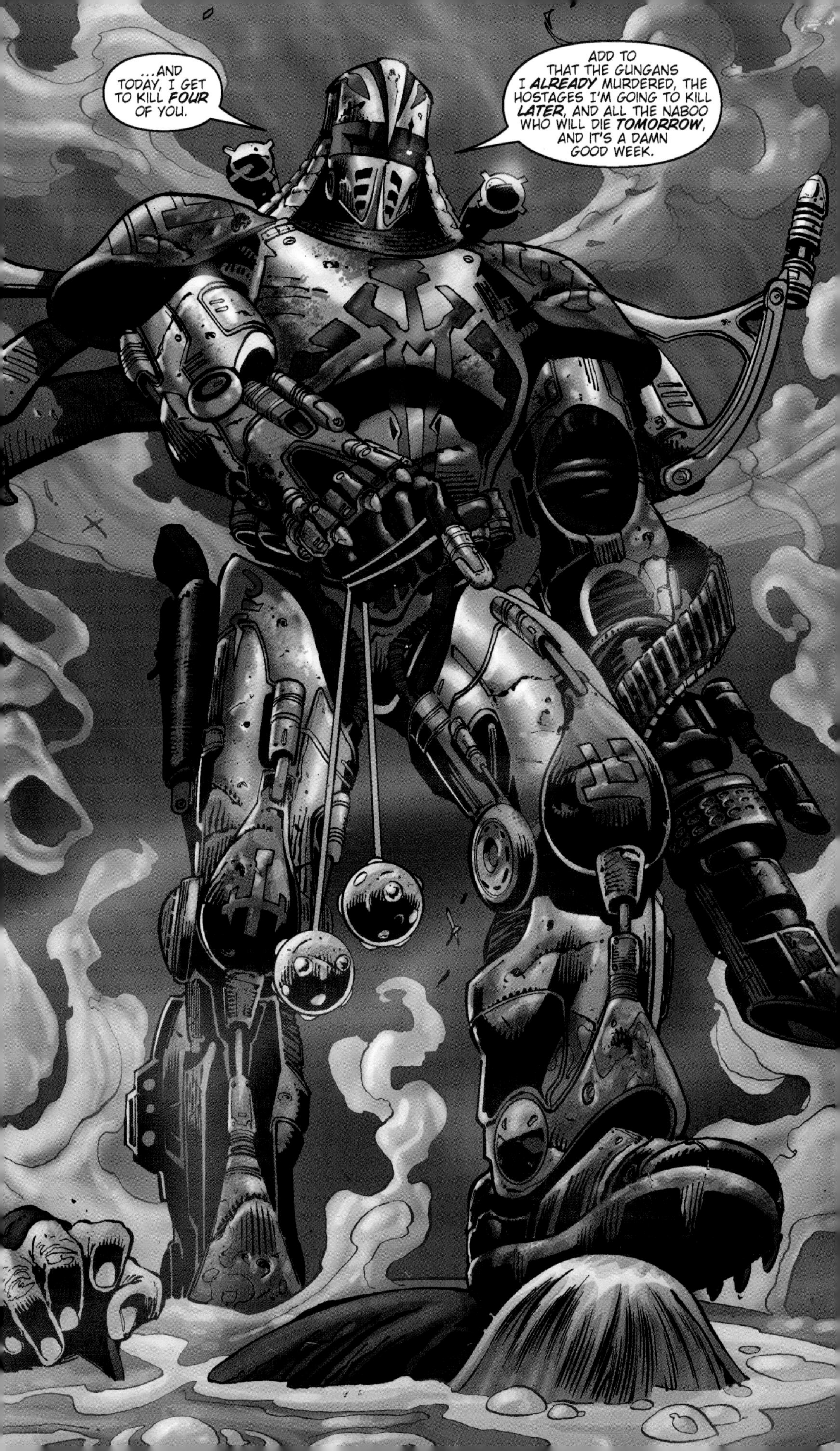
...AND TODAY, I GET TO KILL FOUR OF YOU.
ADD TO THAT THE GUNGANS I ALREADY MURDERED, THE HOSTAGES I'M GOING TO KILL LATER, AND ALL THE NABOO WHO WILL DIE TOMORROW, AND IT'S A DAMN GOOD WEEK.

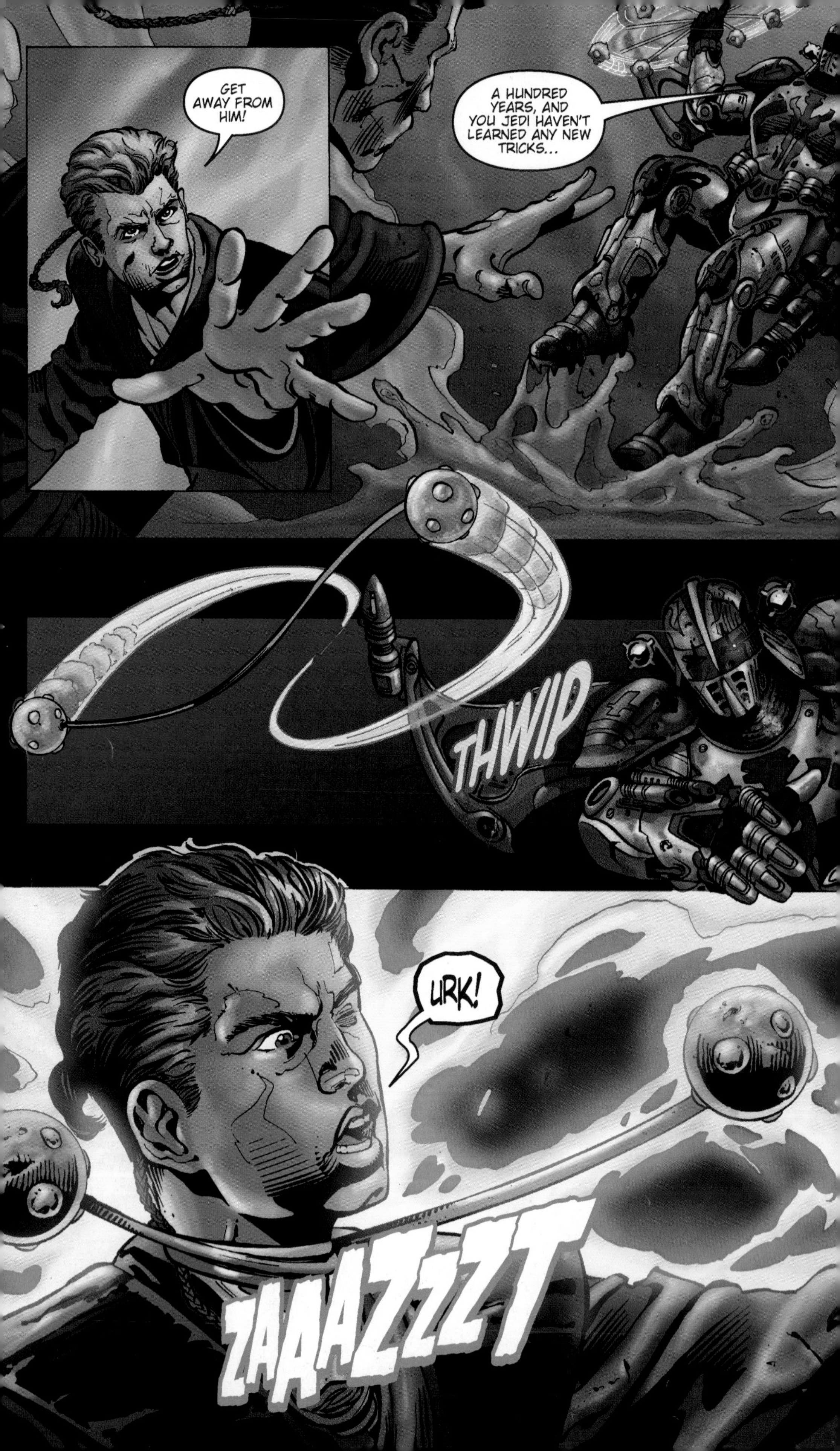
GET AWAY FROM HIM!
A HUNDRED YEARS, AND YOU JEDI HAVEN'T LEARNED ANY NEW TRICKS...
THWIP
URK!
ZAAAZZZT

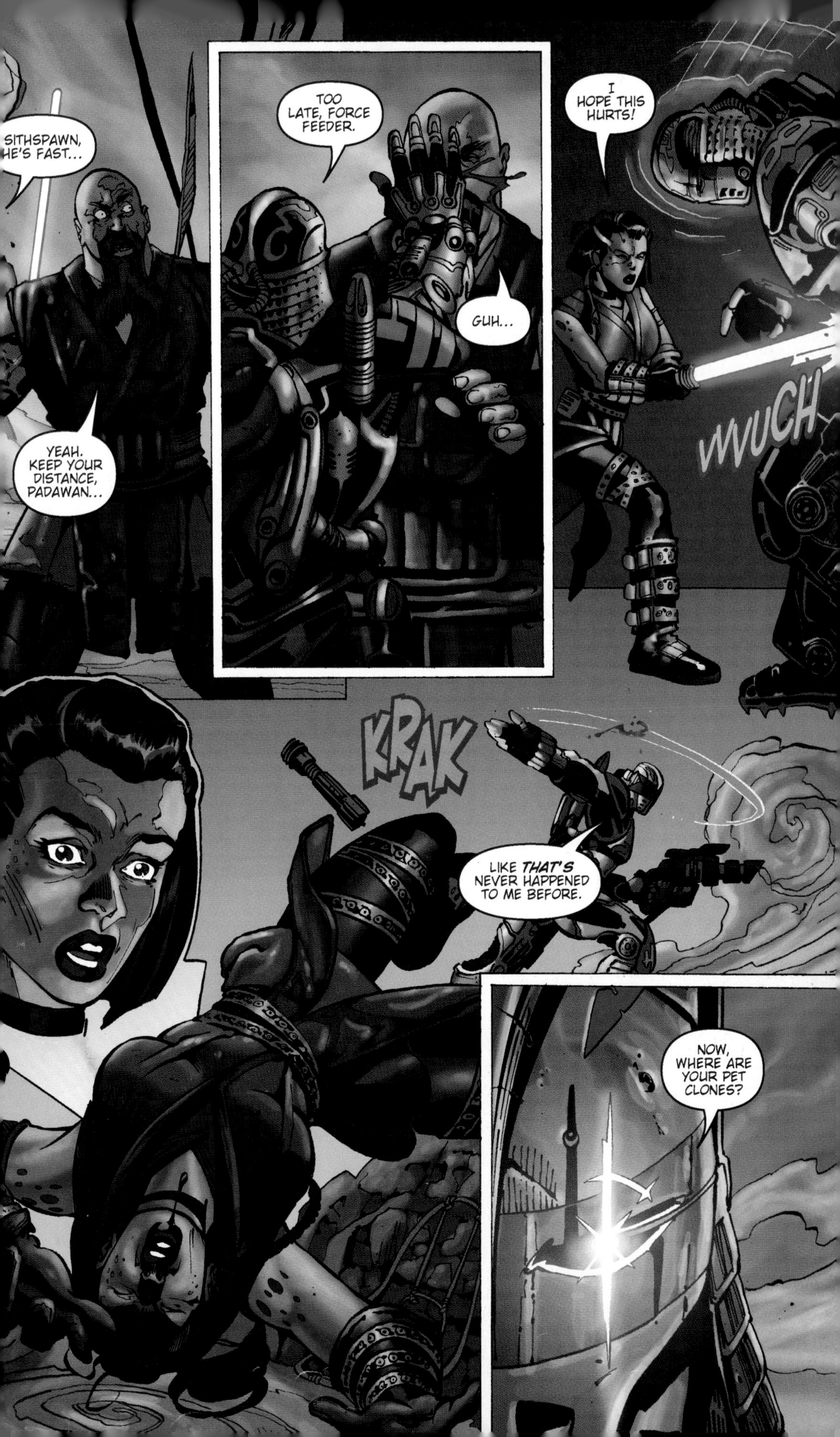
SITHSPAWN, HE'S FAST...
YEAH. KEEP YOUR DISTANCE, PADAWAN...
TOO LATE, FORCE FEEDER.
GUH...
I HOPE THIS HURTS!
VVUCH
KRAK
LIKE *THAT'S* NEVER HAPPENED TO ME BEFORE.
NOW, WHERE ARE YOUR PET CLONES?

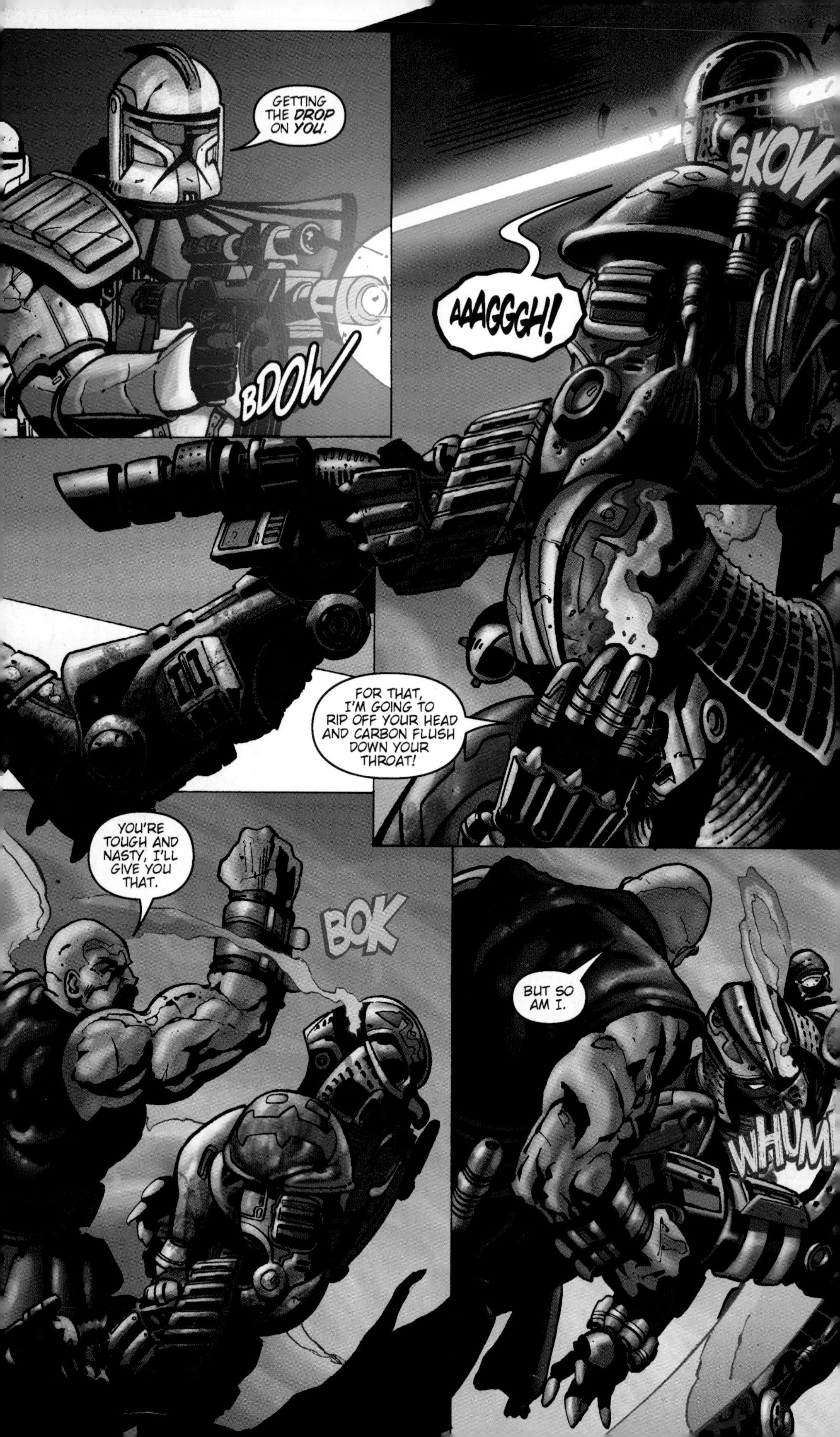
GETTING THE DROP ON YOU.
BDOW
SKOW
AAAGGGH!
FOR THAT, I'M GOING TO RIP OFF YOUR HEAD AND CARBON FLUSH DOWN YOUR THROAT!
YOU'RE TOUGH AND NASTY, I'LL GIVE YOU THAT.
BOK
BUT SO AM I.
WHUM

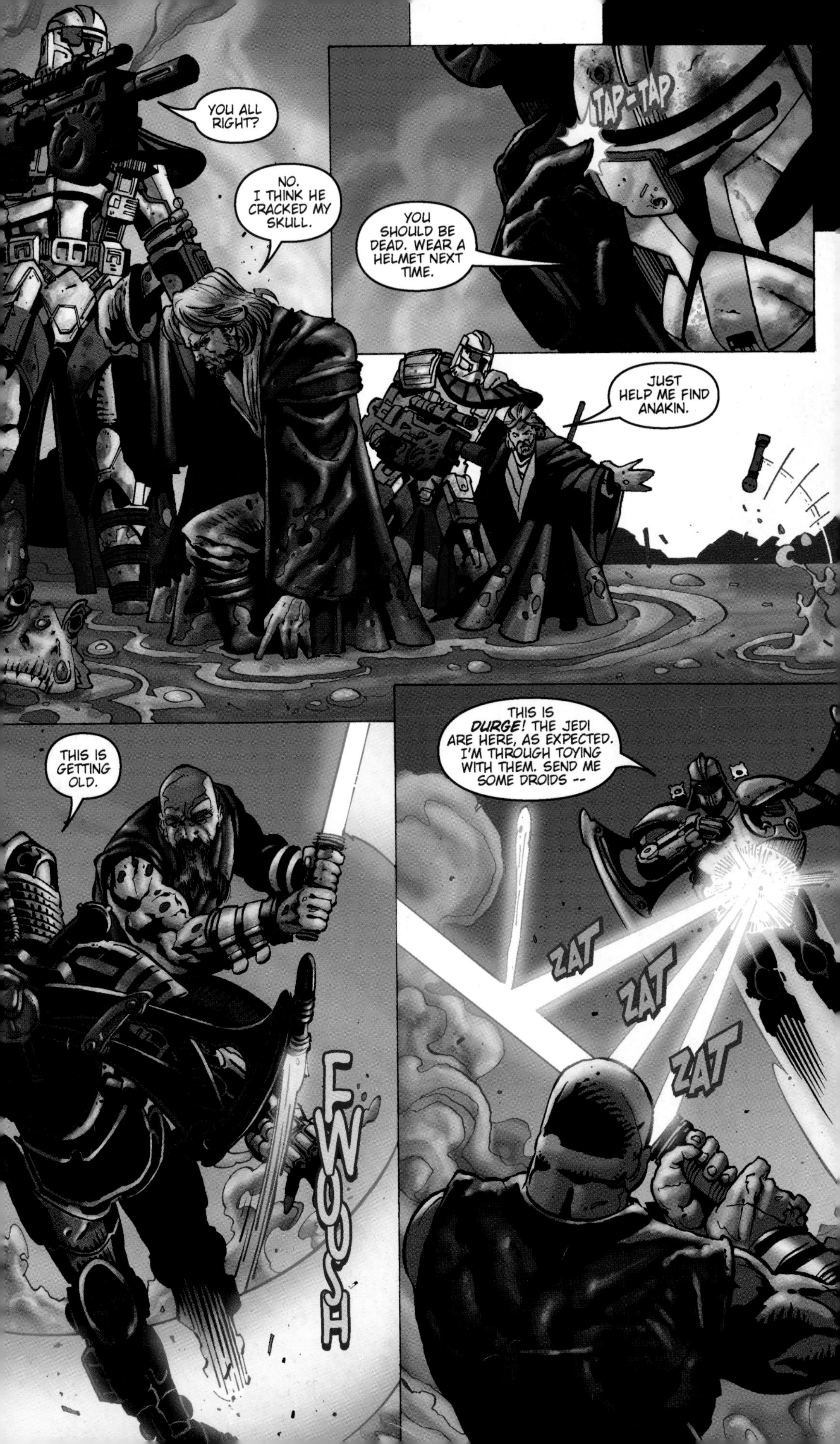
YOU ALL RIGHT?
NO. I THINK HE CRACKED MY SKULL.
YOU SHOULD BE DEAD. WEAR A HELMET NEXT TIME.
TAP-TAP
JUST HELP ME FIND ANAKIN.
THIS IS GETTING OLD.
FWOOSH
THIS IS DURGE! THE JEDI ARE HERE, AS EXPECTED. I'M THROUGH TOYING WITH THEM. SEND ME SOME DROIDS --
ZAT
ZAT
ZAT

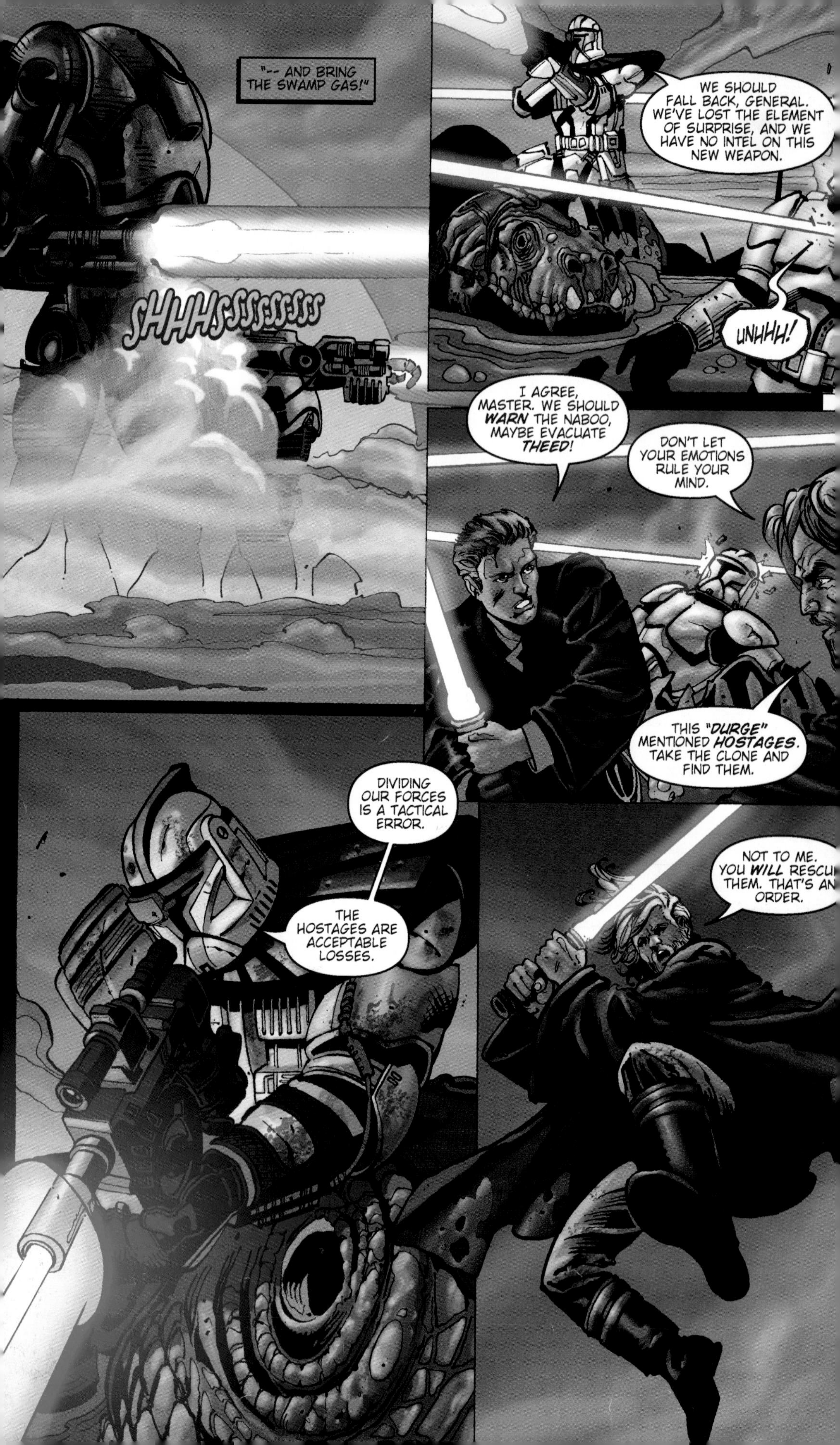
"-- AND BRING THE SWAMP GAS!"
SHHHSSSSSSSSS
WE SHOULD FALL BACK, GENERAL. WE'VE LOST THE ELEMENT OF SURPRISE, AND WE HAVE NO INTEL ON THIS NEW WEAPON.
UNHHH!
I AGREE, MASTER. WE SHOULD WARN THE NABOO, MAYBE EVACUATE THEED!
DON'T LET YOUR EMOTIONS RULE YOUR MIND.
THIS "DURGE" MENTIONED HOSTAGES. TAKE THE CLONE AND FIND THEM.
DIVIDING OUR FORCES IS A TACTICAL ERROR.
THE HOSTAGES ARE ACCEPTABLE LOSSES.
NOT TO ME. YOU WILL RESCU
THEM. THAT'S AN
ORDER.

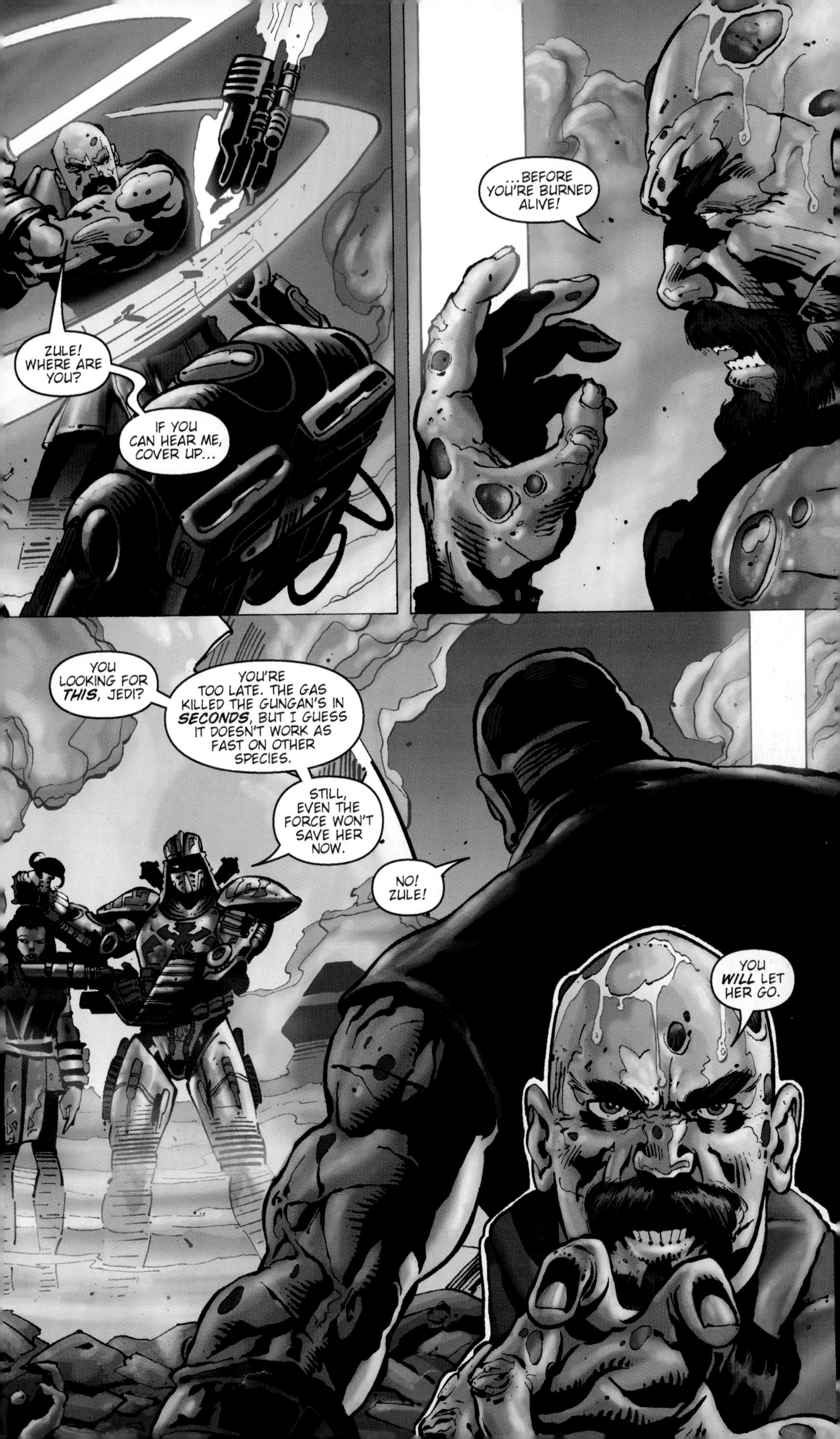
ZULE! WHERE ARE YOU?
IF YOU CAN HEAR ME, COVER UP...
...BEFORE YOU'RE BURNED ALIVE!
YOU LOOKING FOR **THIS**, JEDI?
YOU'RE TOO LATE. THE GAS KILLED THE GUNGAN'S IN **SECONDS**, BUT I GUESS IT DOESN'T WORK AS FAST ON OTHER SPECIES.
STILL, EVEN THE FORCE WON'T SAVE HER NOW.
NO! ZULE!
YOU **WILL** LET HER GO.

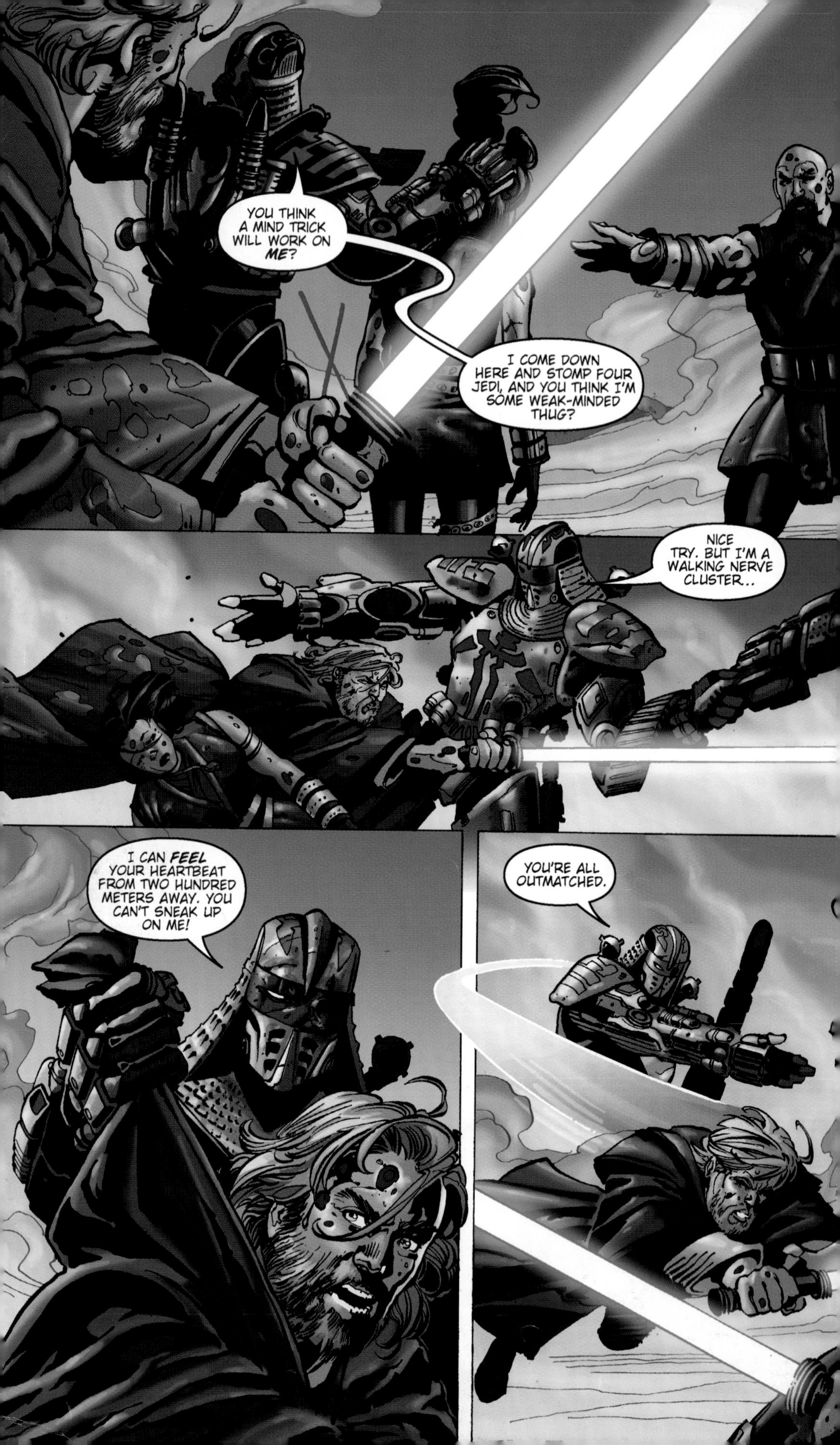
YOU THINK A MIND TRICK WILL WORK ON *ME*?
I COME DOWN HERE AND STOMP FOUR JEDI, AND YOU THINK I'M SOME WEAK-MINDED THUG?
NICE TRY. BUT I'M A WALKING NERVE CLUSTER..
I CAN *FEEL* YOUR HEARTBEAT FROM TWO HUNDRED METERS AWAY. YOU CAN'T SNEAK UP ON ME!
YOU'RE ALL OUTMATCHED.

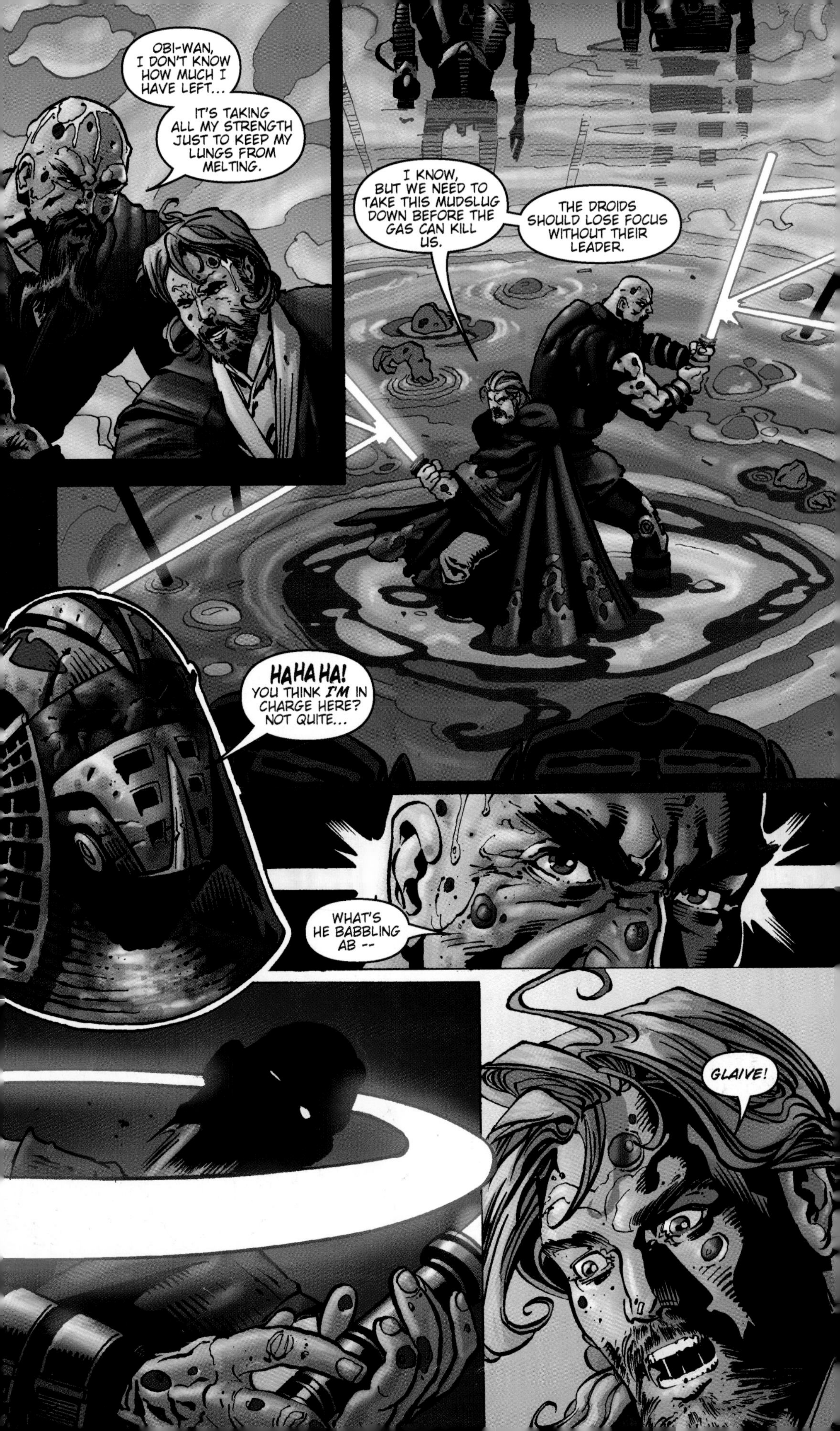
OBI-WAN, I DON'T KNOW HOW MUCH I HAVE LEFT...
IT'S TAKING ALL MY STRENGTH JUST TO KEEP MY LUNGS FROM MELTING.
I KNOW, BUT WE NEED TO TAKE THIS MUDSLUG DOWN BEFORE THE GAS CAN KILL US.
THE DROIDS SHOULD LOSE FOCUS WITHOUT THEIR LEADER.
HAHAHA! YOU THINK *I'M* IN CHARGE HERE? NOT QUITE...
WHAT'S HE BABBLING AB --
GLAIVE!

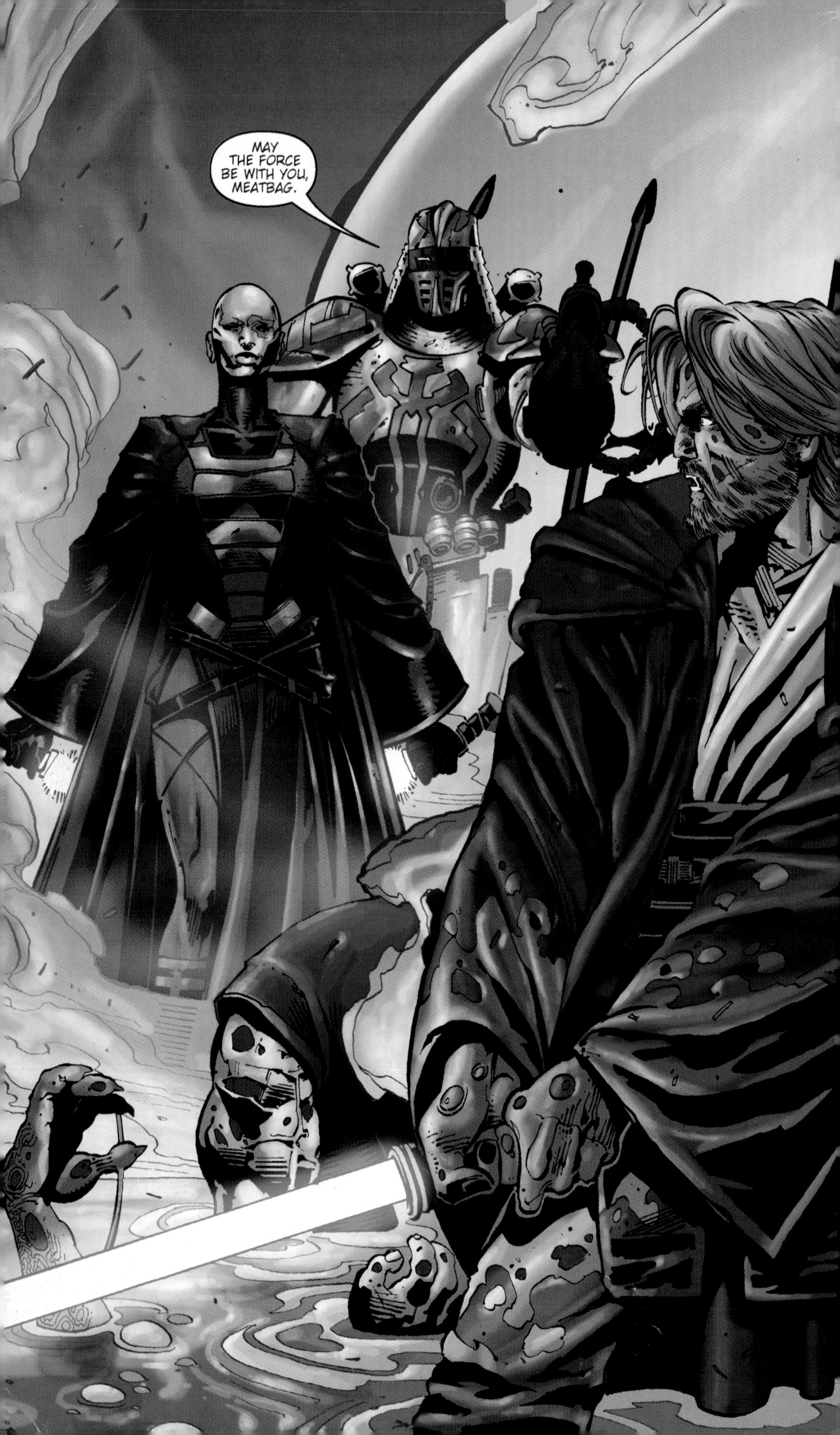
MAY THE FORCE BE WITH YOU, MEATBAG.

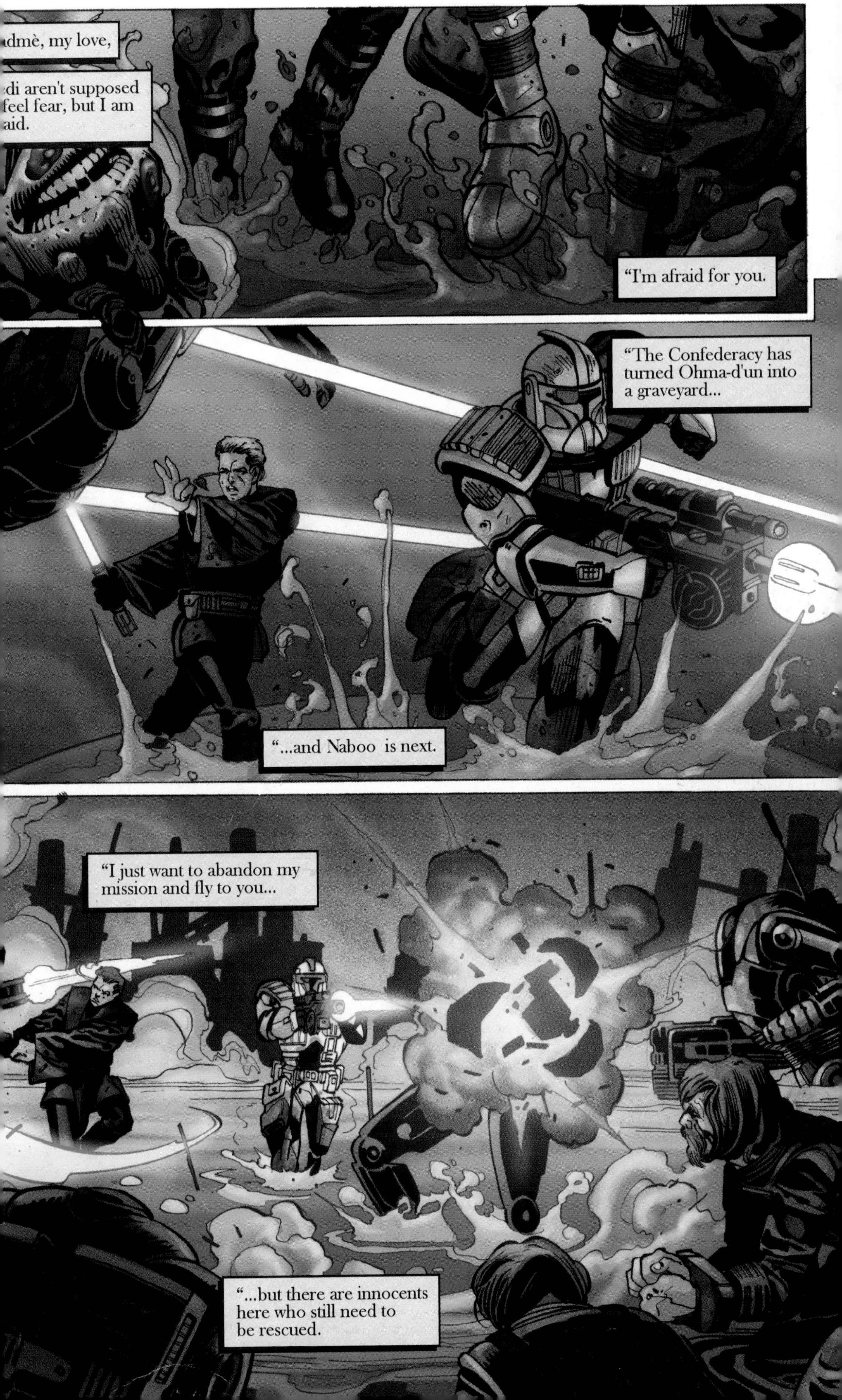
dmè, my love,
di aren't supposed
feel fear, but I am
aid.
"I'm afraid for you.
"The Confederacy has turned Ohma-d'un into a graveyard...
"...and Naboo is next.
"I just want to abandon my mission and fly to you...
"...but there are innocents here who still need to be rescued.

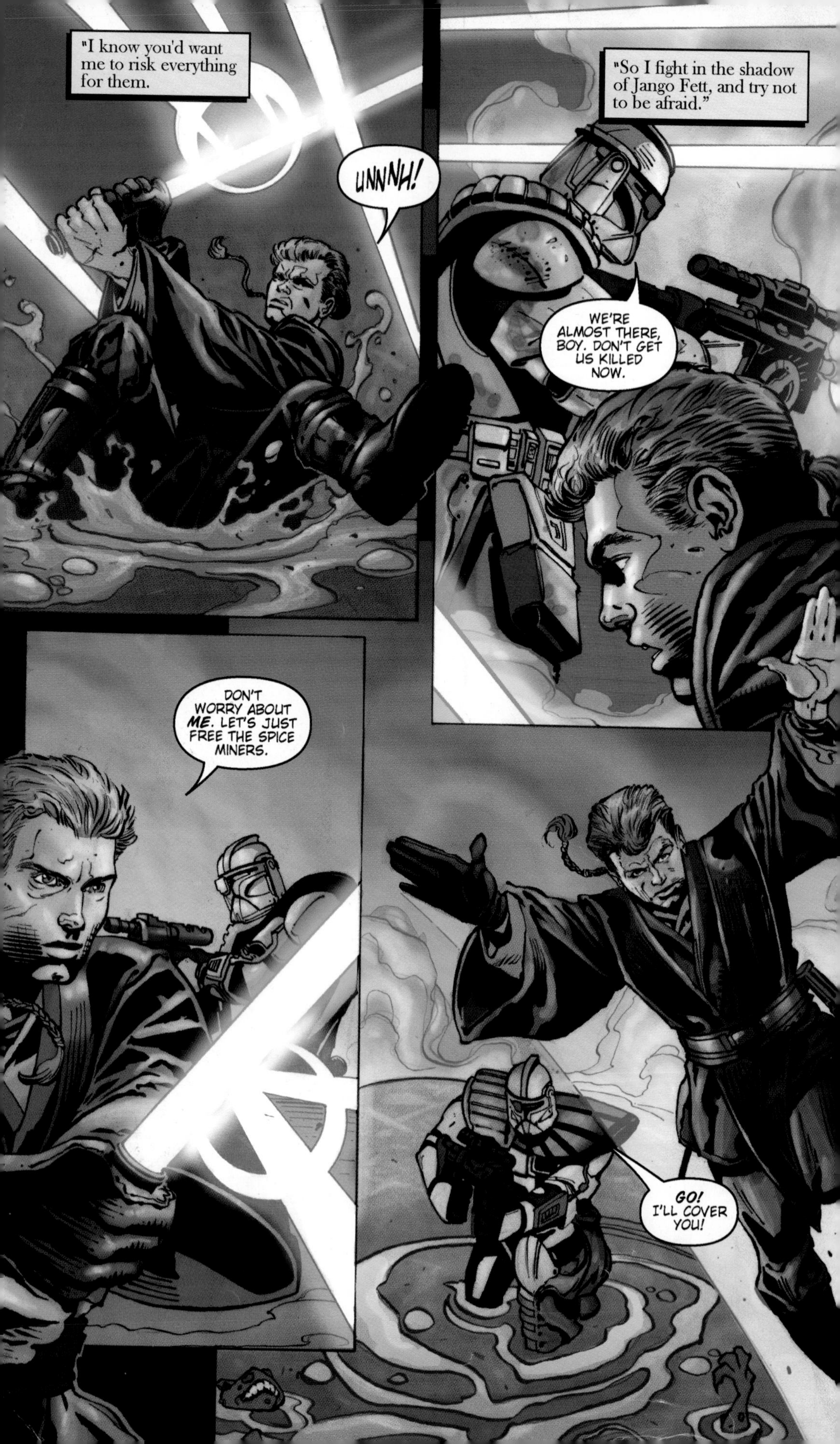
"I know you'd want me to risk everything for them.
UNNNH!
"So I fight in the shadow of Jango Fett, and try not to be afraid."
WE'RE ALMOST THERE, BOY. DON'T GET US KILLED NOW.
DON'T WORRY ABOUT *ME*. LET'S JUST FREE THE SPICE MINERS.
GO! I'LL COVER YOU!

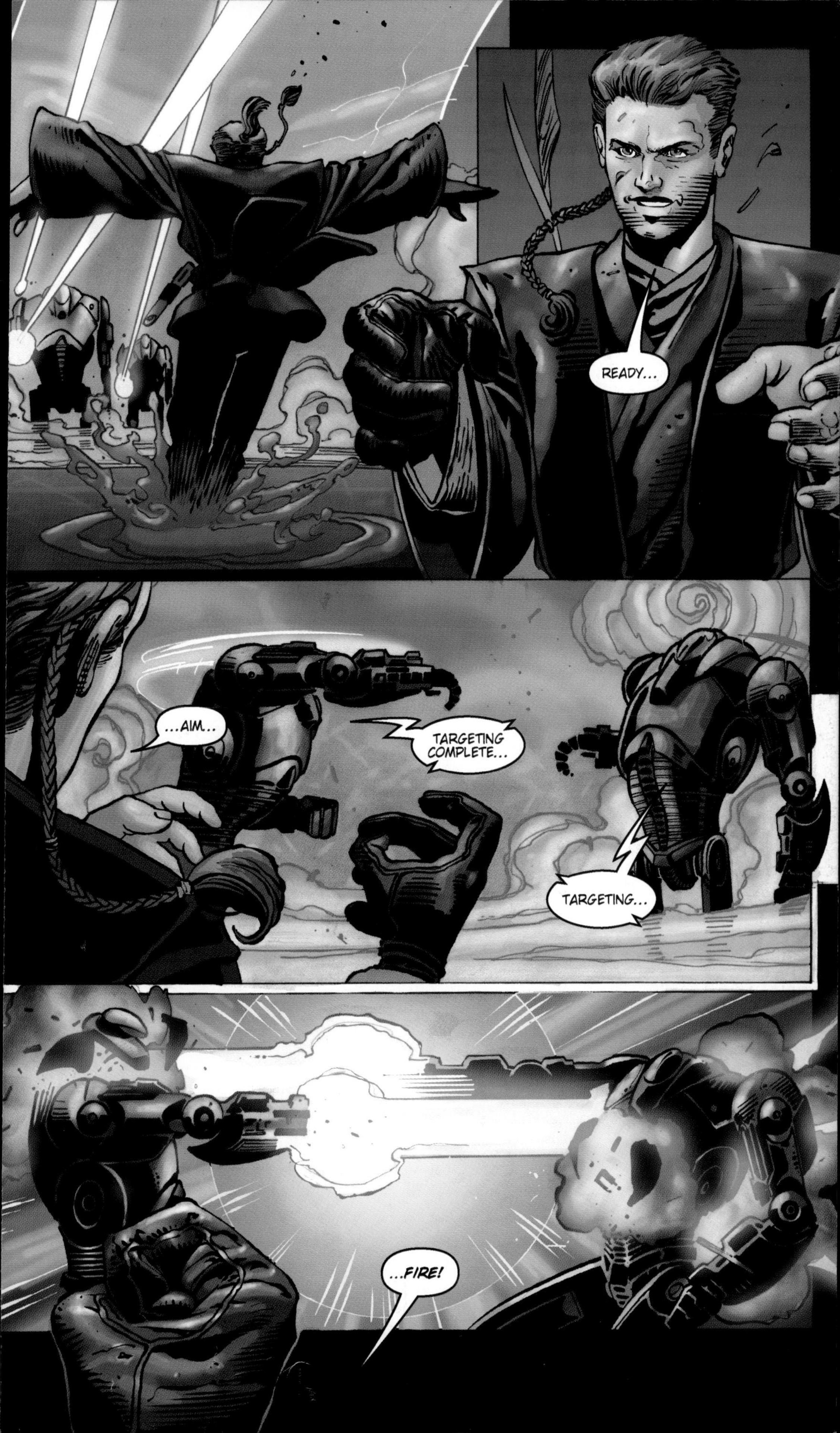
READY...
...AIM...
TARGETING COMPLETE...
TARGETING...
...FIRE!

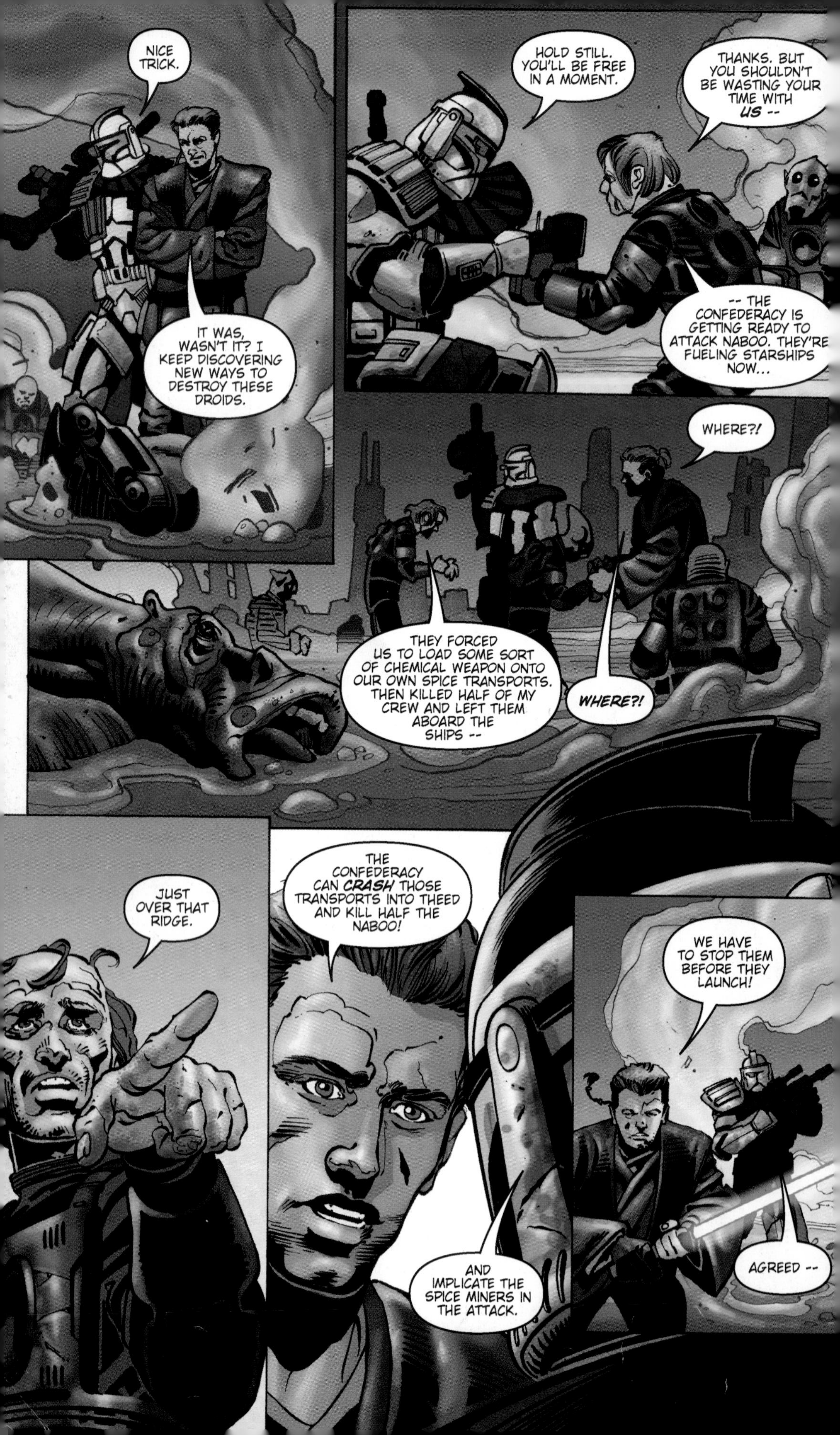
NICE TRICK.
IT WAS, WASN'T IT? I KEEP DISCOVERING NEW WAYS TO DESTROY THESE DROIDS.
HOLD STILL. YOU'LL BE FREE IN A MOMENT.
THANKS. BUT YOU SHOULDN'T BE WASTING YOUR TIME WITH *US* --
-- THE CONFEDERACY IS GETTING READY TO ATTACK NABOO. THEY'RE FUELING STARSHIPS NOW...
WHERE?!
THEY FORCED US TO LOAD SOME SORT OF CHEMICAL WEAPON ONTO OUR OWN SPICE TRANSPORTS. THEN KILLED HALF OF MY CREW AND LEFT THEM ABOARD THE SHIPS --
WHERE?!
JUST OVER THAT RIDGE.
THE CONFEDERACY CAN *CRASH* THOSE TRANSPORTS INTO THEED AND KILL HALF THE NABOO!
AND IMPLICATE THE SPICE MINERS IN THE ATTACK.
WE HAVE TO STOP THEM BEFORE THEY LAUNCH!
AGREED --

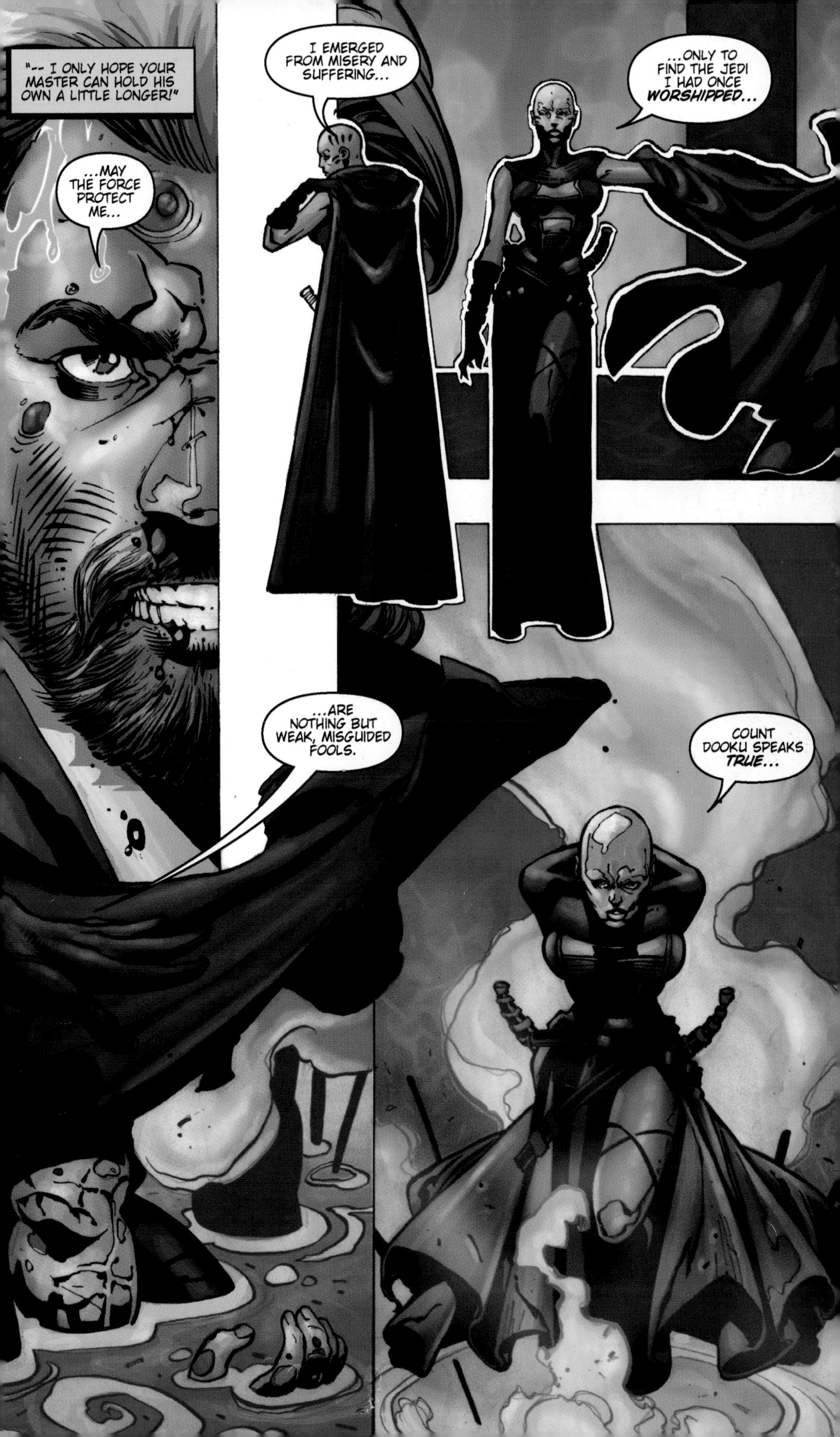
"-- I ONLY HOPE YOUR MASTER CAN HOLD HIS OWN A LITTLE LONGER!"
...MAY THE FORCE PROTECT ME...
I EMERGED FROM MISERY AND SUFFERING...
...ONLY TO FIND THE JEDI I HAD ONCE *WORSHIPPED*...
...ARE NOTHING BUT WEAK, MISGUIDED FOOLS.
COUNT DOOKU SPEAKS *TRUE*...

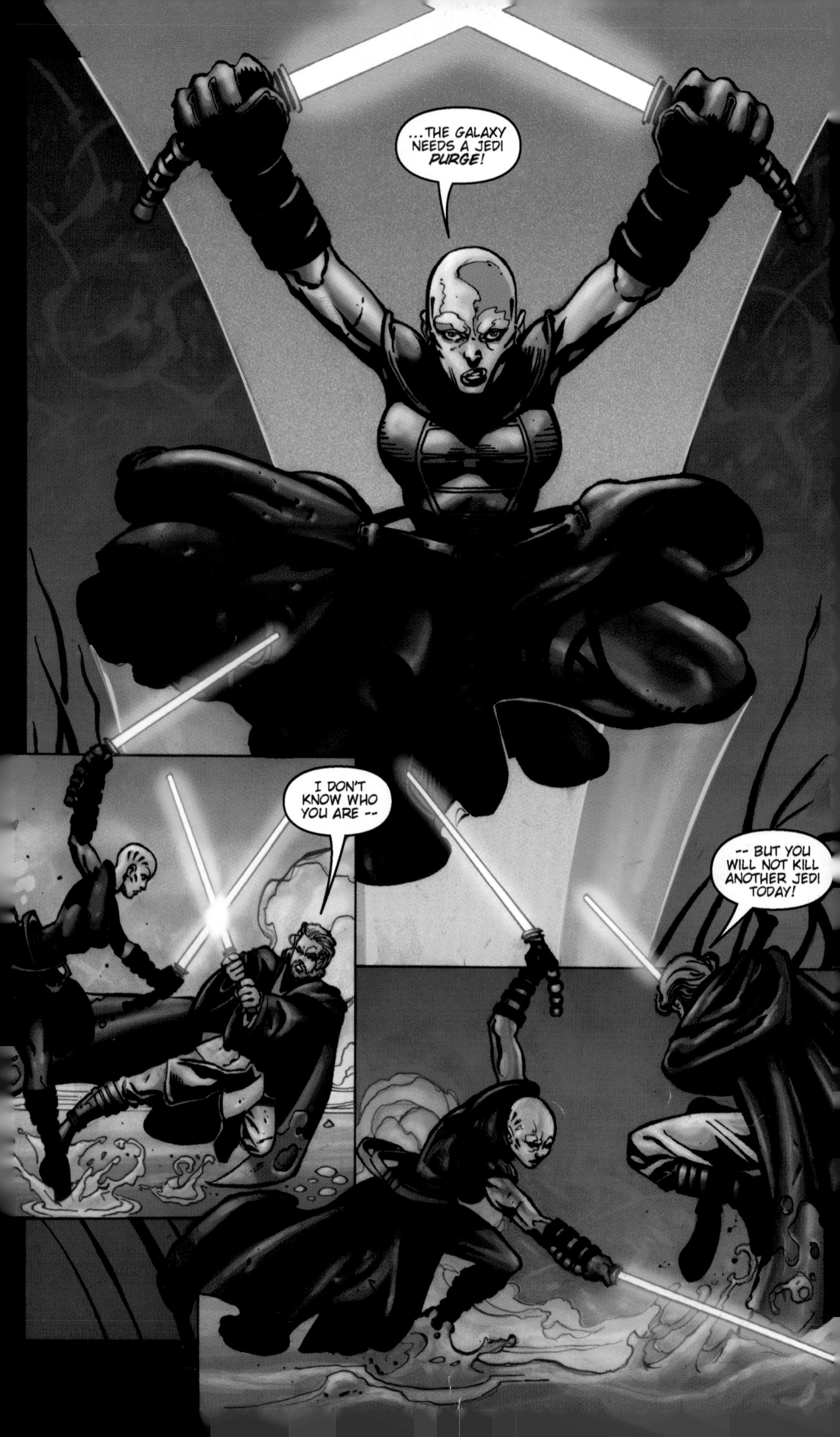
...THE GALAXY NEEDS A JEDI PURGE!
I DON'T KNOW WHO YOU ARE --
-- BUT YOU WILL NOT KILL ANOTHER JEDI TODAY!

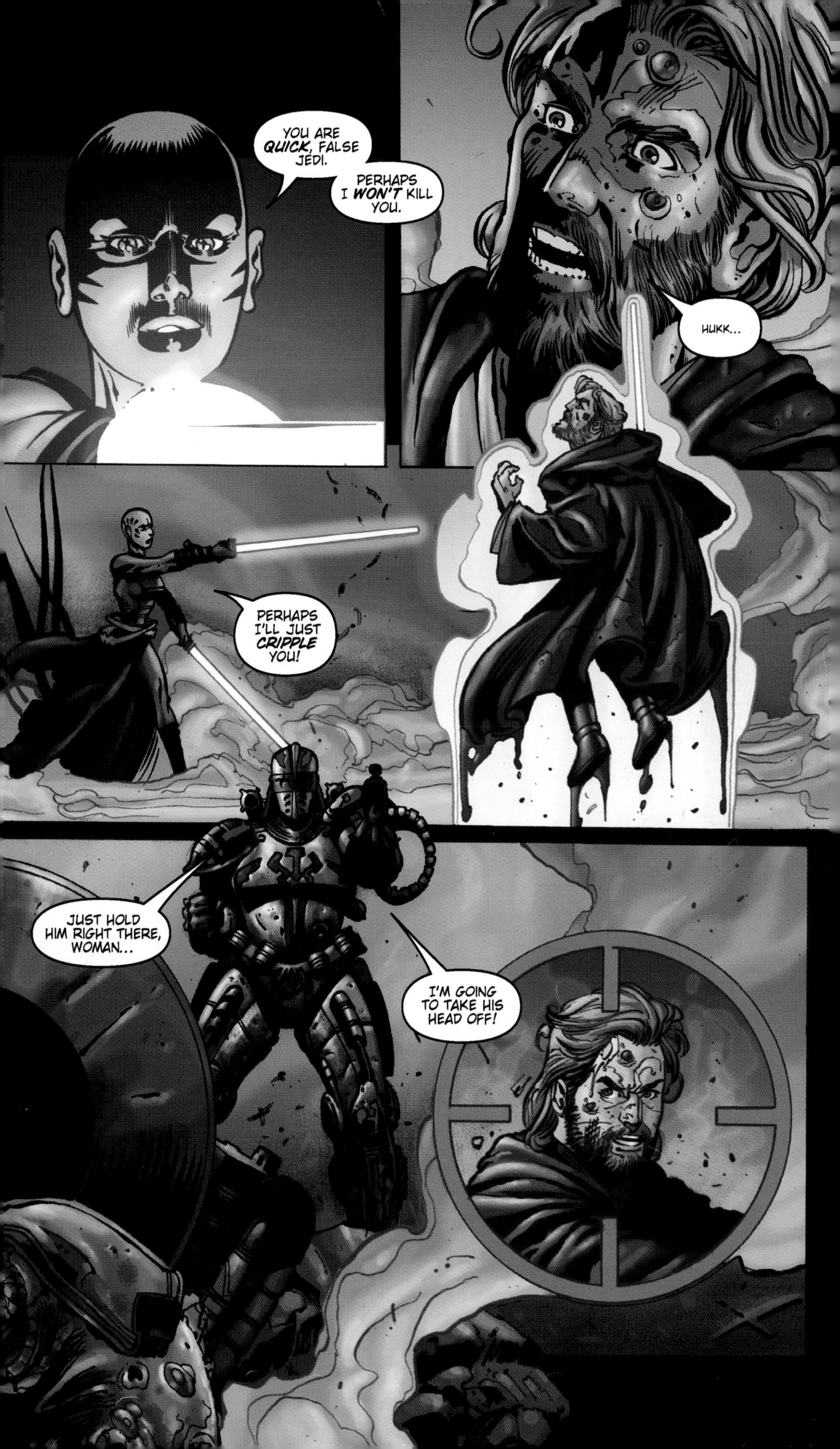
YOU ARE QUICK, FALSE JEDI.
PERHAPS I WON'T KILL YOU.
HUKK...
PERHAPS I'LL JUST CRIPPLE YOU!
JUST HOLD HIM RIGHT THERE, WOMAN...
I'M GOING TO TAKE HIS HEAD OFF!

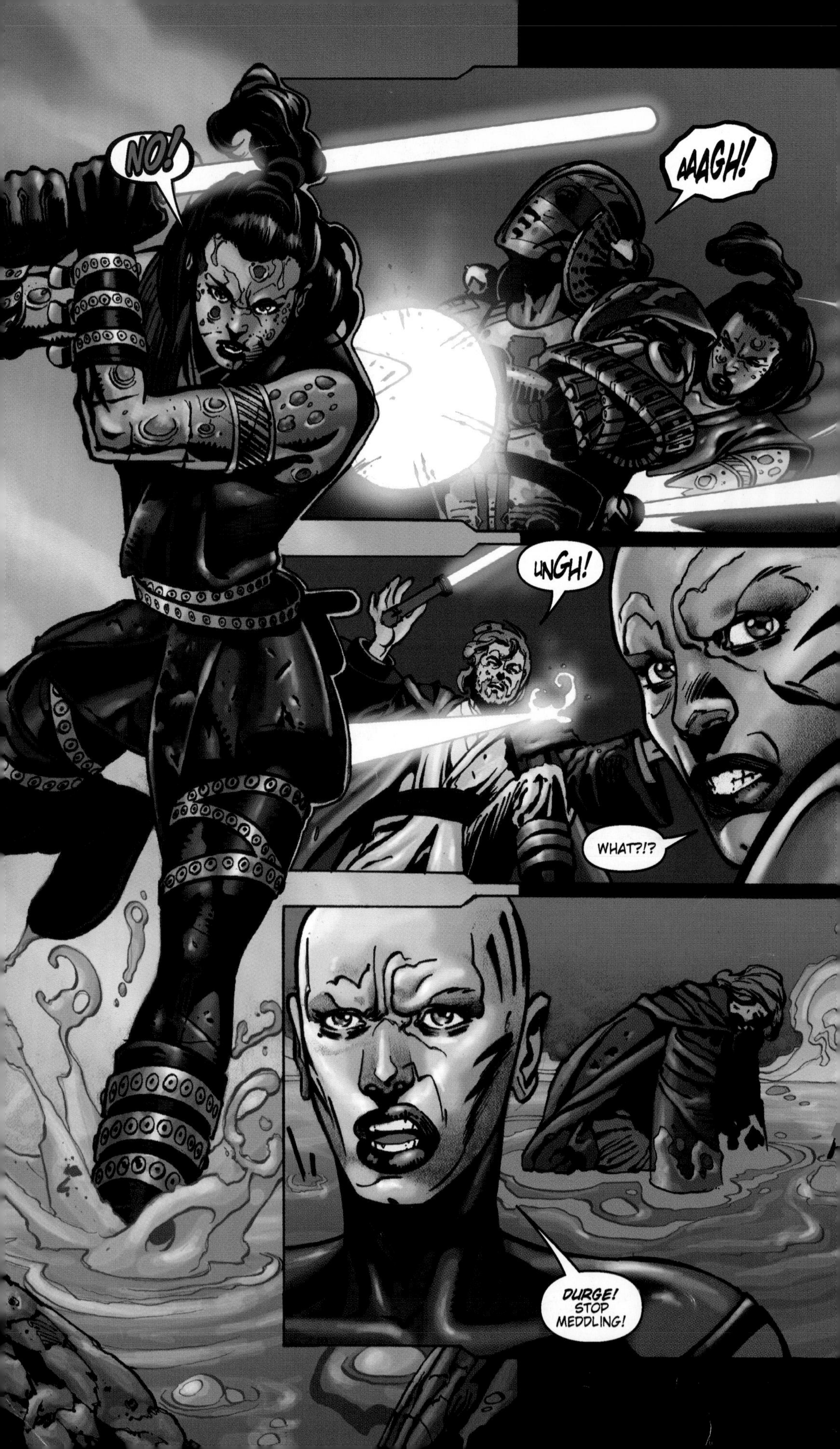
NO!
AAAGH!
UNGH!
WHAT?!?
DURGE! STOP MEDDLING!

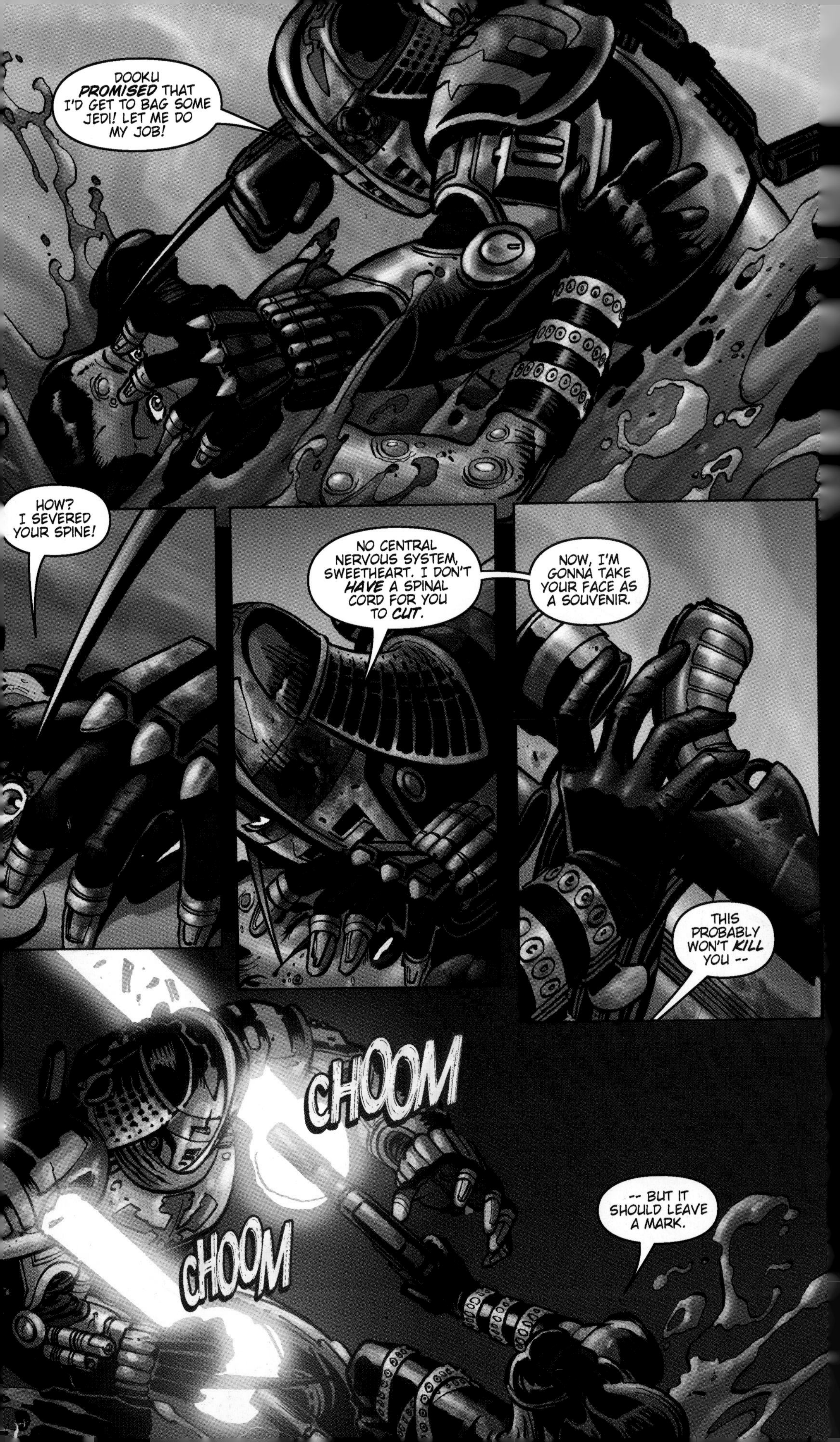
DOOKU PROMISED THAT I'D GET TO BAG SOME JEDI! LET ME DO MY JOB!
HOW? I SEVERED YOUR SPINE!
NO CENTRAL NERVOUS SYSTEM, SWEETHEART. I DON'T HAVE A SPINAL CORD FOR YOU TO CUT.
NOW, I'M GONNA TAKE YOUR FACE AS A SOUVENIR.
THIS PROBABLY WON'T KILL YOU --
CHOOM
CHOOM
-- BUT IT SHOULD LEAVE A MARK.

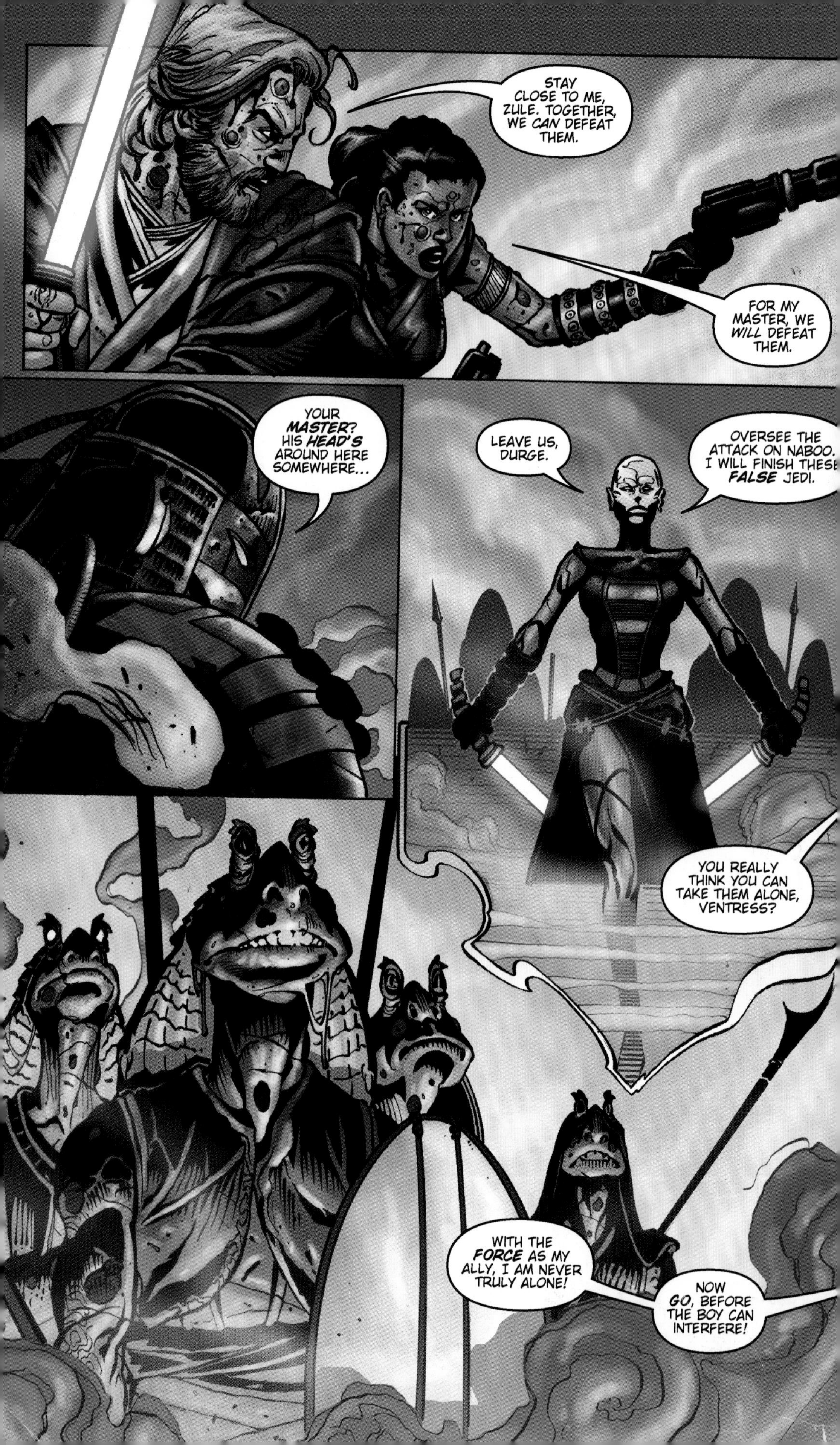

STAY CLOSE TO ME, ZULE. TOGETHER, WE CAN DEFEAT THEM.
FOR MY MASTER, WE WILL DEFEAT THEM.
YOUR MASTER? HIS HEAD'S AROUND HERE SOMEWHERE...
LEAVE US, DURGE.
OVERSEE THE ATTACK ON NABOO. I WILL FINISH THESE FALSE JEDI.
YOU REALLY THINK YOU CAN TAKE THEM ALONE, VENTRESS?
WITH THE FORCE AS MY ALLY, I AM NEVER TRULY ALONE!
NOW GO, BEFORE THE BOY CAN INTERFERE!

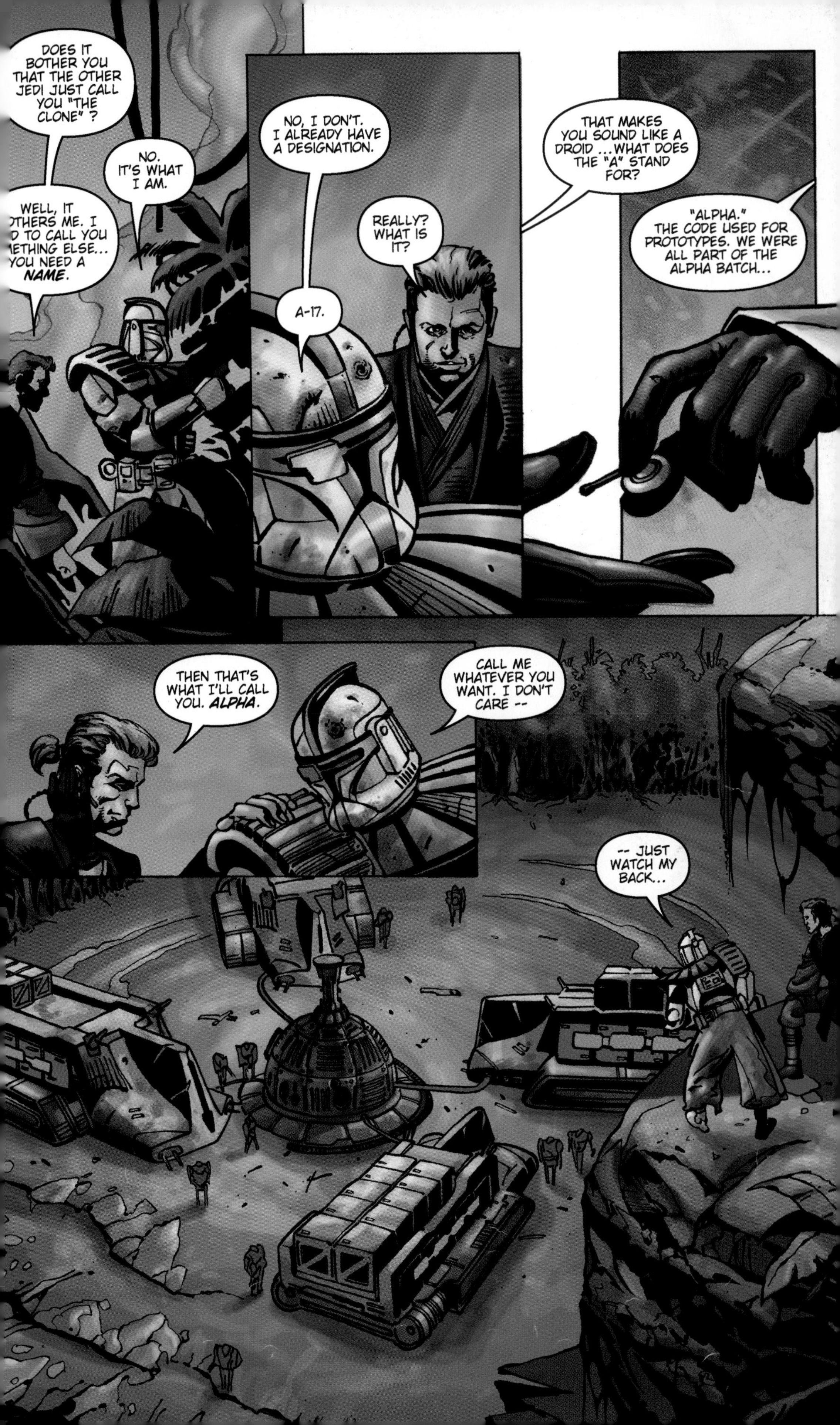
DOES IT BOTHER YOU THAT THE OTHER JEDI JUST CALL YOU "THE CLONE" ?
NO. IT'S WHAT I AM.
WELL, IT OTHERS ME. I D TO CALL YOU METHING ELSE... YOU NEED A ***NAME***.
NO, I DON'T. I ALREADY HAVE A DESIGNATION.
REALLY? WHAT IS IT?
A-17.
THAT MAKES YOU SOUND LIKE A DROID ...WHAT DOES THE "A" STAND FOR?
"ALPHA." THE CODE USED FOR PROTOTYPES. WE WERE ALL PART OF THE ALPHA BATCH...
THEN THAT'S WHAT I'LL CALL YOU. ***ALPHA***.
CALL ME WHATEVER YOU WANT. I DON'T CARE --
-- JUST WATCH MY BACK...

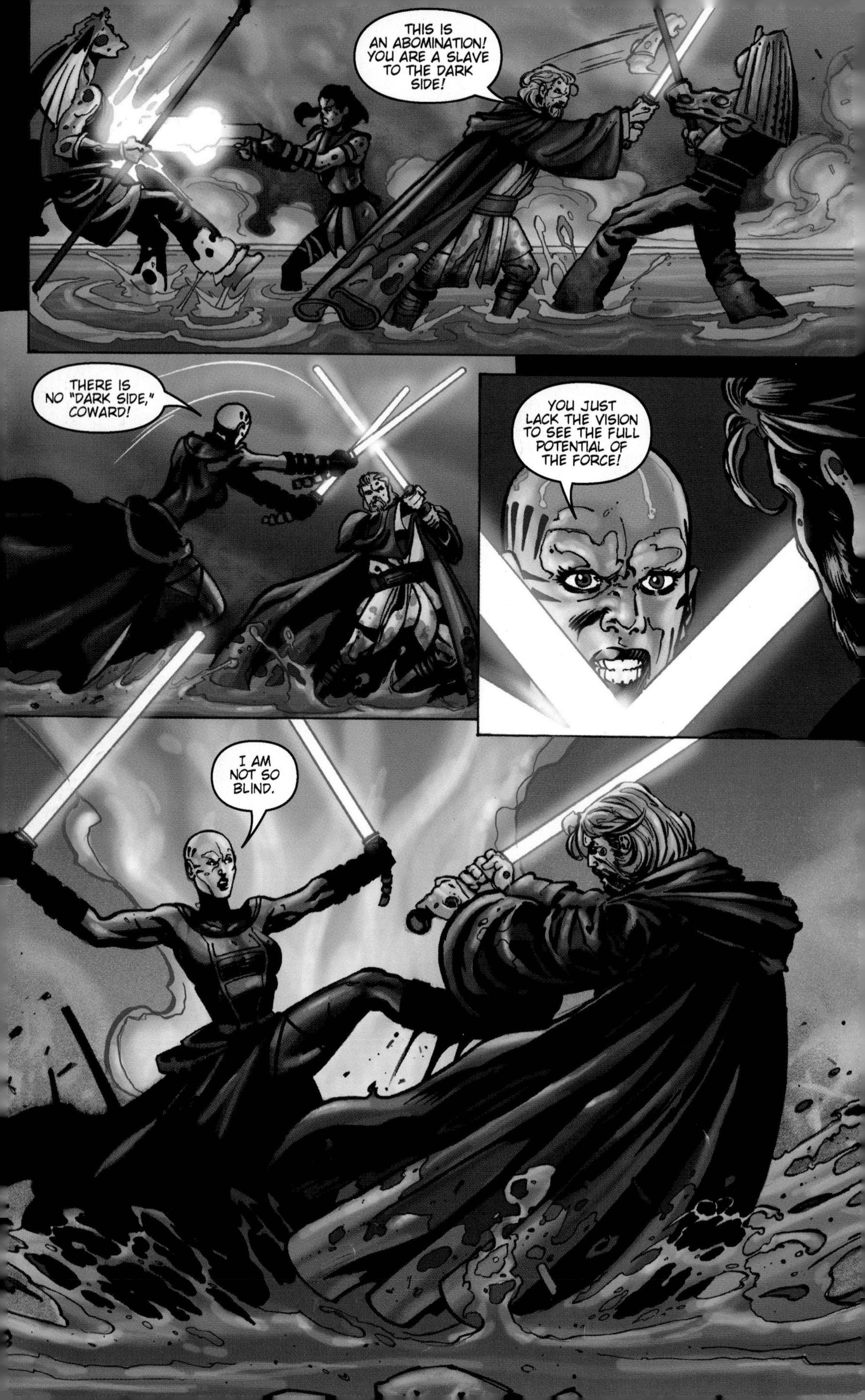
THIS IS AN ABOMINATION! YOU ARE A SLAVE TO THE DARK SIDE!
THERE IS NO "DARK SIDE," COWARD!
YOU JUST LACK THE VISION TO SEE THE FULL POTENTIAL OF THE FORCE!
I AM NOT SO BLIND.

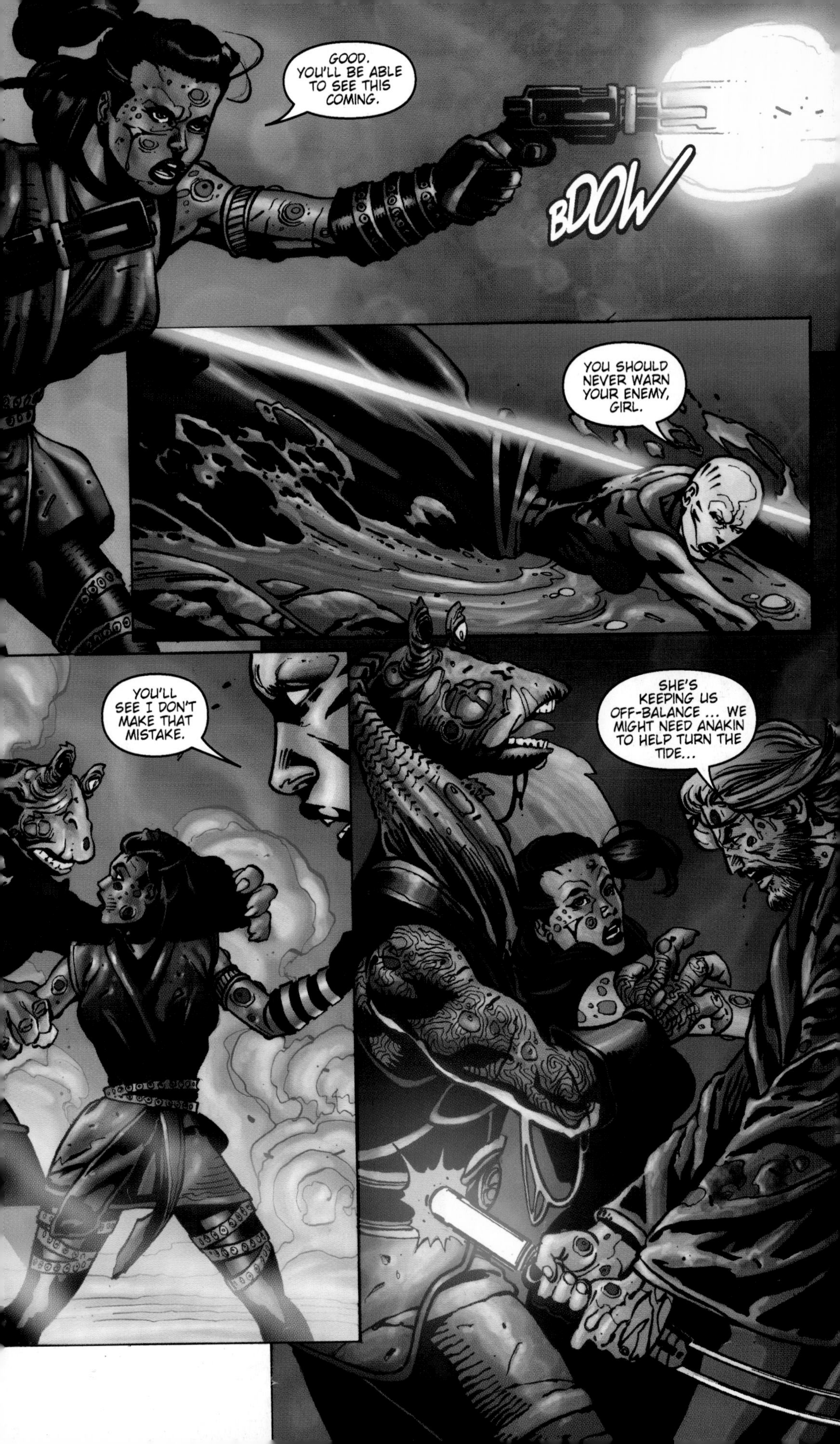
GOOD. YOU'LL BE ABLE TO SEE THIS COMING.
BDOW
YOU SHOULD NEVER WARN YOUR ENEMY, GIRL.
YOU'LL SEE I DON'T MAKE THAT MISTAKE.
SHE'S KEEPING US OFF-BALANCE ... WE MIGHT NEED ANAKIN TO HELP TURN THE TIDE...

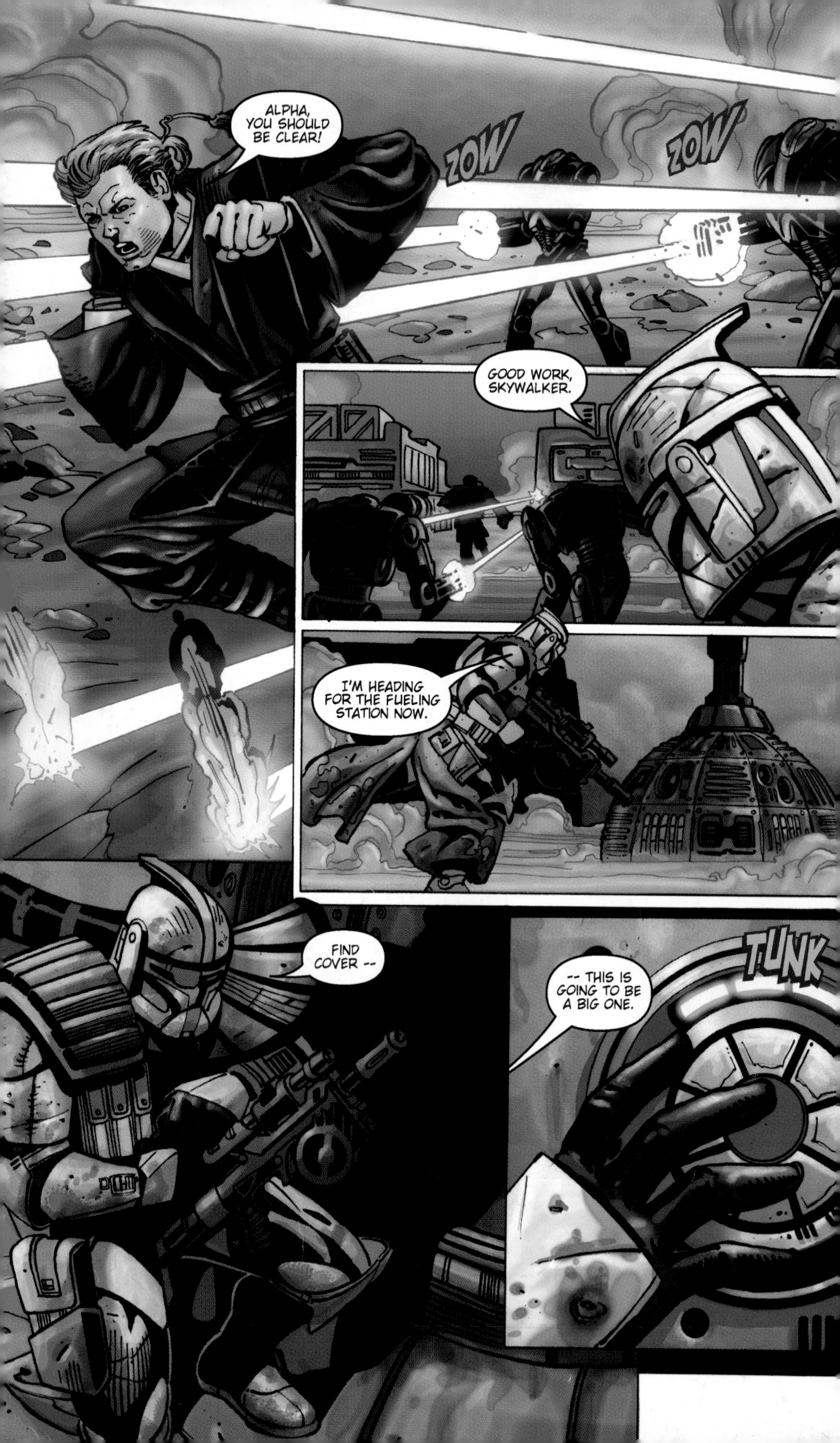
ALPHA, YOU SHOULD BE CLEAR!
ZOW
ZOW
GOOD WORK, SKYWALKER.
I'M HEADING FOR THE FUELING STATION NOW.
FIND COVER --
TUNK
-- THIS IS GOING TO BE A BIG ONE.

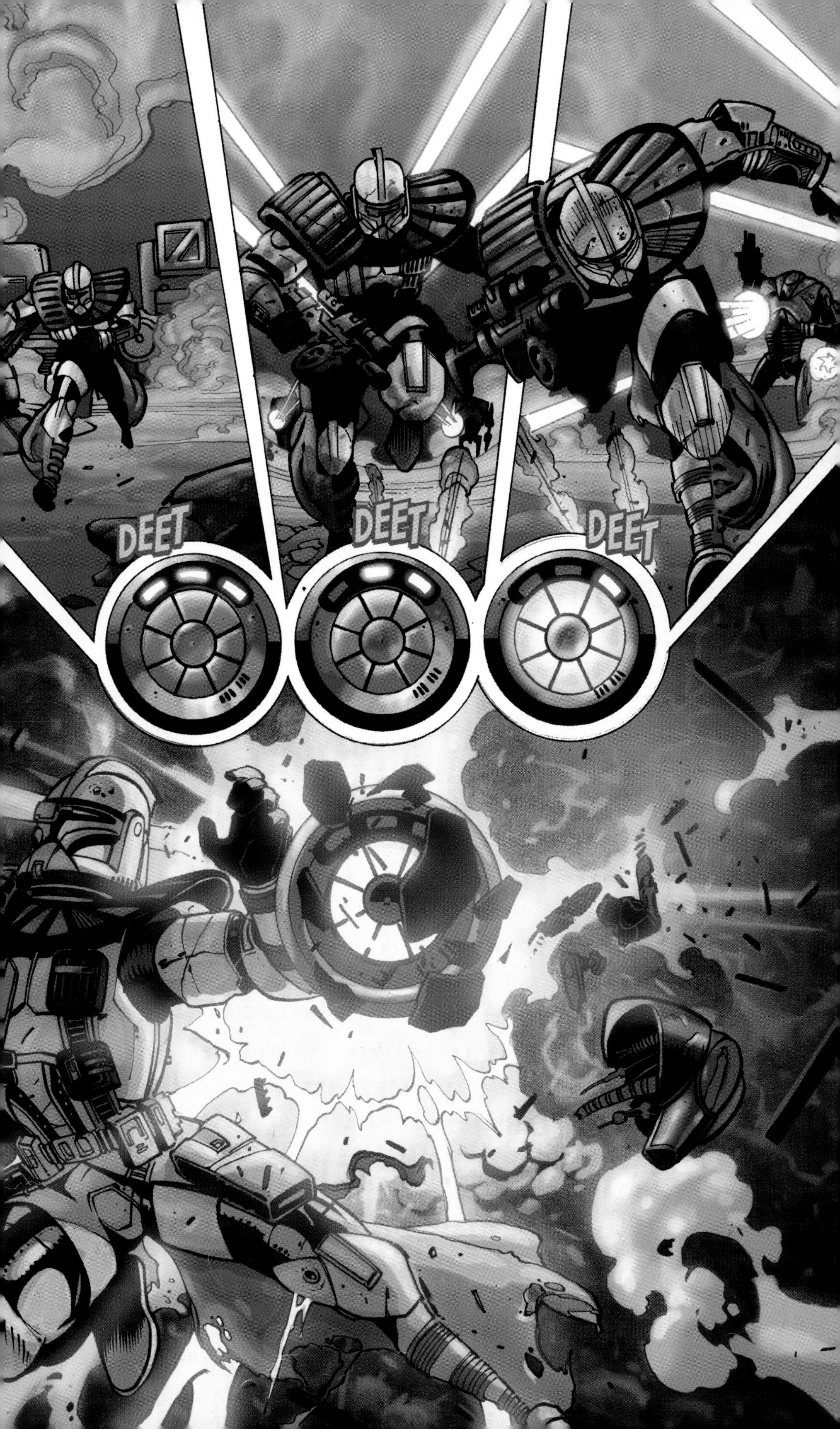
DEET
DEET
DEET

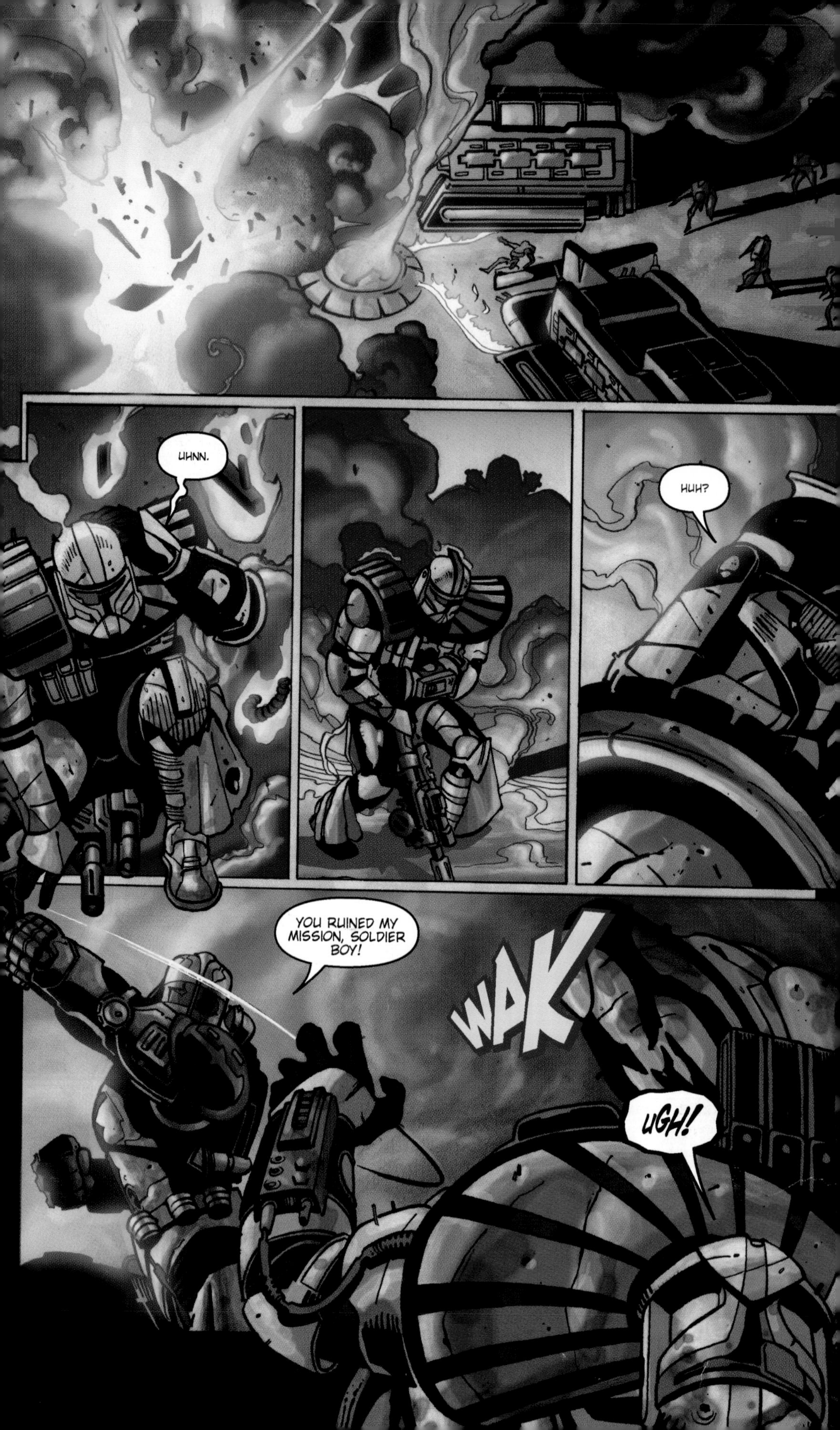
UHNN.
HUH?
YOU RUINED MY MISSION, SOLDIER BOY!
WAK
UGH!

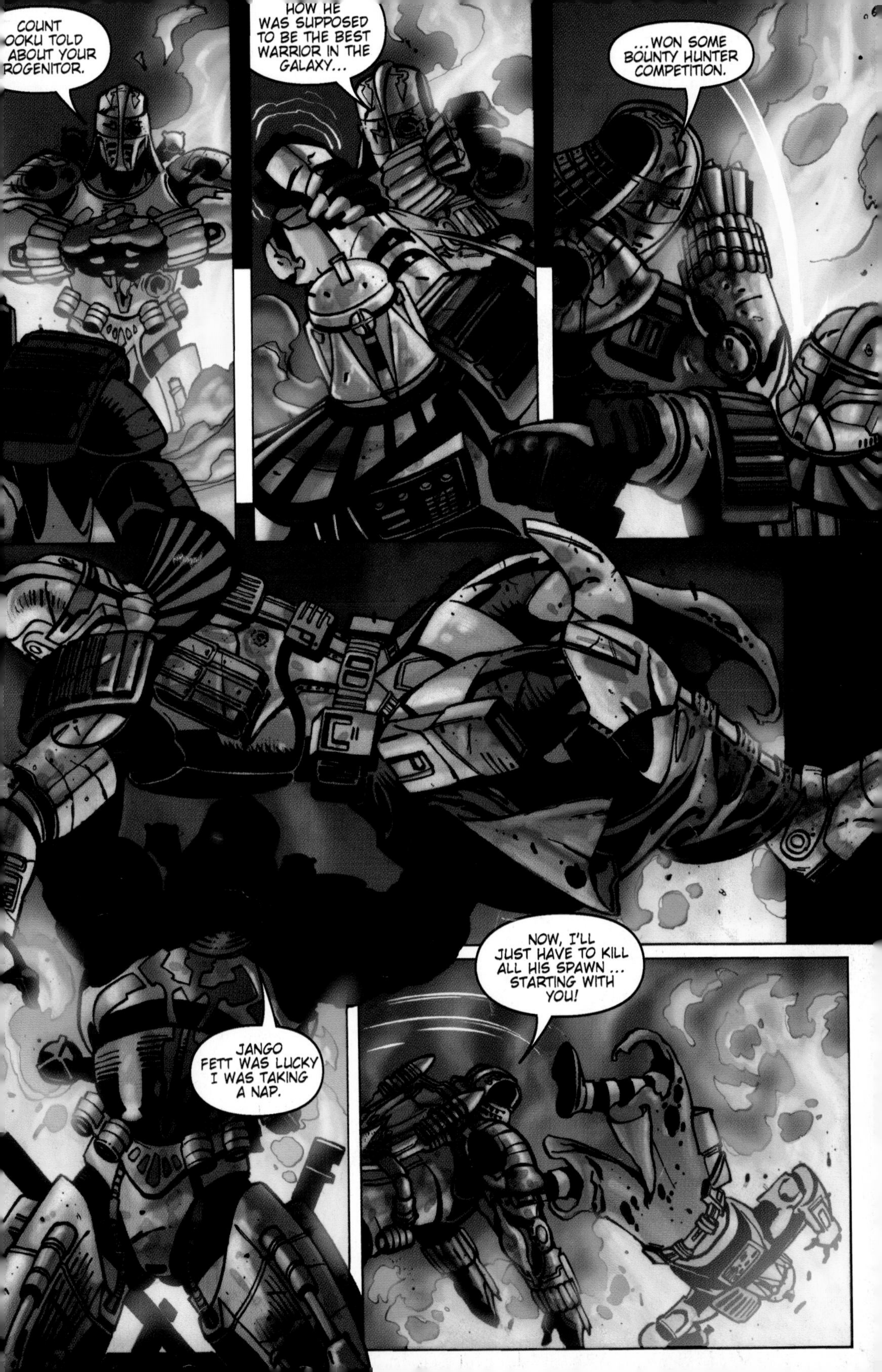
COUNT OOKU TOLD ABOUT YOUR ROGENITOR.
HOW HE WAS SUPPOSED TO BE THE BEST WARRIOR IN THE GALAXY...
...WON SOME BOUNTY HUNTER COMPETITION.
JANGO FETT WAS LUCKY I WAS TAKING A NAP.
NOW, I'LL JUST HAVE TO KILL ALL HIS SPAWN ... STARTING WITH YOU!

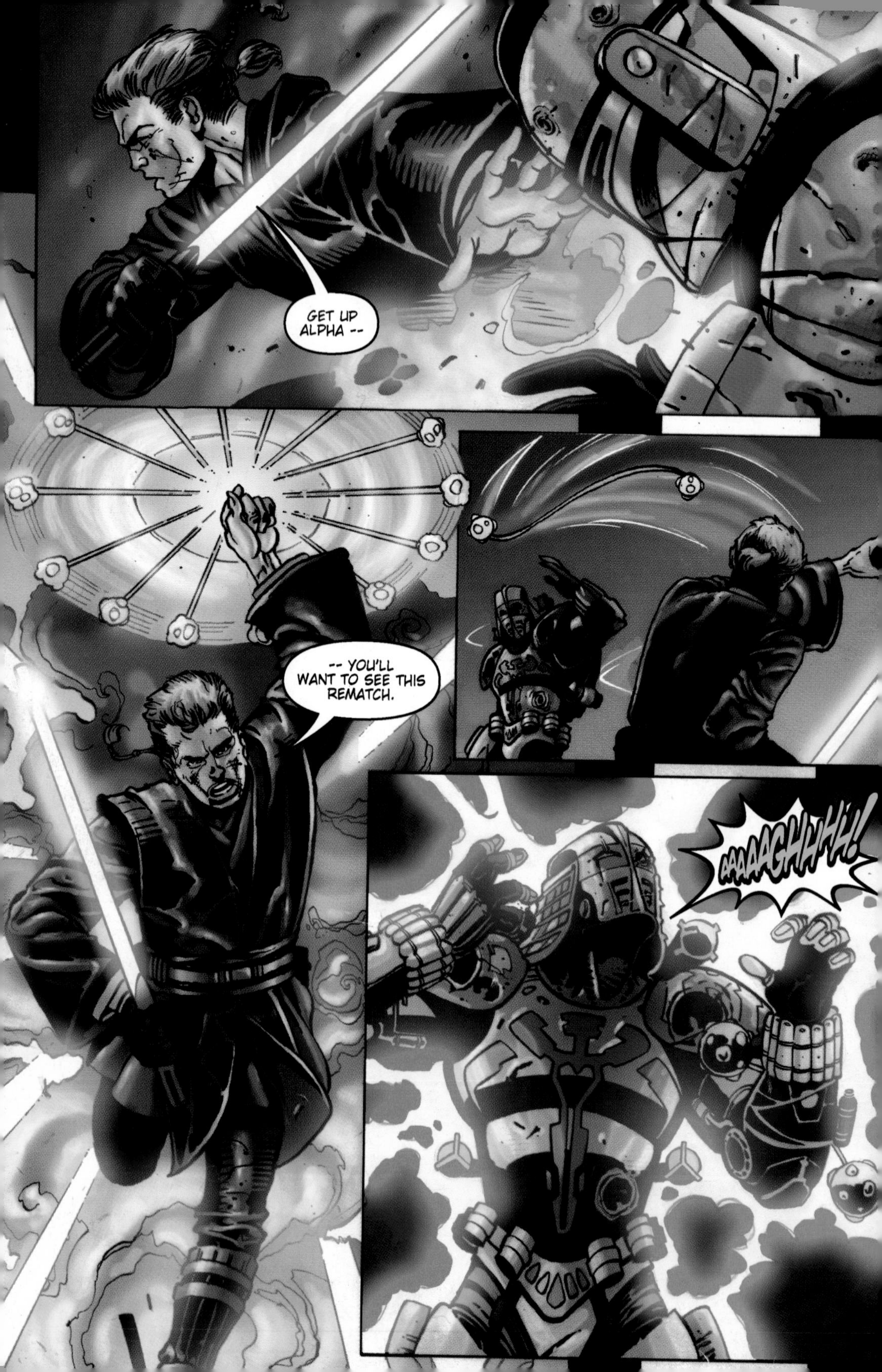
GET UP ALPHA --
-- YOU'LL WANT TO SEE THIS REMATCH.
AAAAAGHHHH!

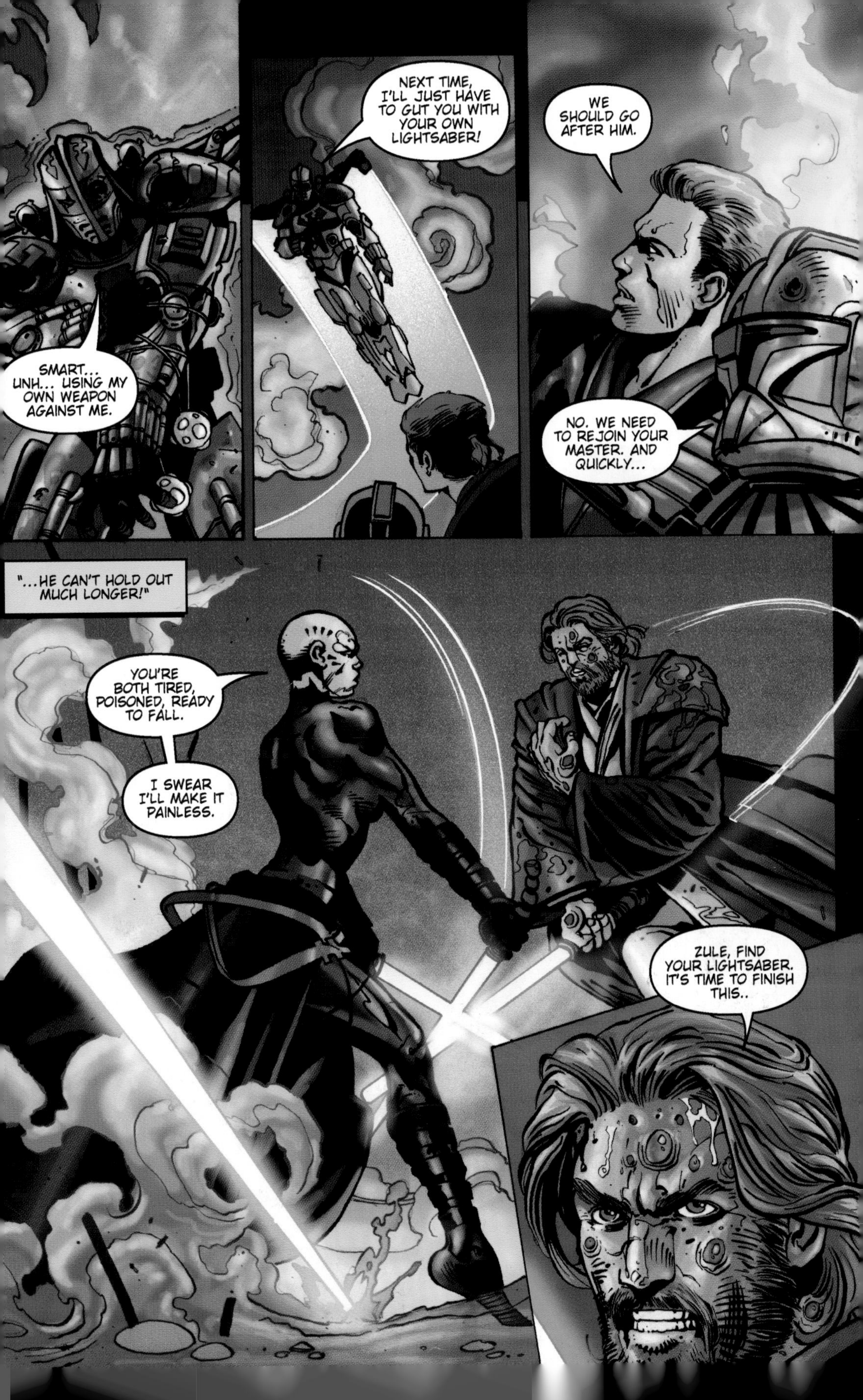

SMART... UNH... USING MY OWN WEAPON AGAINST ME.
NEXT TIME, I'LL JUST HAVE TO GUT YOU WITH YOUR OWN LIGHTSABER!
WE SHOULD GO AFTER HIM.
NO. WE NEED TO REJOIN YOUR MASTER. AND QUICKLY...
"...HE CAN'T HOLD OUT MUCH LONGER!"
YOU'RE BOTH TIRED, POISONED, READY TO FALL.
I SWEAR I'LL MAKE IT PAINLESS.
ZULE, FIND YOUR LIGHTSABER. IT'S TIME TO FINISH THIS..

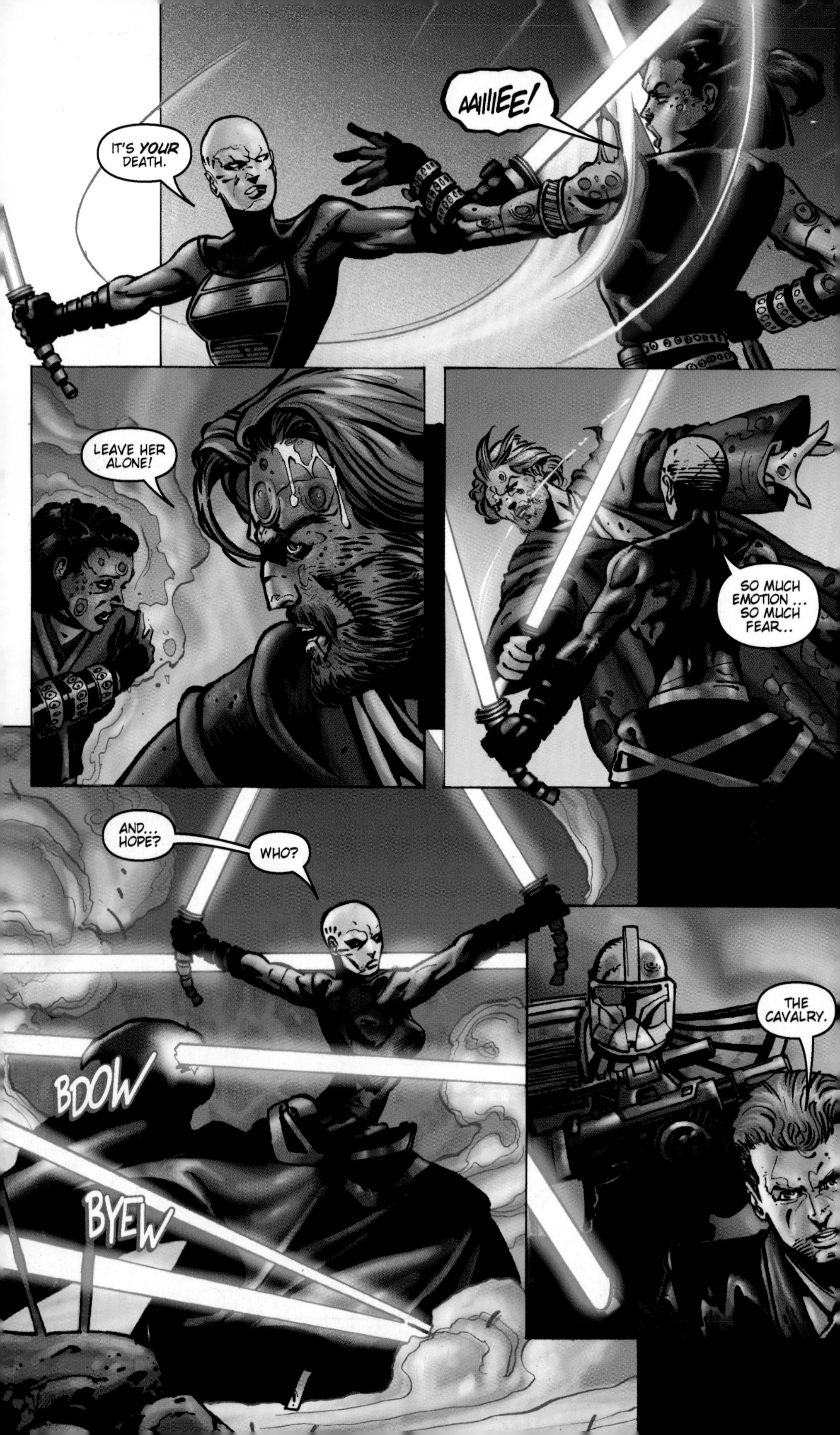
IT'S YOUR DEATH.
AAIIIIEE!
LEAVE HER ALONE!
SO MUCH EMOTION... SO MUCH FEAR...
AND... HOPE?
WHO?
BDOW
BYEW
THE CAVALRY.

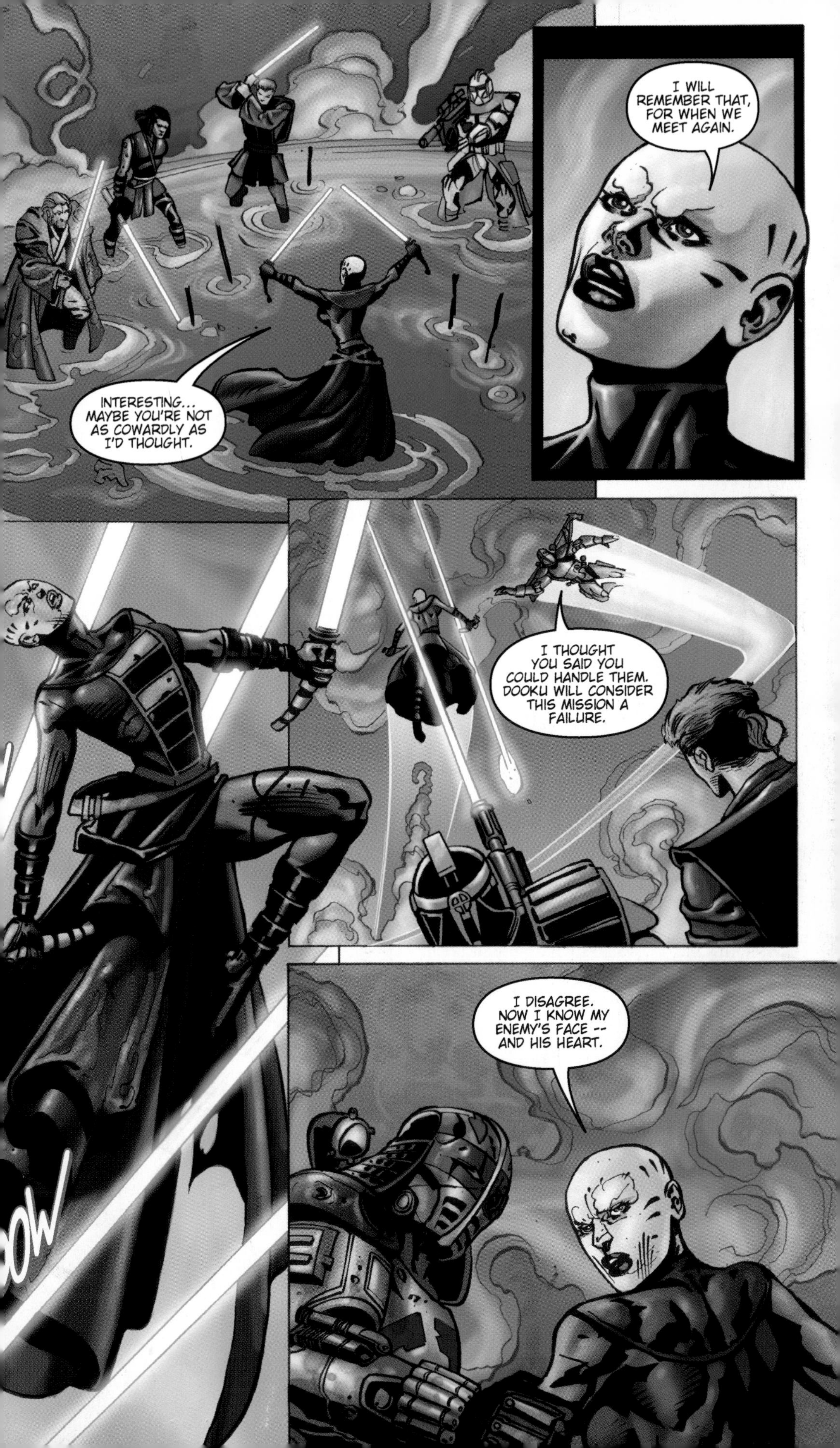
INTERESTING... MAYBE YOU'RE NOT AS COWARDLY AS I'D THOUGHT.
I WILL REMEMBER THAT, FOR WHEN WE MEET AGAIN.
I THOUGHT YOU SAID YOU COULD HANDLE THEM. DOOKU WILL CONSIDER THIS MISSION A FAILURE.
I DISAGREE. NOW I KNOW MY ENEMY'S FACE -- AND HIS HEART.

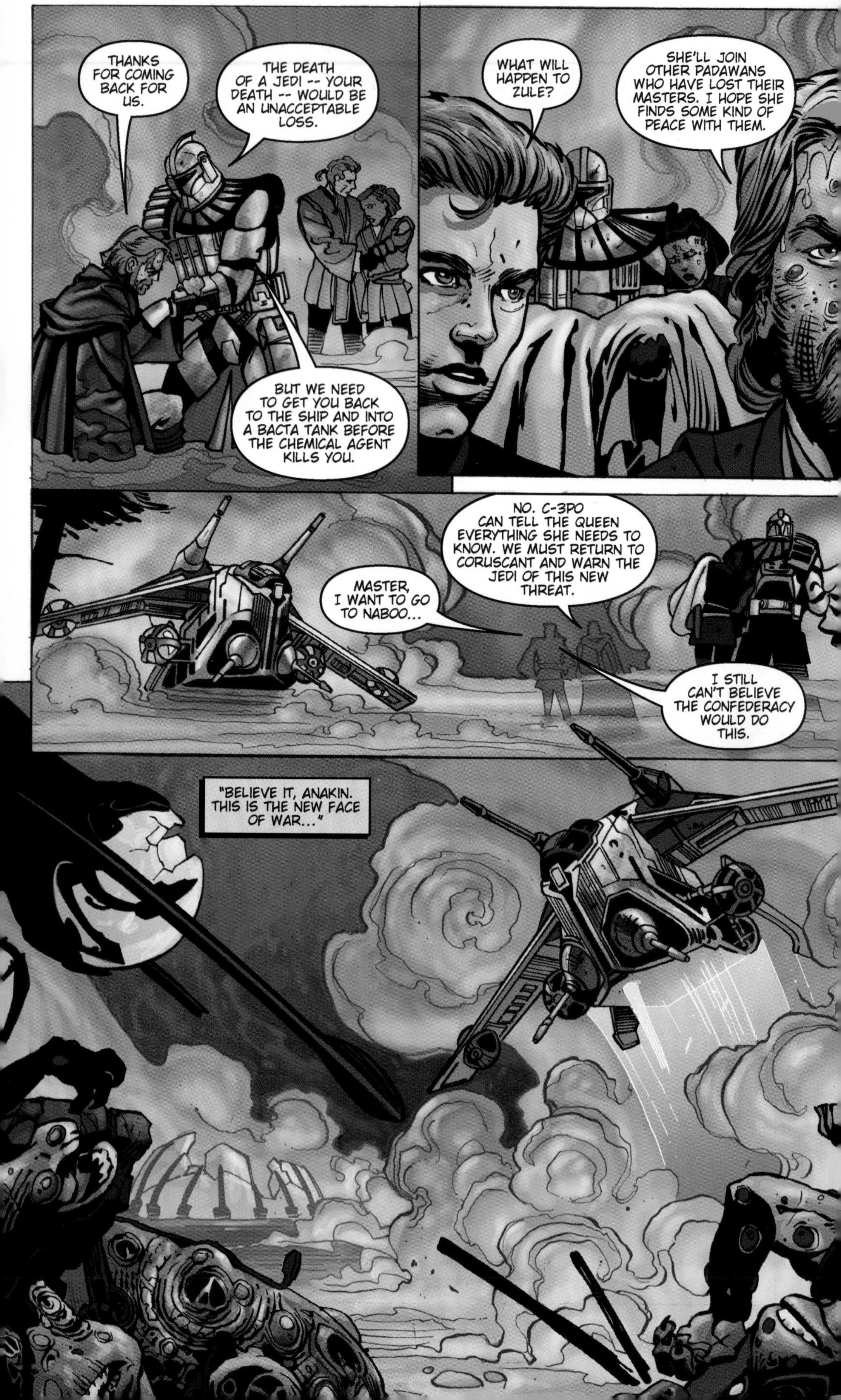
THANKS FOR COMING BACK FOR US.
THE DEATH OF A JEDI -- YOUR DEATH -- WOULD BE AN UNACCEPTABLE LOSS.
BUT WE NEED TO GET YOU BACK TO THE SHIP AND INTO A BACTA TANK BEFORE THE CHEMICAL AGENT KILLS YOU.
WHAT WILL HAPPEN TO ZULE?
SHE'LL JOIN OTHER PADAWANS WHO HAVE LOST THEIR MASTERS. I HOPE SHE FINDS SOME KIND OF PEACE WITH THEM.
MASTER, I WANT TO GO TO NABOO...
NO. C-3PO CAN TELL THE QUEEN EVERYTHING SHE NEEDS TO KNOW. WE MUST RETURN TO CORUSCANT AND WARN THE JEDI OF THIS NEW THREAT.
I STILL CAN'T BELIEVE THE CONFEDERACY WOULD DO THIS.
"BELIEVE IT, ANAKIN. THIS IS THE NEW FACE OF WAR..."

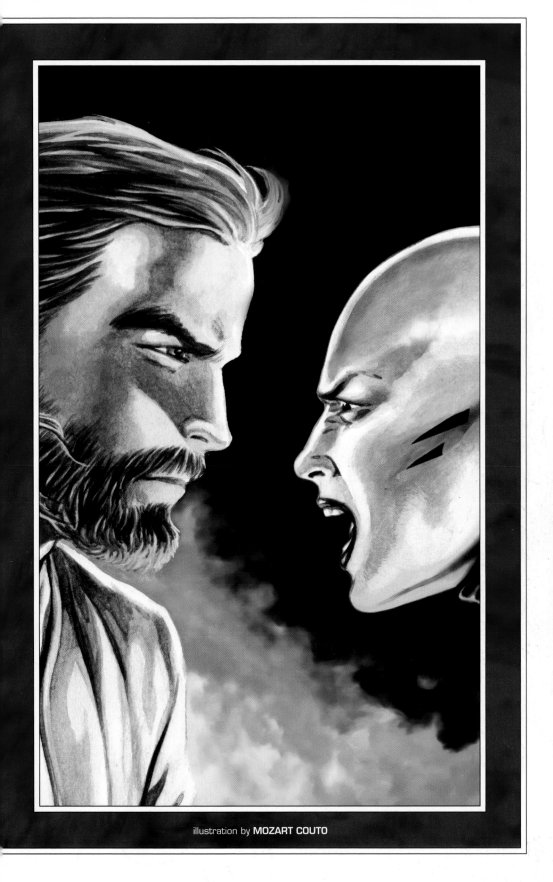

illustration by **MOZART COUTO**

BLAST RADIUS

APPROXIMATELY FOUR MONTHS
AFTER THE BATTLE OF GEONOSIS...

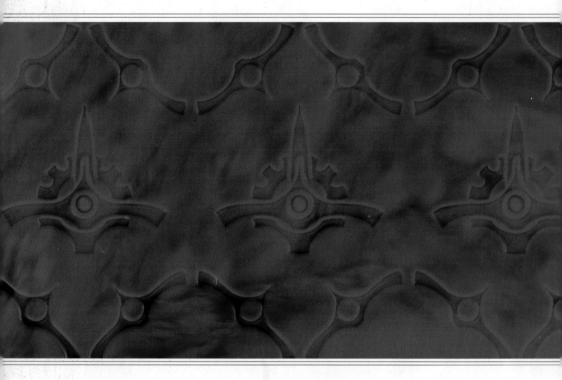

"Blast Radius"
written by **Haden Blackman**
pencilled by **Brian Ching**
inks by **Joe Weems**

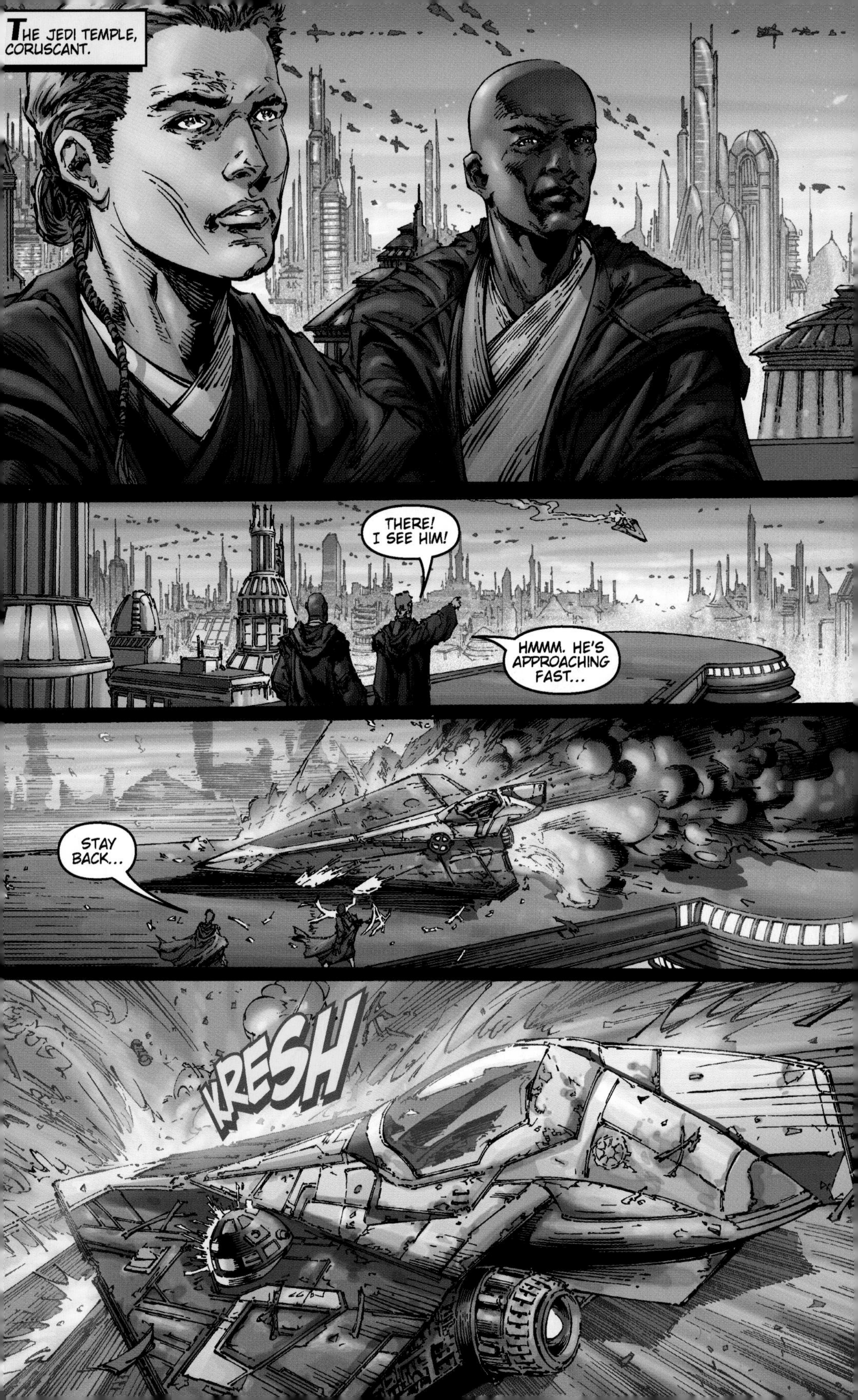
THE JEDI TEMPLE, CORUSCANT.
THERE! I SEE HIM!
HMMM. HE'S APPROACHING FAST...
STAY BACK...
KRESH

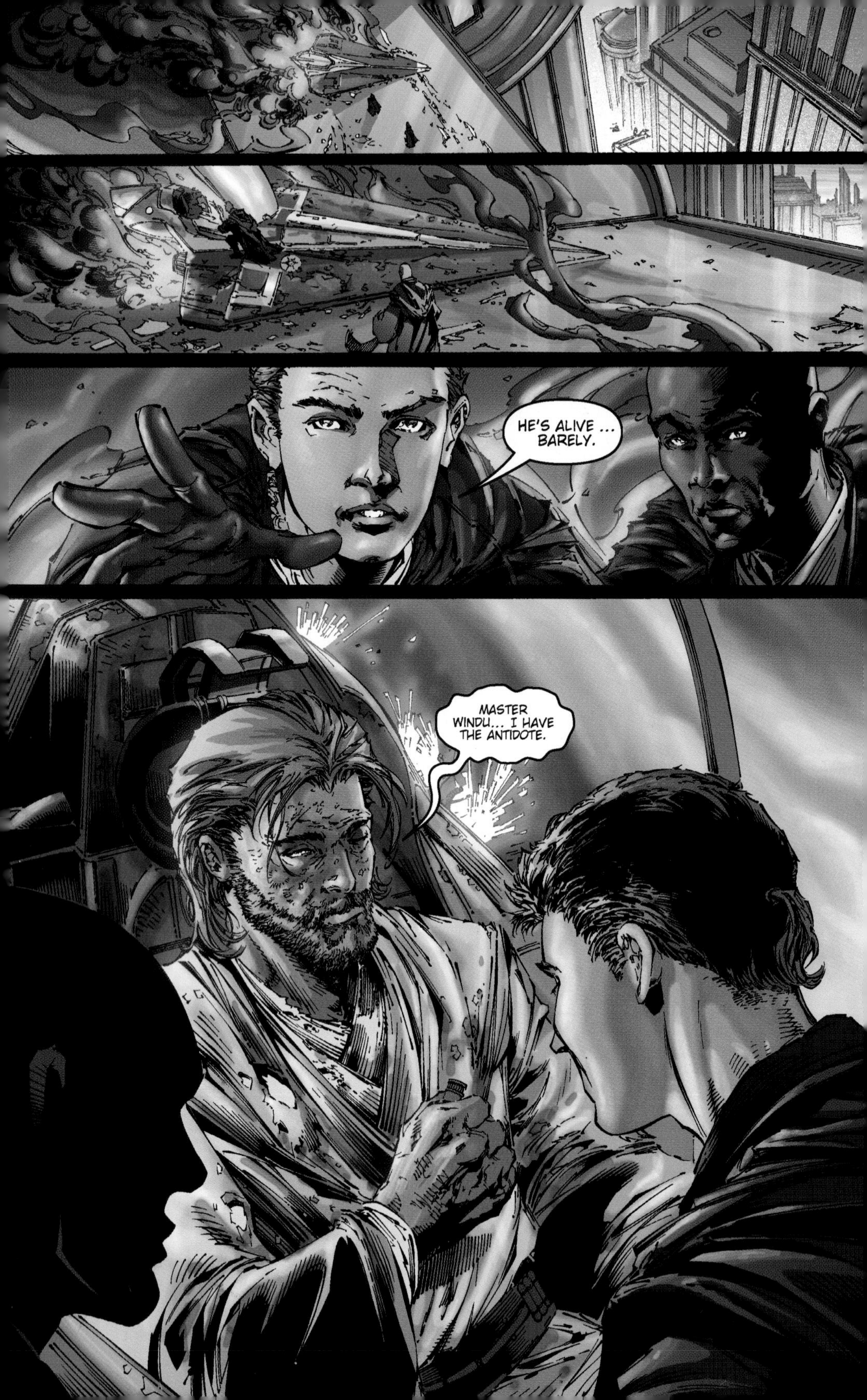
HE'S ALIVE ... BARELY.
MASTER WINDU... I HAVE THE ANTIDOTE.

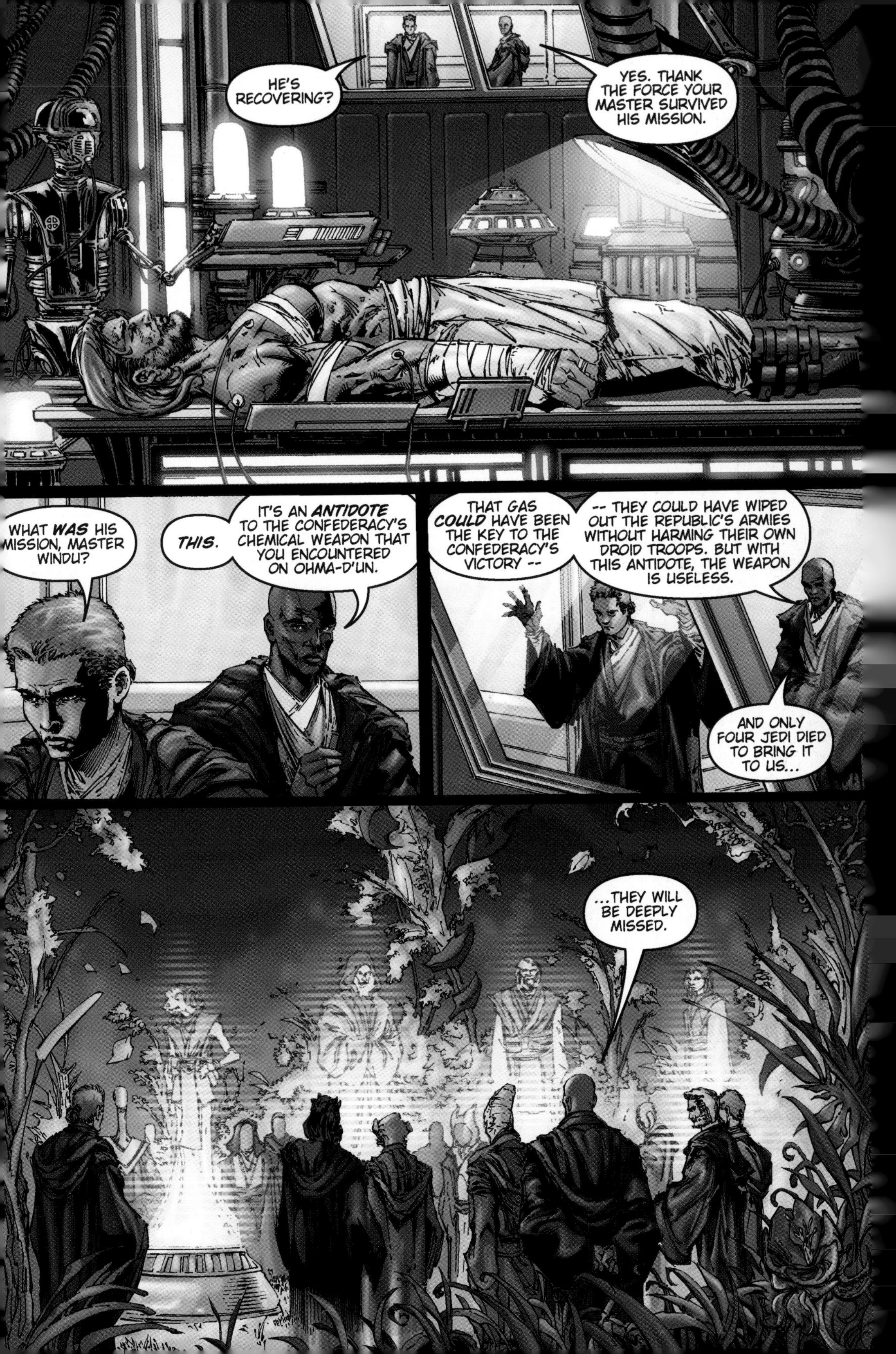

HE'S RECOVERING?
YES. THANK THE FORCE YOUR MASTER SURVIVED HIS MISSION.
WHAT WAS HIS MISSION, MASTER WINDU?
THIS.
IT'S AN ANTIDOTE TO THE CONFEDERACY'S CHEMICAL WEAPON THAT YOU ENCOUNTERED ON OHMA-D'UN.
THAT GAS COULD HAVE BEEN THE KEY TO THE CONFEDERACY'S VICTORY --
-- THEY COULD HAVE WIPED OUT THE REPUBLIC'S ARMIES WITHOUT HARMING THEIR OWN DROID TROOPS. BUT WITH THIS ANTIDOTE, THE WEAPON IS USELESS.
AND ONLY FOUR JEDI DIED TO BRING IT TO US...
...THEY WILL BE DEEPLY MISSED.

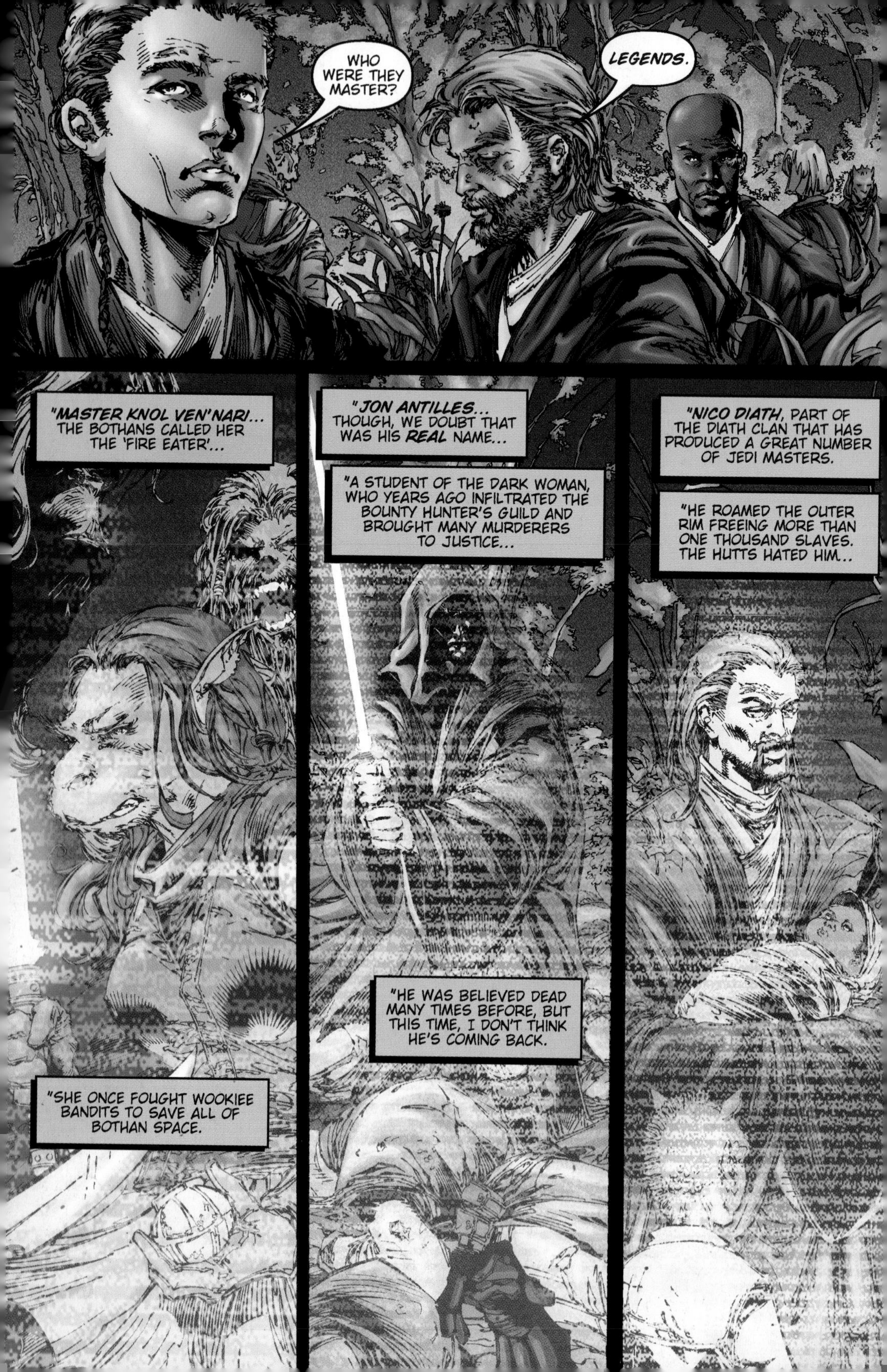
WHO WERE THEY MASTER?
LEGENDS.
"MASTER KNOL VEN'NARI... THE BOTHANS CALLED HER THE 'FIRE EATER'...
"SHE ONCE FOUGHT WOOKIEE BANDITS TO SAVE ALL OF BOTHAN SPACE.
"JON ANTILLES... THOUGH, WE DOUBT THAT WAS HIS REAL NAME...
"A STUDENT OF THE DARK WOMAN, WHO YEARS AGO INFILTRATED THE BOUNTY HUNTER'S GUILD AND BROUGHT MANY MURDERERS TO JUSTICE...
"HE WAS BELIEVED DEAD MANY TIMES BEFORE, BUT THIS TIME, I DON'T THINK HE'S COMING BACK.
"NICO DIATH, PART OF THE DIATH CLAN THAT HAS PRODUCED A GREAT NUMBER OF JEDI MASTERS.
"HE ROAMED THE OUTER RIM FREEING MORE THAN ONE THOUSAND SLAVES. THE HUTTS HATED HIM...

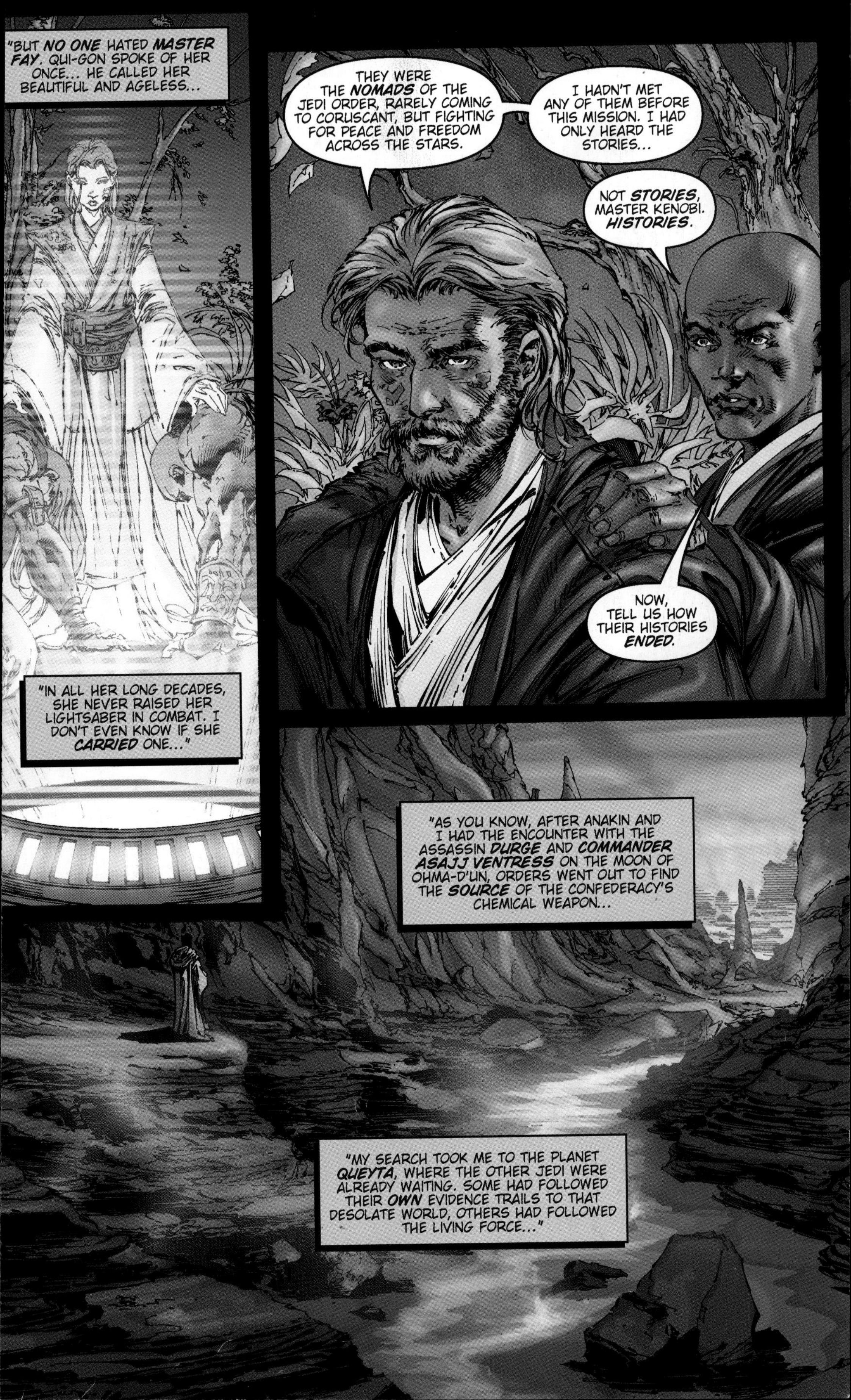
"BUT NO ONE HATED MASTER FAY. QUI-GON SPOKE OF HER ONCE... HE CALLED HER BEAUTIFUL AND AGELESS...
"IN ALL HER LONG DECADES, SHE NEVER RAISED HER LIGHTSABER IN COMBAT. I DON'T EVEN KNOW IF SHE CARRIED ONE..."
THEY WERE THE NOMADS OF THE JEDI ORDER, RARELY COMING TO CORUSCANT, BUT FIGHTING FOR PEACE AND FREEDOM ACROSS THE STARS.
I HADN'T MET ANY OF THEM BEFORE THIS MISSION. I HAD ONLY HEARD THE STORIES...
NOT STORIES, MASTER KENOBI. HISTORIES.
NOW, TELL US HOW THEIR HISTORIES ENDED.
"AS YOU KNOW, AFTER ANAKIN AND I HAD THE ENCOUNTER WITH THE ASSASSIN DURGE AND COMMANDER ASAJJ VENTRESS ON THE MOON OF OHMA-D'UN, ORDERS WENT OUT TO FIND THE SOURCE OF THE CONFEDERACY'S CHEMICAL WEAPON...
"MY SEARCH TOOK ME TO THE PLANET QUEYTA, WHERE THE OTHER JEDI WERE ALREADY WAITING. SOME HAD FOLLOWED THEIR OWN EVIDENCE TRAILS TO THAT DESOLATE WORLD, OTHERS HAD FOLLOWED THE LIVING FORCE..."

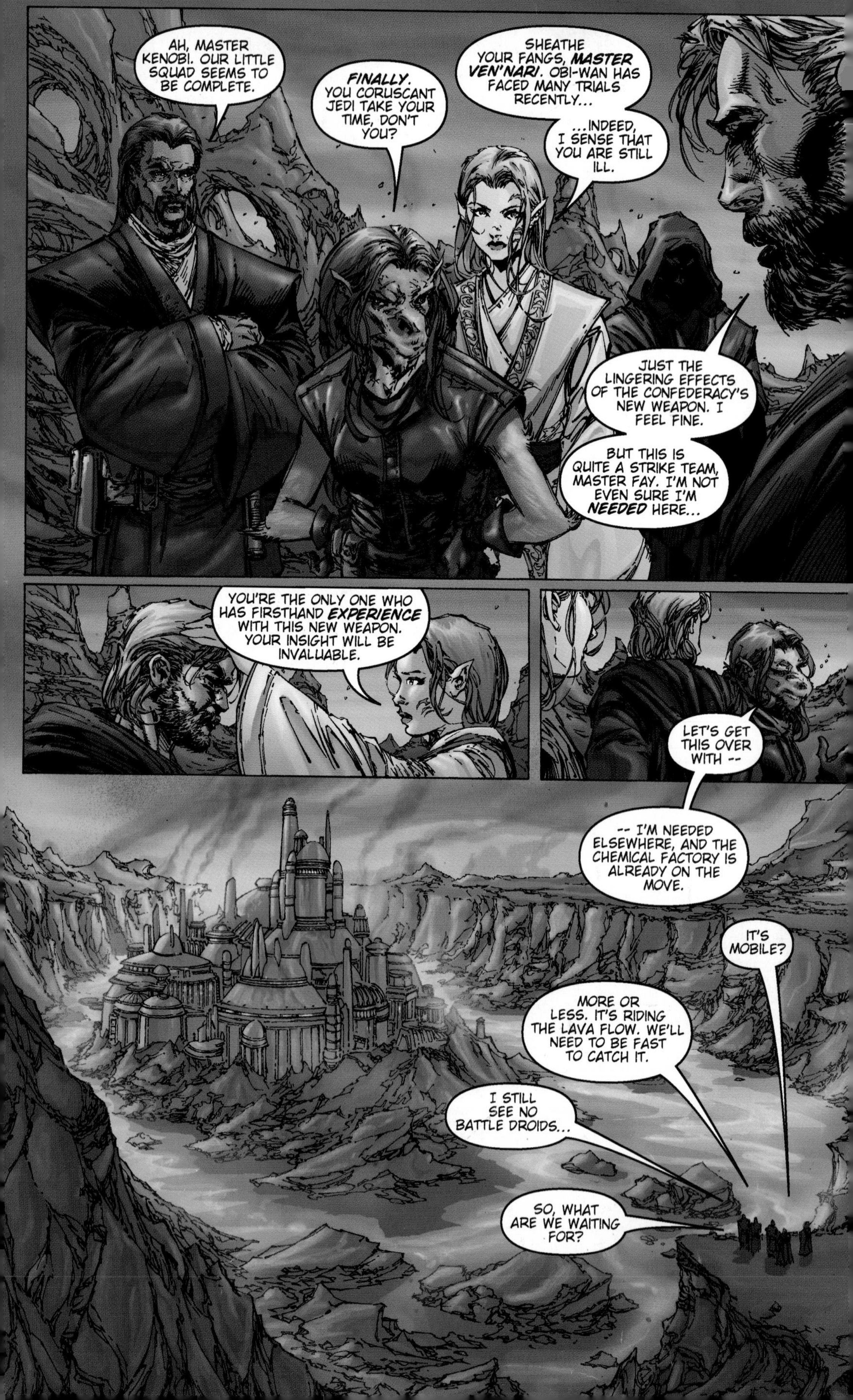
AH, MASTER KENOBI. OUR LITTLE SQUAD SEEMS TO BE COMPLETE.
FINALLY. YOU CORUSCANT JEDI TAKE YOUR TIME, DON'T YOU?
SHEATHE YOUR FANGS, MASTER VEN'NARI. OBI-WAN HAS FACED MANY TRIALS RECENTLY...
...INDEED, I SENSE THAT YOU ARE STILL ILL.
JUST THE LINGERING EFFECTS OF THE CONFEDERACY'S NEW WEAPON. I FEEL FINE.
BUT THIS IS QUITE A STRIKE TEAM, MASTER FAY. I'M NOT EVEN SURE I'M NEEDED HERE...
YOU'RE THE ONLY ONE WHO HAS FIRSTHAND EXPERIENCE WITH THIS NEW WEAPON. YOUR INSIGHT WILL BE INVALUABLE.
LET'S GET THIS OVER WITH --
-- I'M NEEDED ELSEWHERE, AND THE CHEMICAL FACTORY IS ALREADY ON THE MOVE.
IT'S MOBILE?
MORE OR LESS. IT'S RIDING THE LAVA FLOW. WE'LL NEED TO BE FAST TO CATCH IT.
I STILL SEE NO BATTLE DROIDS...
SO, WHAT ARE WE WAITING FOR?

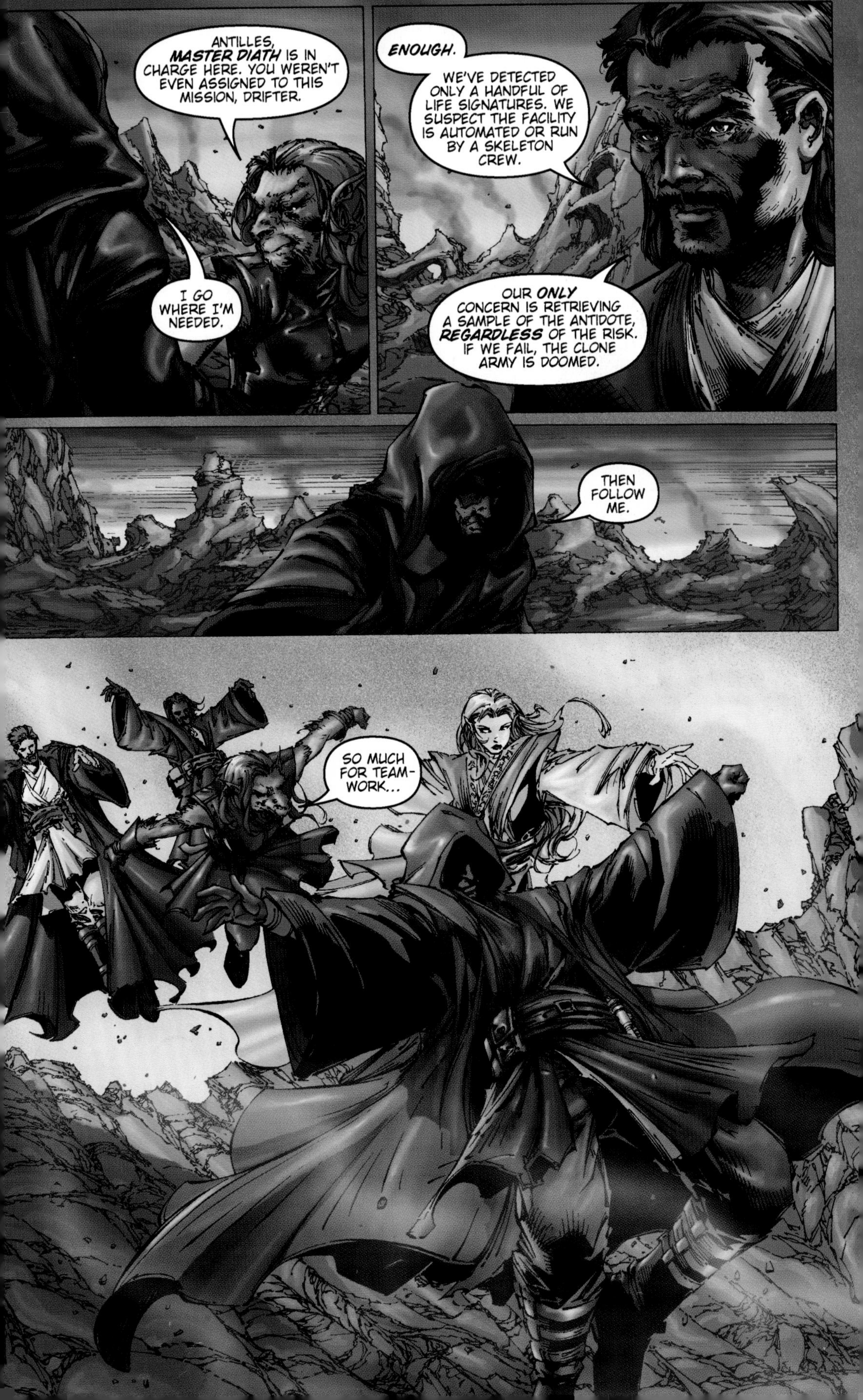
ANTILLES, MASTER DIATH IS IN CHARGE HERE. YOU WEREN'T EVEN ASSIGNED TO THIS MISSION, DRIFTER.
I GO WHERE I'M NEEDED.
ENOUGH.
WE'VE DETECTED ONLY A HANDFUL OF LIFE SIGNATURES. WE SUSPECT THE FACILITY IS AUTOMATED OR RUN BY A SKELETON CREW.
OUR ONLY CONCERN IS RETRIEVING A SAMPLE OF THE ANTIDOTE, REGARDLESS OF THE RISK. IF WE FAIL, THE CLONE ARMY IS DOOMED.
THEN FOLLOW ME.
SO MUCH FOR TEAM-WORK...

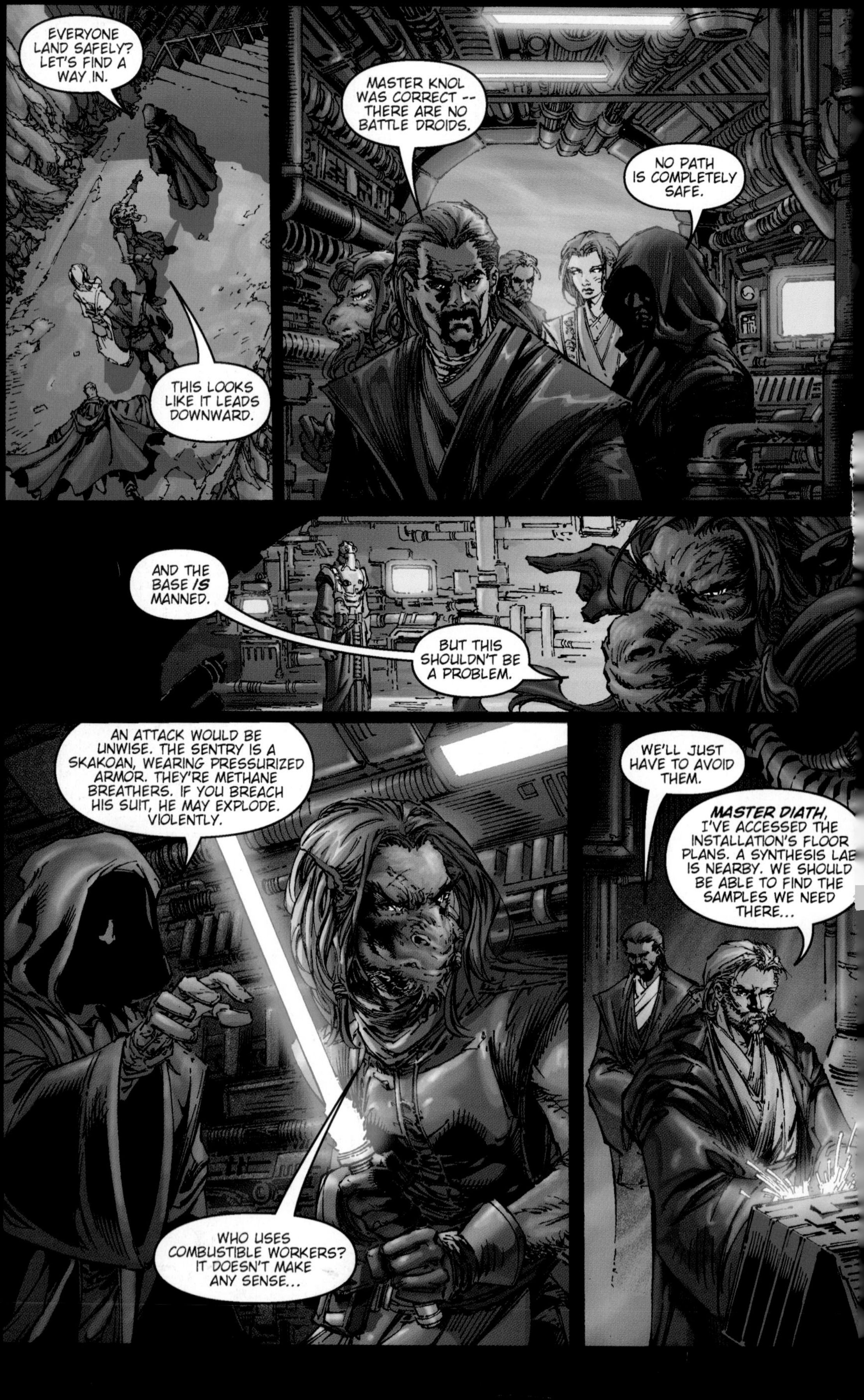
EVERYONE LAND SAFELY? LET'S FIND A WAY IN.
THIS LOOKS LIKE IT LEADS DOWNWARD.
MASTER KNOL WAS CORRECT -- THERE ARE NO BATTLE DROIDS.
NO PATH IS COMPLETELY SAFE.
AND THE BASE *IS* MANNED.
BUT THIS SHOULDN'T BE A PROBLEM.
AN ATTACK WOULD BE UNWISE. THE SENTRY IS A SKAKOAN, WEARING PRESSURIZED ARMOR. THEY'RE METHANE BREATHERS. IF YOU BREACH HIS SUIT, HE MAY EXPLODE. VIOLENTLY.
WHO USES COMBUSTIBLE WORKERS? IT DOESN'T MAKE ANY SENSE...
WE'LL JUST HAVE TO AVOID THEM.
MASTER DIATH, I'VE ACCESSED THE INSTALLATION'S FLOOR PLANS. A SYNTHESIS LAB IS NEARBY. WE SHOULD BE ABLE TO FIND THE SAMPLES WE NEED THERE...

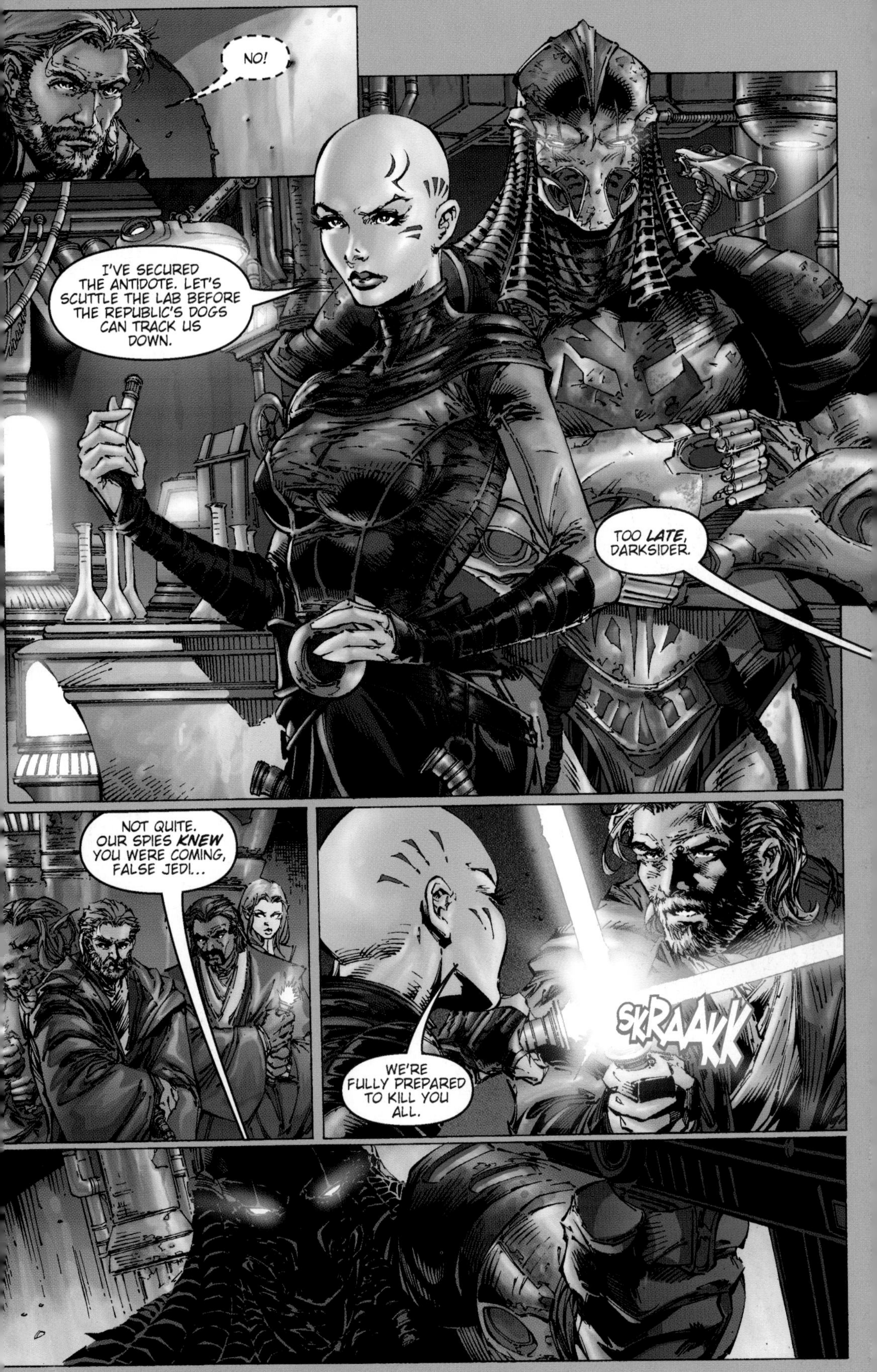
NO!
I'VE SECURED THE ANTIDOTE. LET'S SCUTTLE THE LAB BEFORE THE REPUBLIC'S DOGS CAN TRACK US DOWN.
TOO *LATE*, DARKSIDER.
NOT QUITE. OUR SPIES *KNEW* YOU WERE COMING, FALSE JEDI...
WE'RE FULLY PREPARED TO KILL YOU ALL.
SKRAAKK

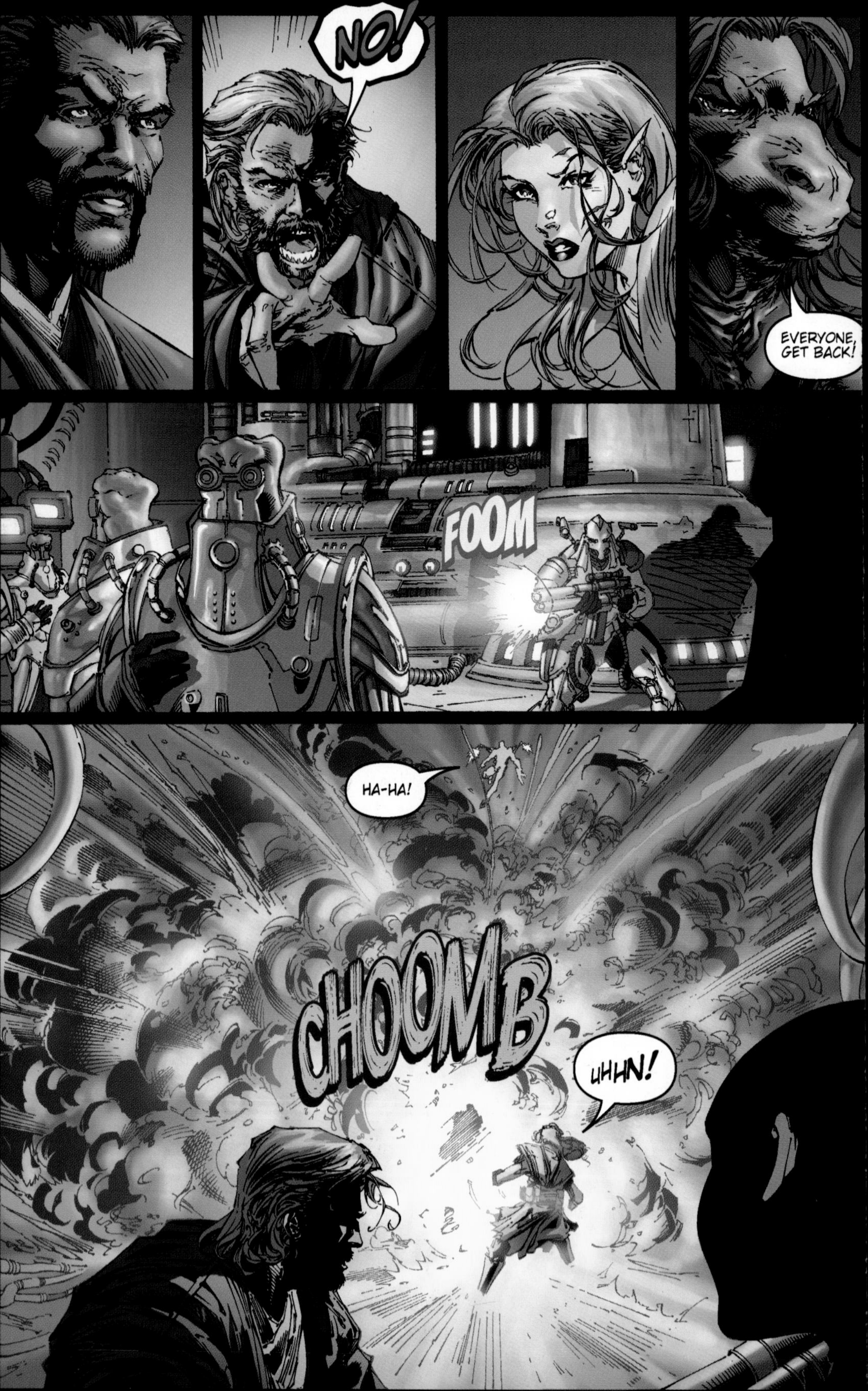
NO!
EVERYONE, GET BACK!
FOOM
HA-HA!
CHOOMB
UHHN!

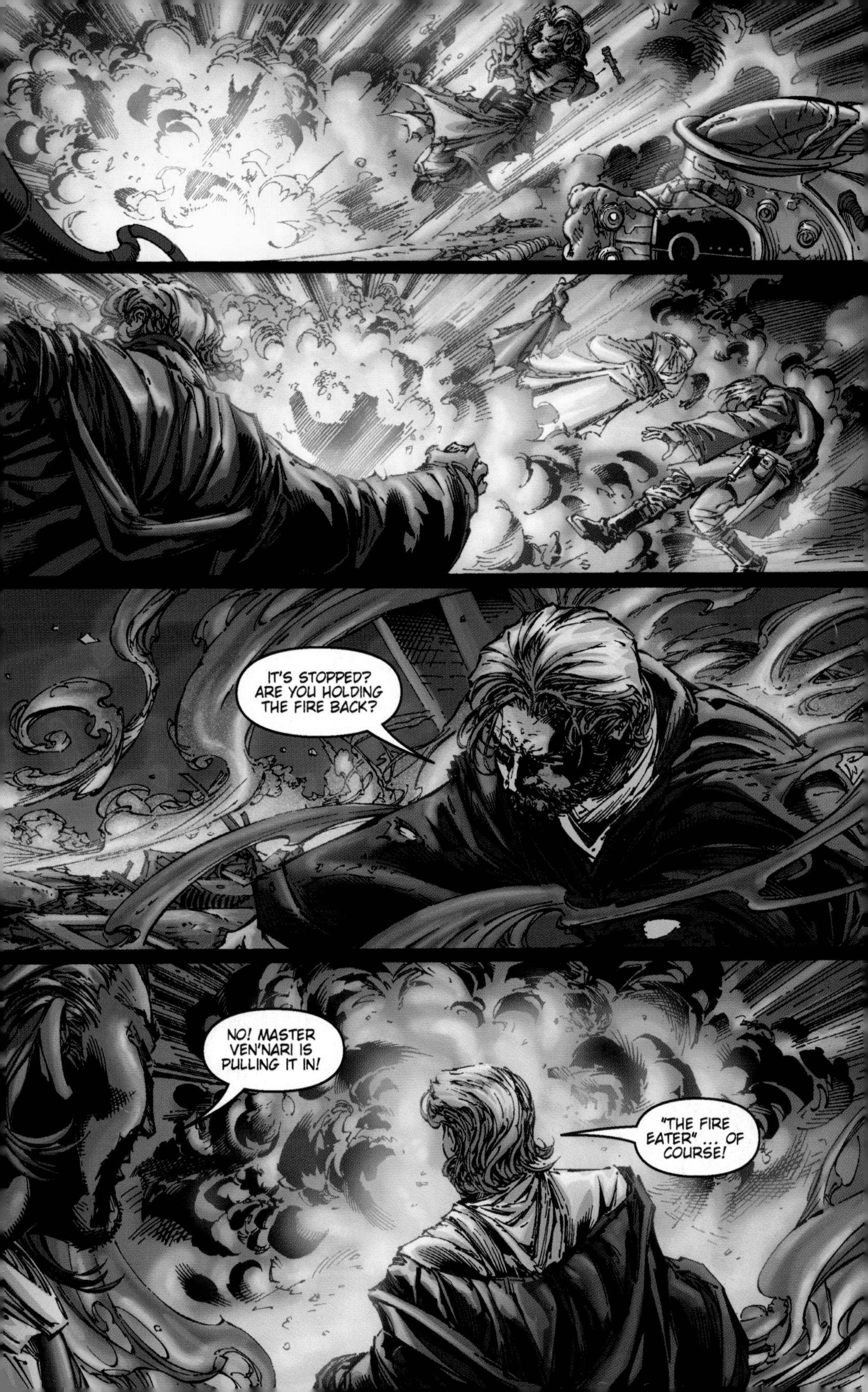

IT'S STOPPED? ARE YOU HOLDING THE FIRE BACK?
NO! MASTER VEN'NARI IS PULLING IT IN!
"THE FIRE EATER"... OF COURSE!

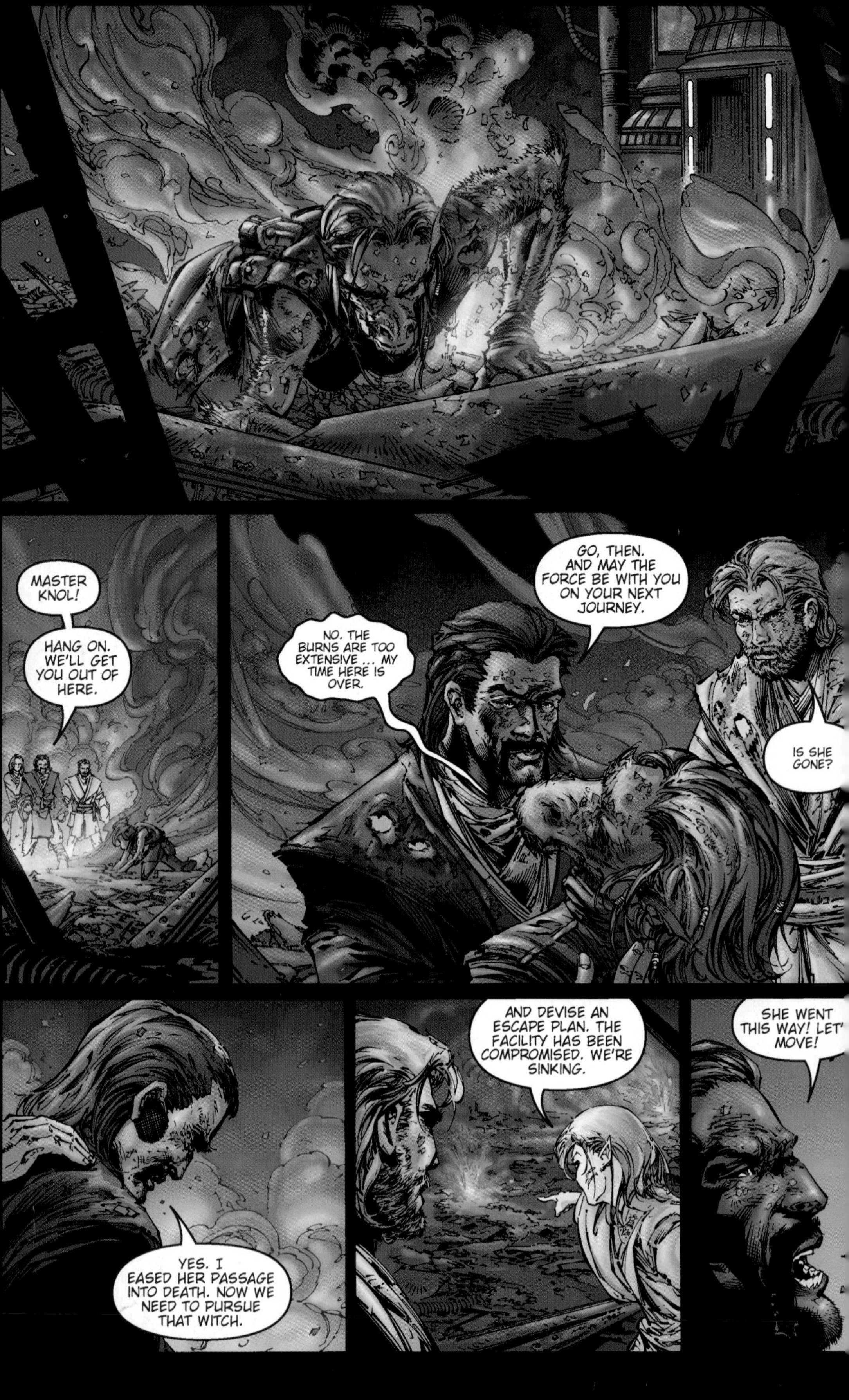
MASTER KNOL!
HANG ON. WE'LL GET YOU OUT OF HERE.
NO. THE BURNS ARE TOO EXTENSIVE ... MY TIME HERE IS OVER.
GO, THEN. AND MAY THE FORCE BE WITH YOU ON YOUR NEXT JOURNEY.
IS SHE GONE?
YES. I EASED HER PASSAGE INTO DEATH. NOW WE NEED TO PURSUE THAT WITCH.
AND DEVISE AN ESCAPE PLAN. THE FACILITY HAS BEEN COMPROMISED. WE'RE SINKING.
SHE WENT THIS WAY! LET'
MOVE!

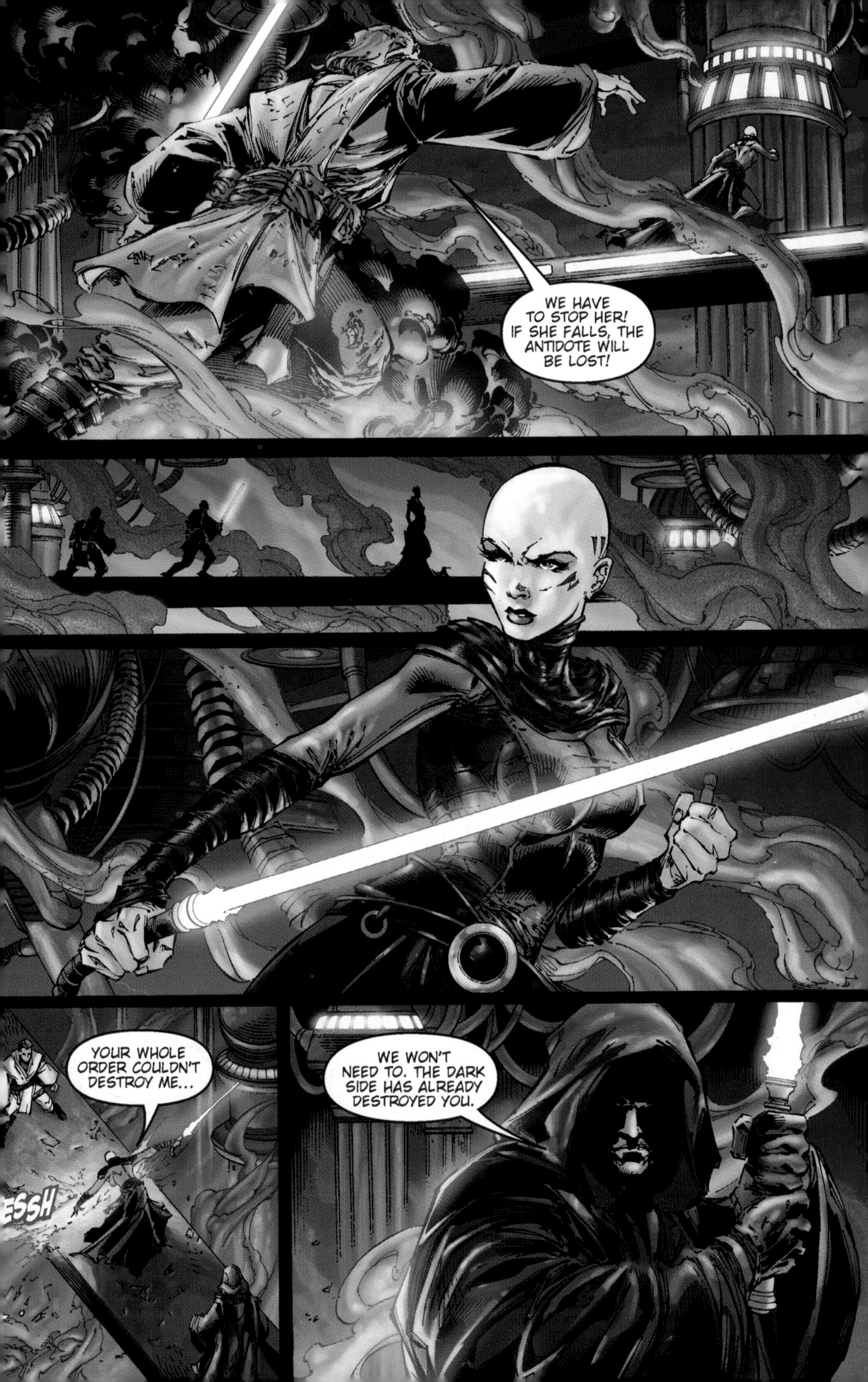

WE HAVE TO STOP HER! IF SHE FALLS, THE ANTIDOTE WILL BE LOST!
YOUR WHOLE ORDER COULDN'T DESTROY ME...
ESSH
WE WON'T NEED TO. THE DARK SIDE HAS ALREADY DESTROYED YOU.

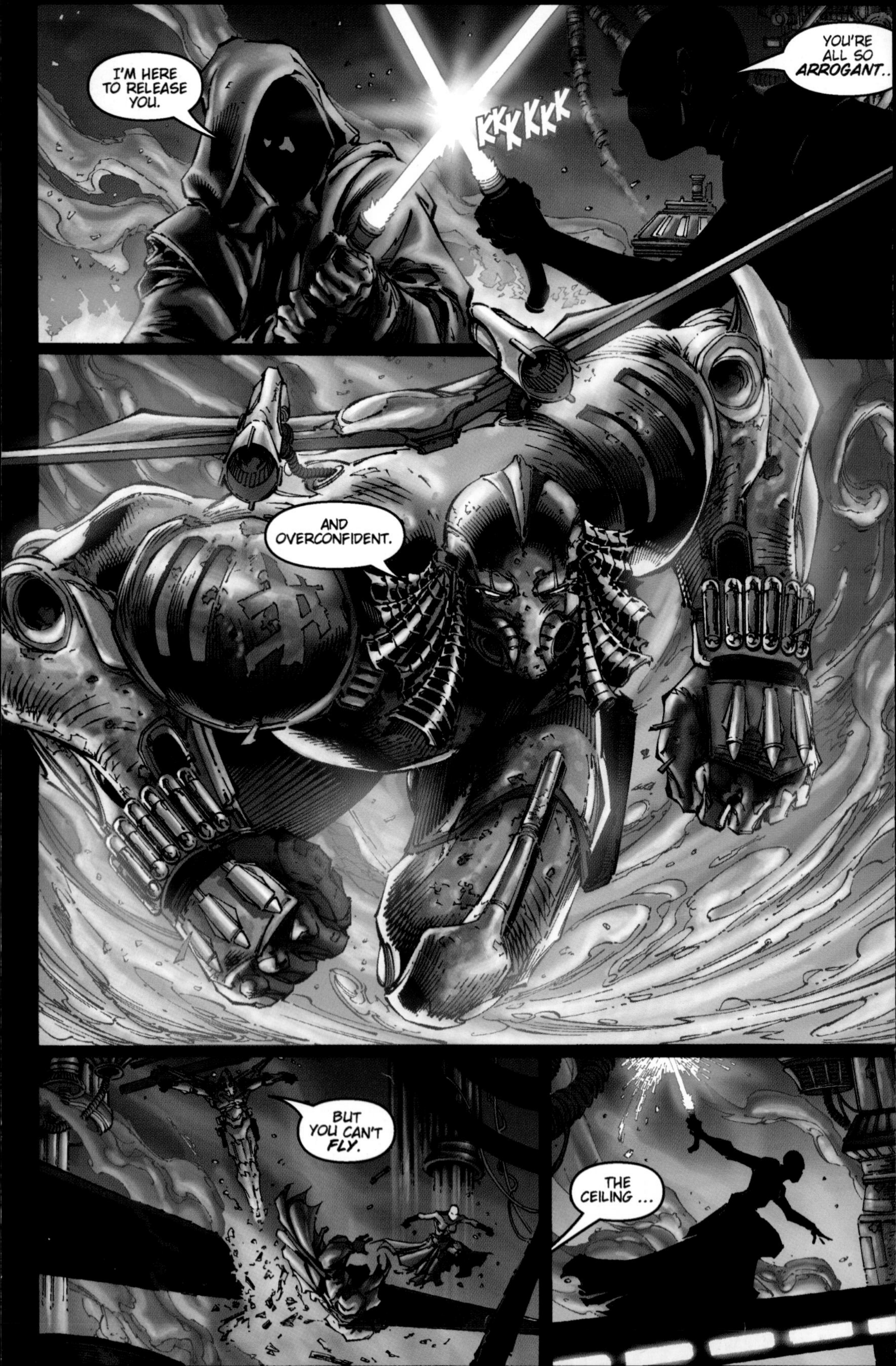
I'M HERE TO RELEASE YOU.
KKKKKK
YOU'RE ALL SO ARROGANT..
AND OVERCONFIDENT.
BUT YOU CAN'T FLY.
THE CEILING ...

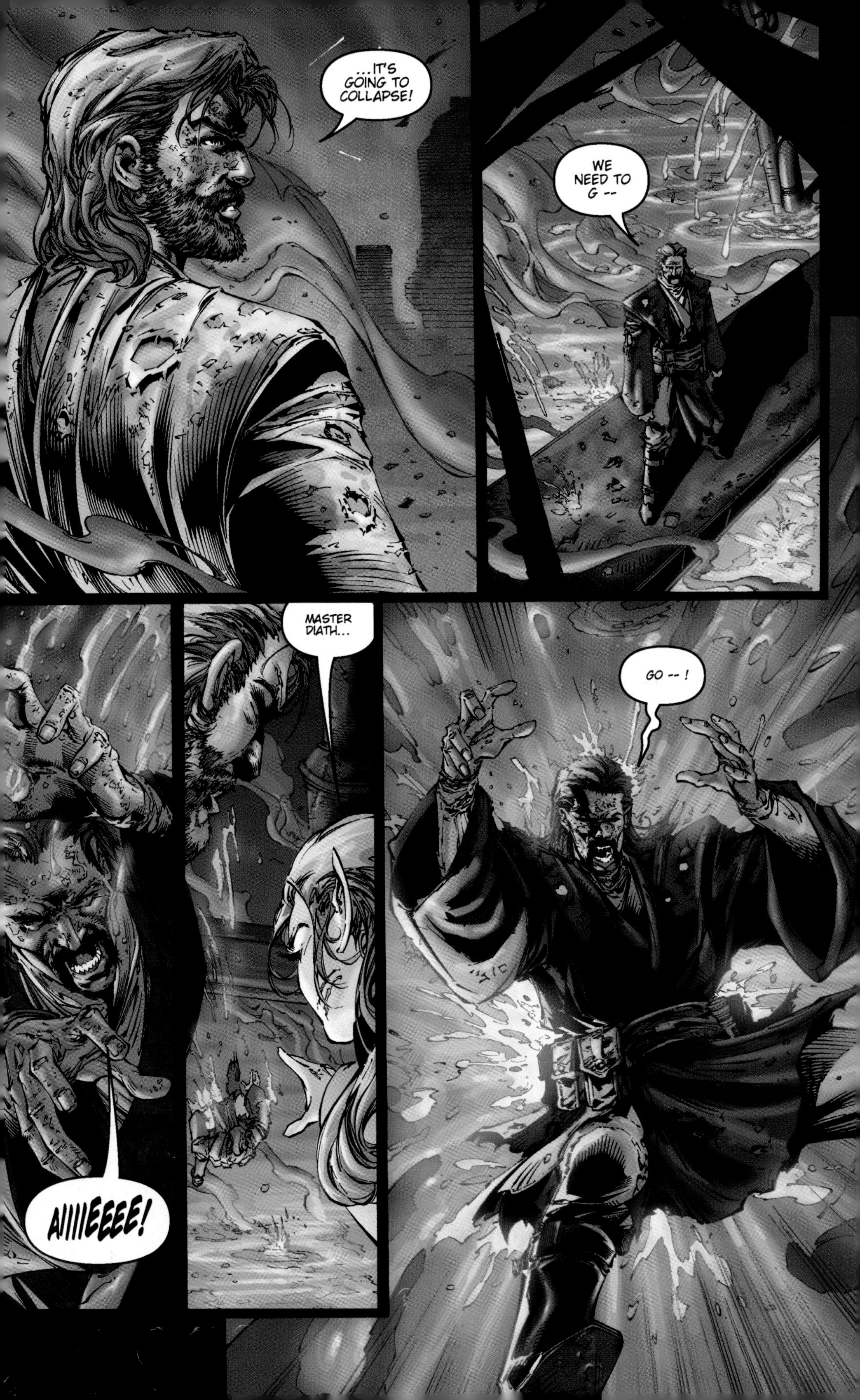
...IT'S GOING TO COLLAPSE!
WE NEED TO G --
MASTER DIATH...
AIIIIEEEE!
GO -- !

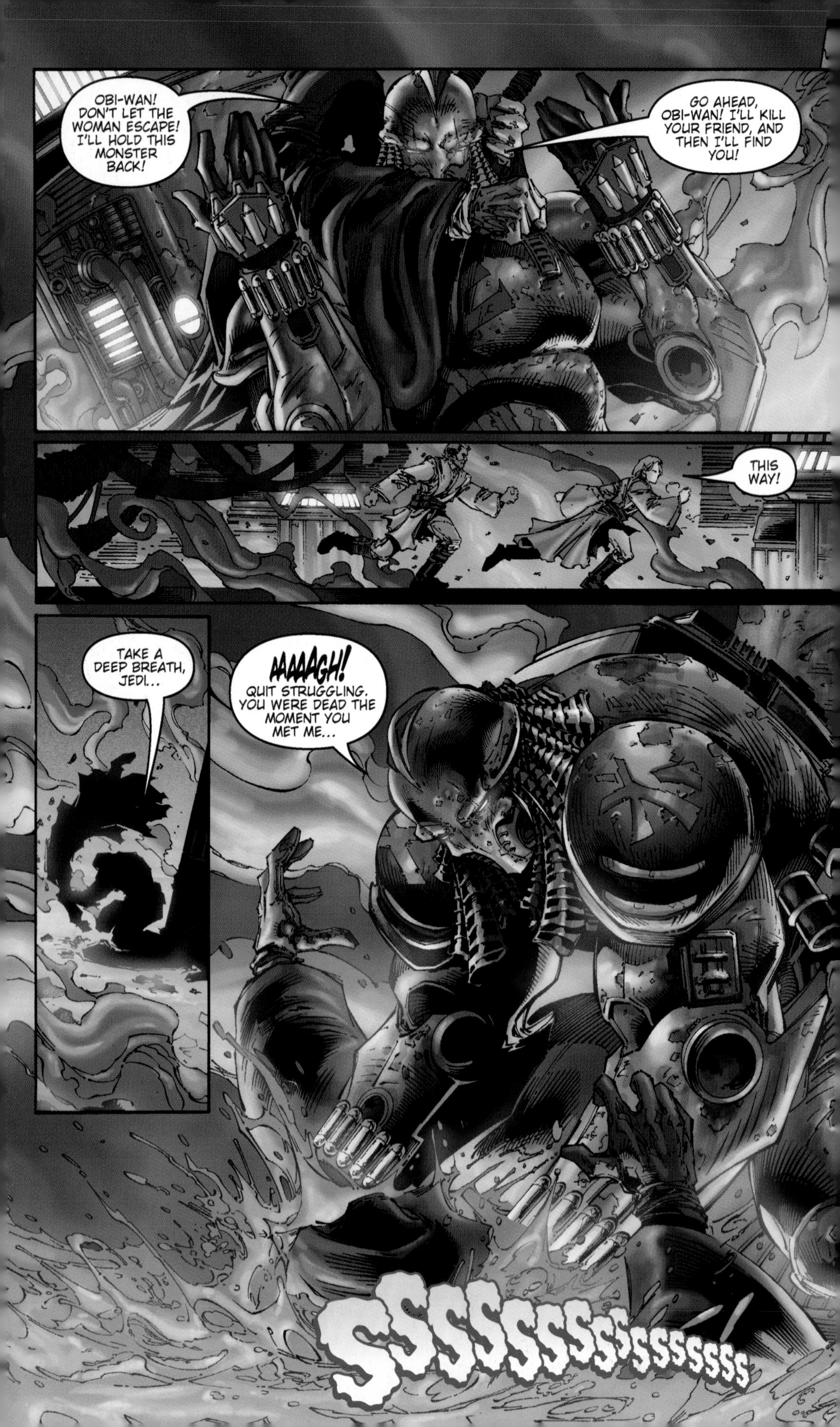
OBI-WAN! DON'T LET THE WOMAN ESCAPE! I'LL HOLD THIS MONSTER BACK!
GO AHEAD, OBI-WAN! I'LL KILL YOUR FRIEND, AND THEN I'LL FIND YOU!
THIS WAY!
TAKE A DEEP BREATH, JEDI...
AAAAAGH!
QUIT STRUGGLING. YOU WERE DEAD THE MOMENT YOU MET ME...
SSSSSSSSSSSSSSSS

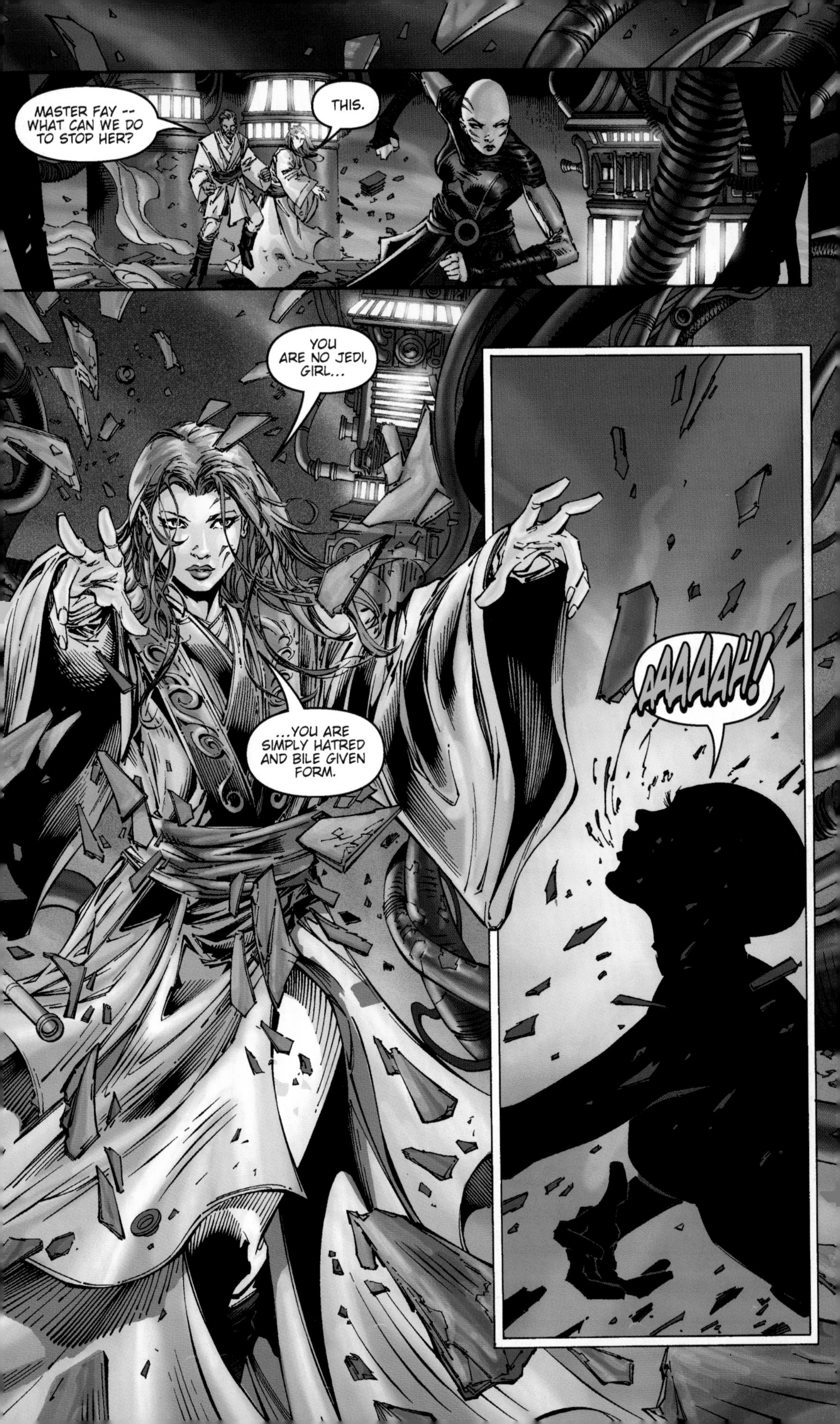
MASTER FAY -- WHAT CAN WE DO TO STOP HER?
THIS.
YOU ARE NO JEDI, GIRL...
...YOU ARE SIMPLY HATRED AND BILE GIVEN FORM.
AAAAAH!

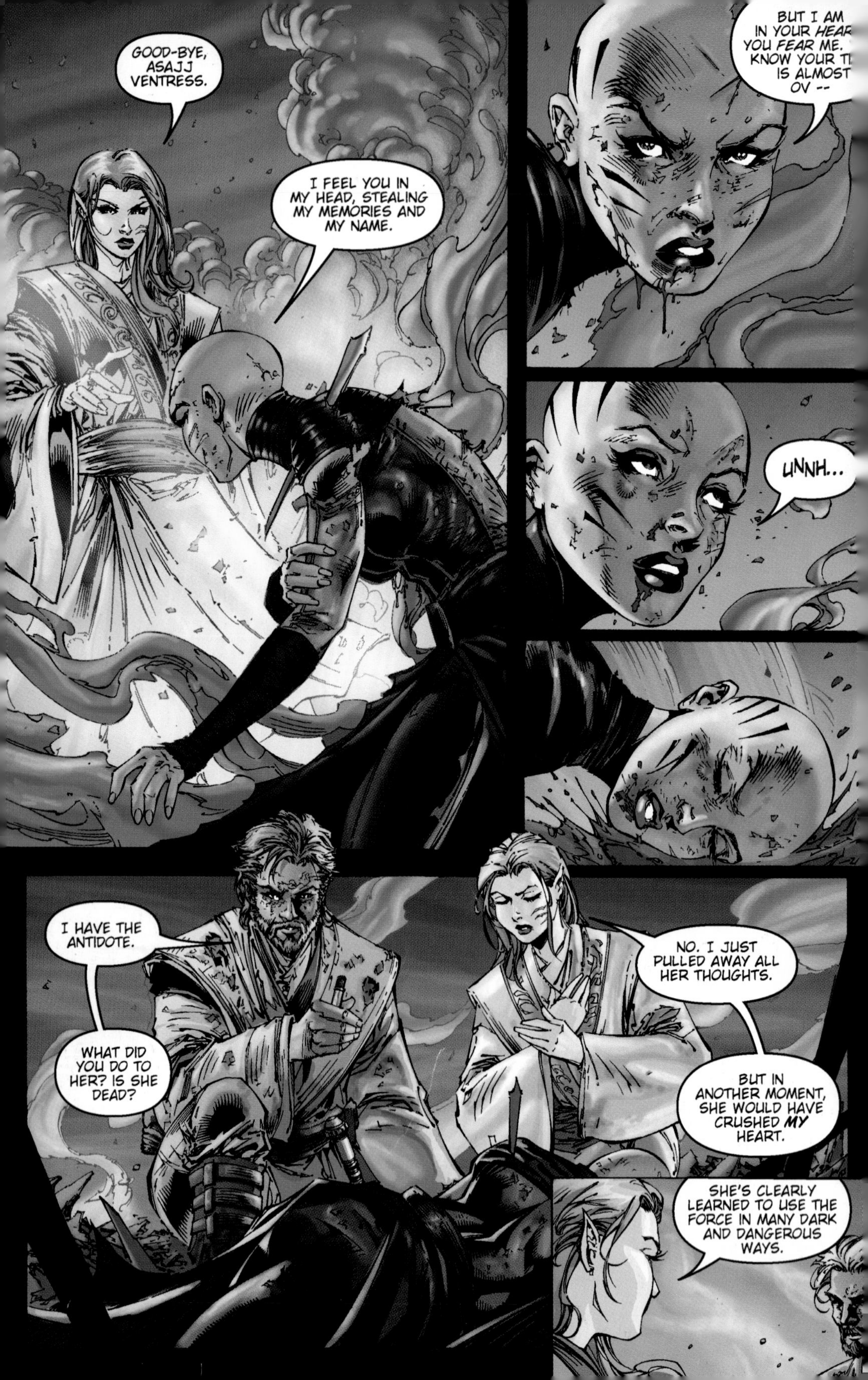
GOOD-BYE, ASAJJ VENTRESS.
I FEEL YOU IN MY HEAD, STEALING MY MEMORIES AND MY NAME.
BUT I AM IN YOUR HEAR YOU FEAR ME. KNOW YOUR TI IS ALMOST OV --
UNNH...
I HAVE THE ANTIDOTE.
WHAT DID YOU DO TO HER? IS SHE DEAD?
NO. I JUST PULLED AWAY ALL HER THOUGHTS.
BUT IN ANOTHER MOMENT, SHE WOULD HAVE CRUSHED MY HEART.
SHE'S CLEARLY LEARNED TO USE THE FORCE IN MANY DARK AND DANGEROUS WAYS.

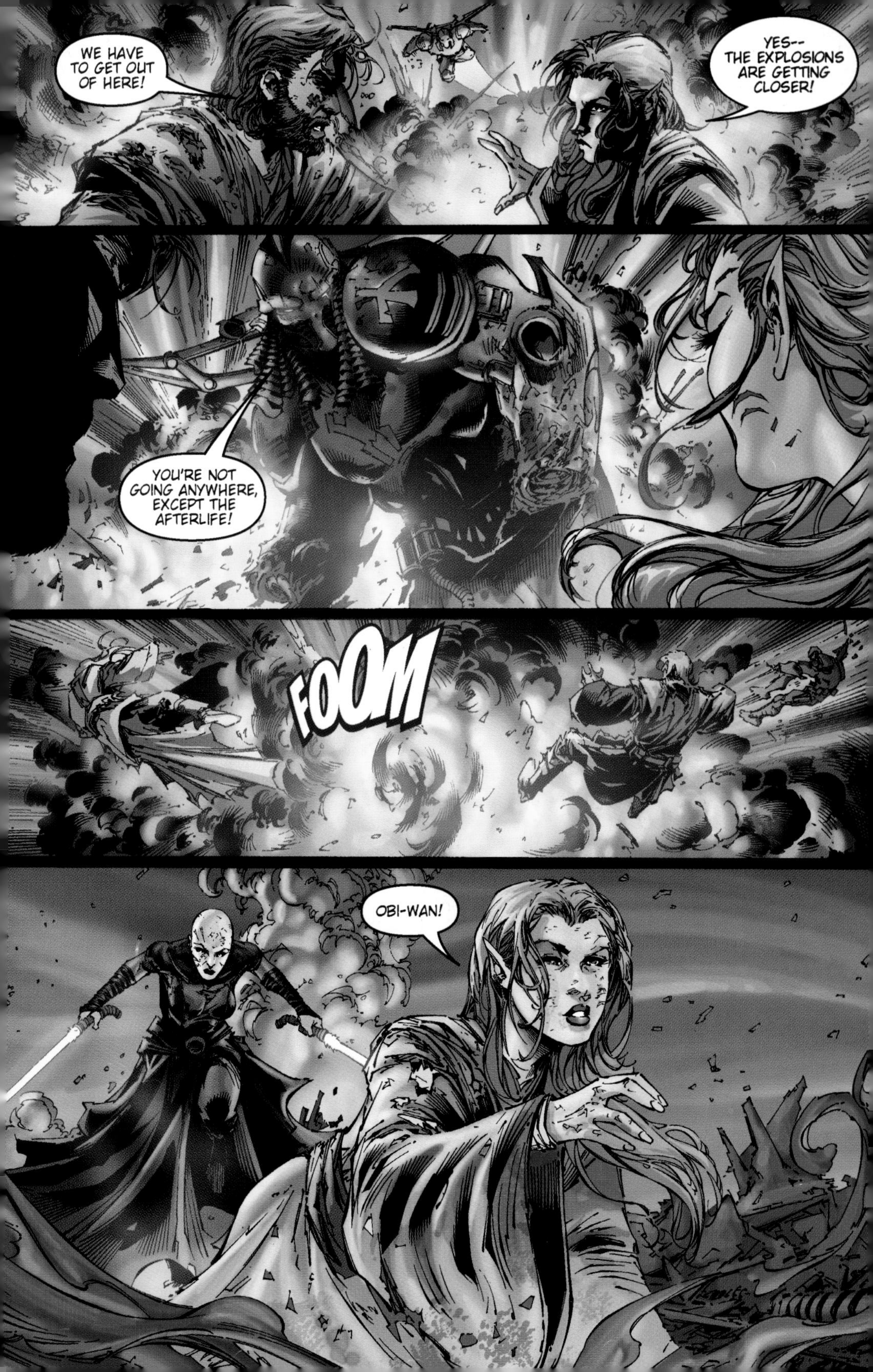
WE HAVE TO GET OUT OF HERE!
YES-- THE EXPLOSIONS ARE GETTING CLOSER!
YOU'RE NOT GOING ANYWHERE, EXCEPT THE AFTERLIFE!
FOOM
OBI-WAN!

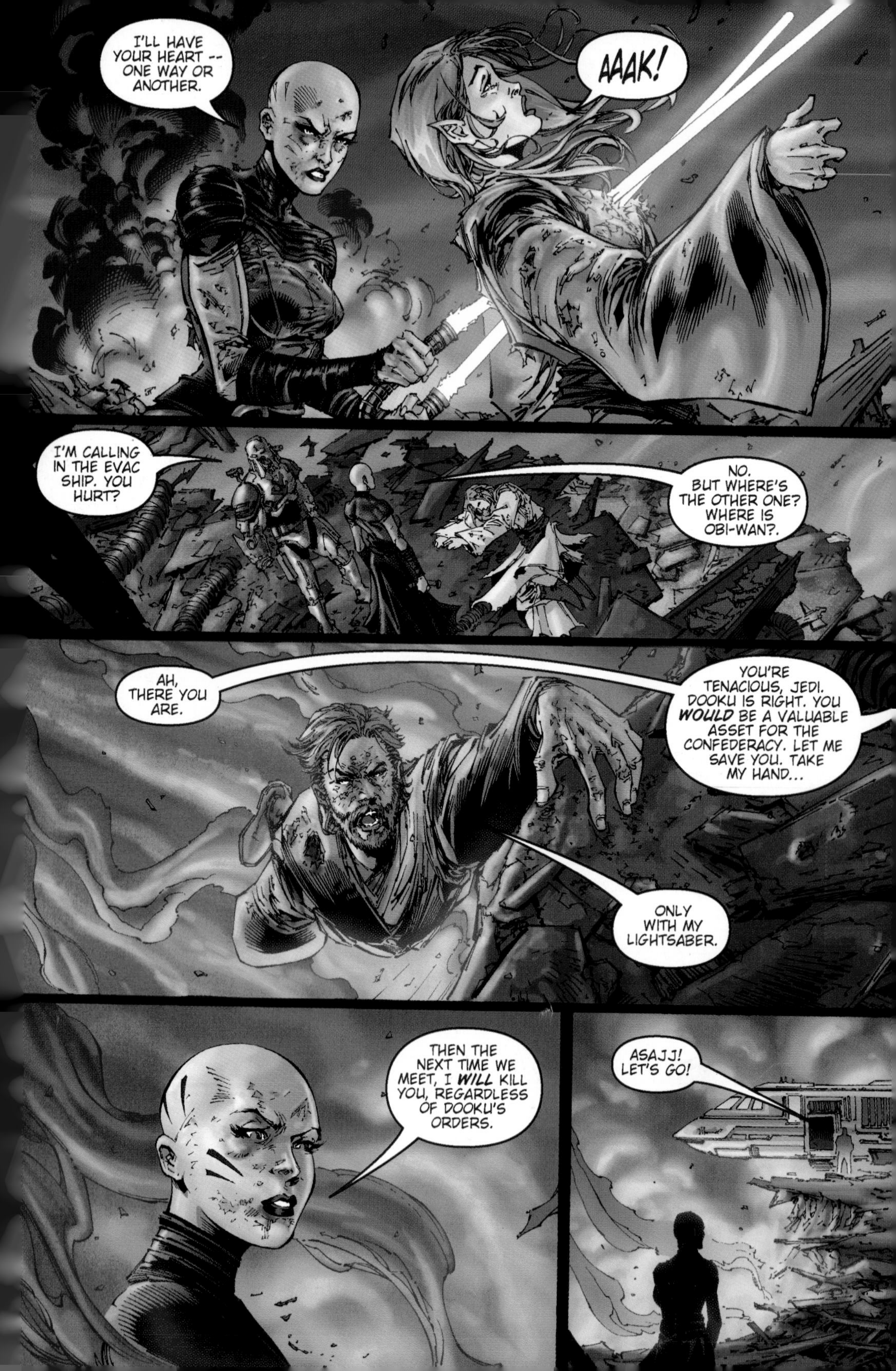
I'LL HAVE YOUR HEART -- ONE WAY OR ANOTHER.
AAAK!
I'M CALLING IN THE EVAC SHIP. YOU HURT?
NO. BUT WHERE'S THE OTHER ONE? WHERE IS OBI-WAN?.
AH, THERE YOU ARE.
YOU'RE TENACIOUS, JEDI. DOOKU IS RIGHT. YOU WOULD BE A VALUABLE ASSET FOR THE CONFEDERACY. LET ME SAVE YOU. TAKE MY HAND...
ONLY WITH MY LIGHTSABER.
THEN THE NEXT TIME WE MEET, I WILL KILL YOU, REGARDLESS OF DOOKU'S ORDERS.
ASAJJ! LET'S GO!

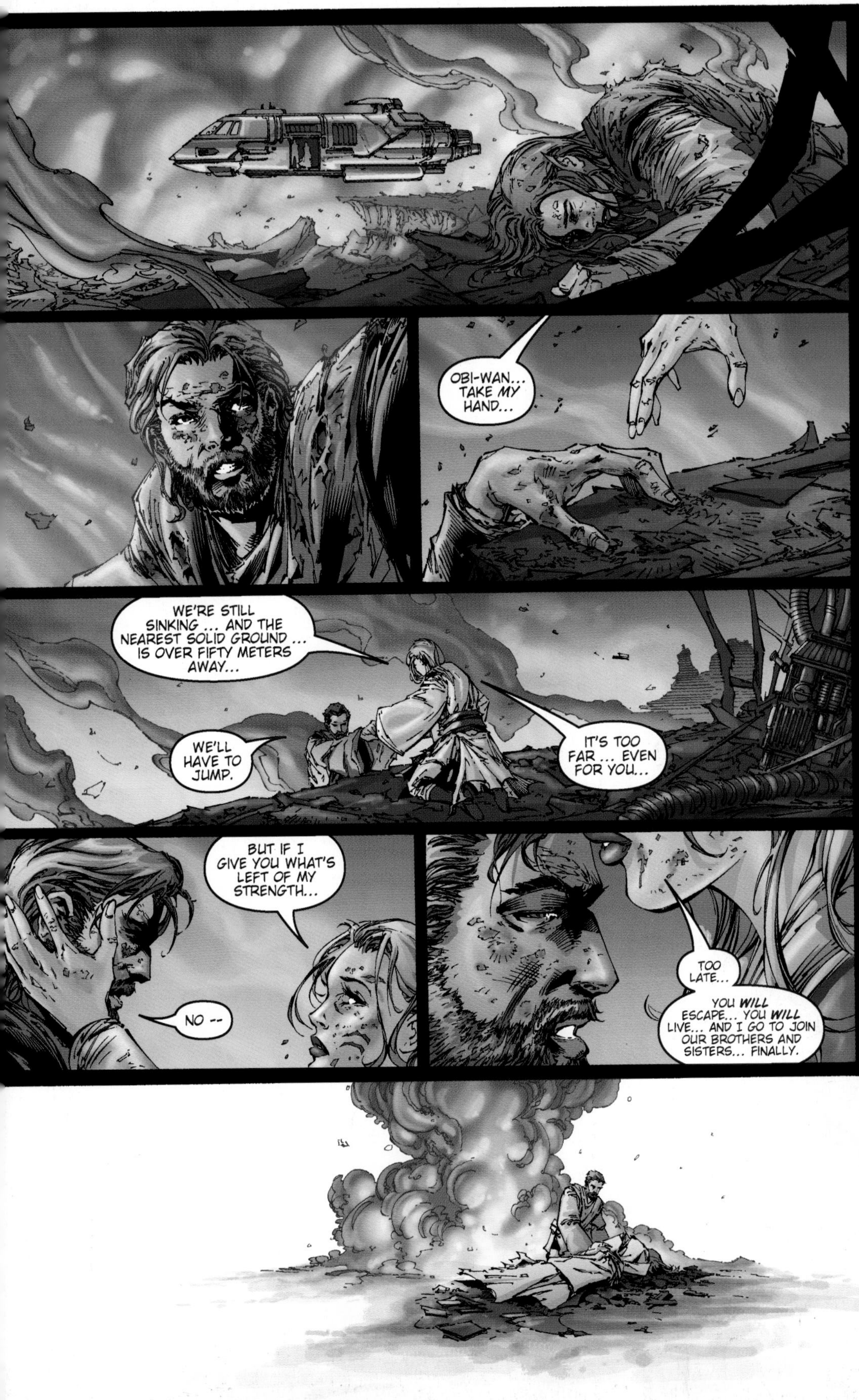
OBI-WAN... TAKE MY HAND...
WE'RE STILL SINKING ... AND THE NEAREST SOLID GROUND ... IS OVER FIFTY METERS AWAY...
WE'LL HAVE TO JUMP.
IT'S TOO FAR ... EVEN FOR YOU...
BUT IF I GIVE YOU WHAT'S LEFT OF MY STRENGTH...
NO --
TOO LATE...
YOU **WILL** ESCAPE... YOU **WILL** LIVE... AND I GO TO JOIN OUR BROTHERS AND SISTERS... FINALLY.

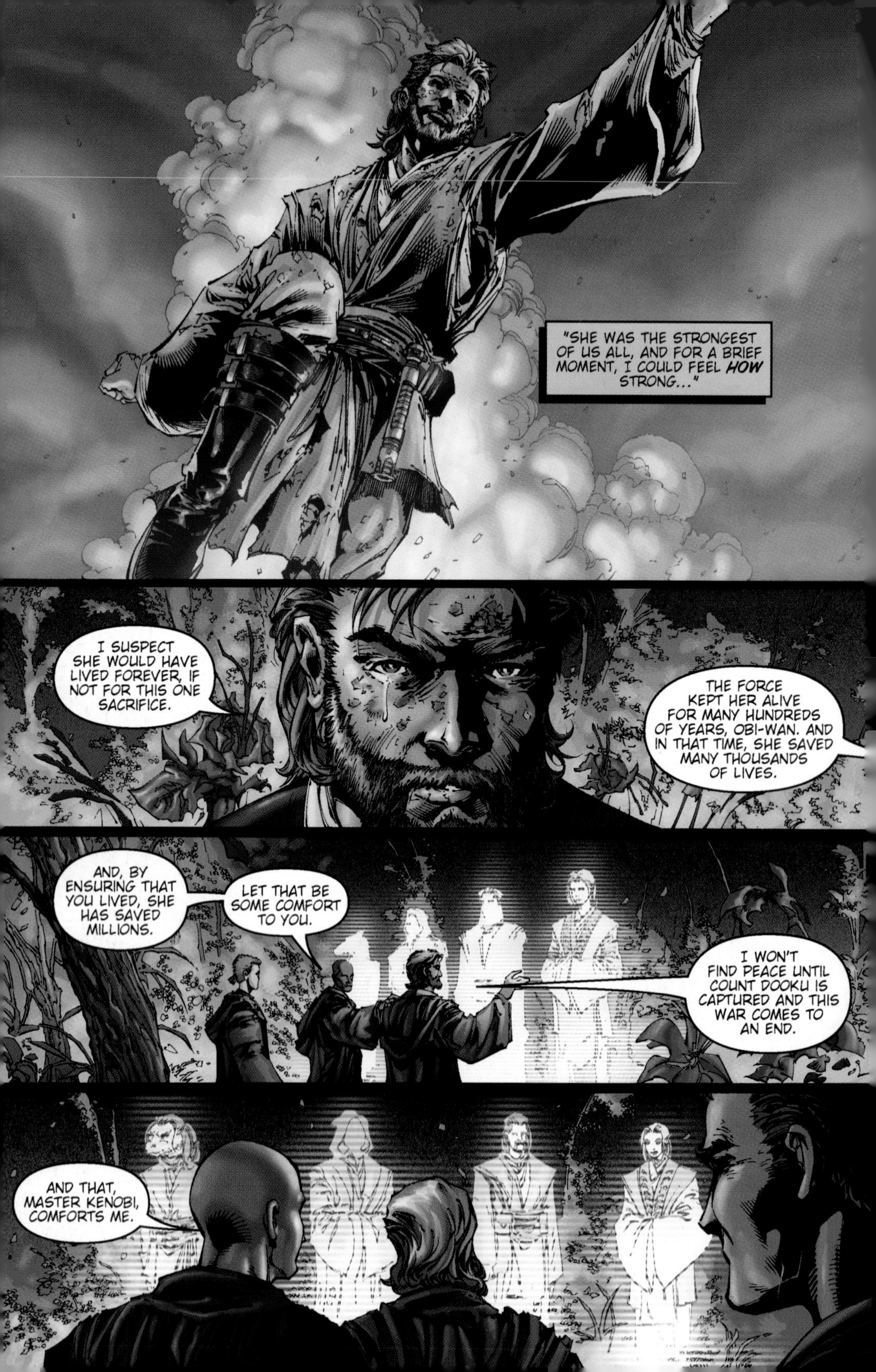
"SHE WAS THE STRONGEST OF US ALL, AND FOR A BRIEF MOMENT, I COULD FEEL **HOW** STRONG..."
I SUSPECT SHE WOULD HAVE LIVED FOREVER, IF NOT FOR THIS ONE SACRIFICE.
THE FORCE KEPT HER ALIVE FOR MANY HUNDREDS OF YEARS, OBI-WAN. AND IN THAT TIME, SHE SAVED MANY THOUSANDS OF LIVES.
AND, BY ENSURING THAT YOU LIVED, SHE HAS SAVED MILLIONS.
LET THAT BE SOME COMFORT TO YOU.
I WON'T FIND PEACE UNTIL COUNT DOOKU IS CAPTURED AND THIS WAR COMES TO AN END.
AND THAT, MASTER KENOBI, COMFORTS ME.

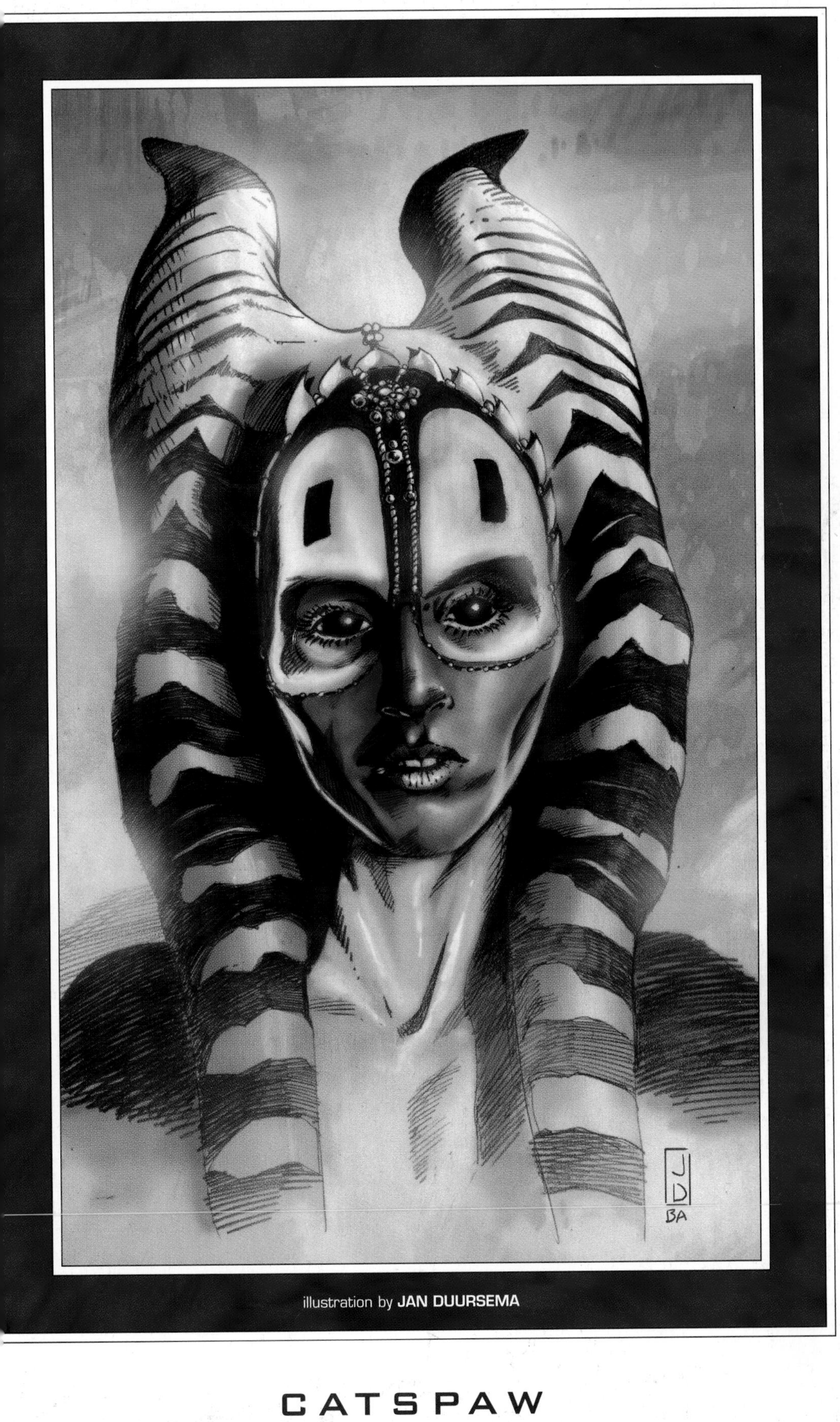
JD
BA

illustration by **JAN DUURSEMA**

CATSPAW

APPROXIMATELY FIVE MONTHS
AFTER THE BATTLE OF GEONOSIS...

"Catspaw"
written by **John Ostrander**
pencilled by **Jan Duursema**
inked by **Dan Parsons**

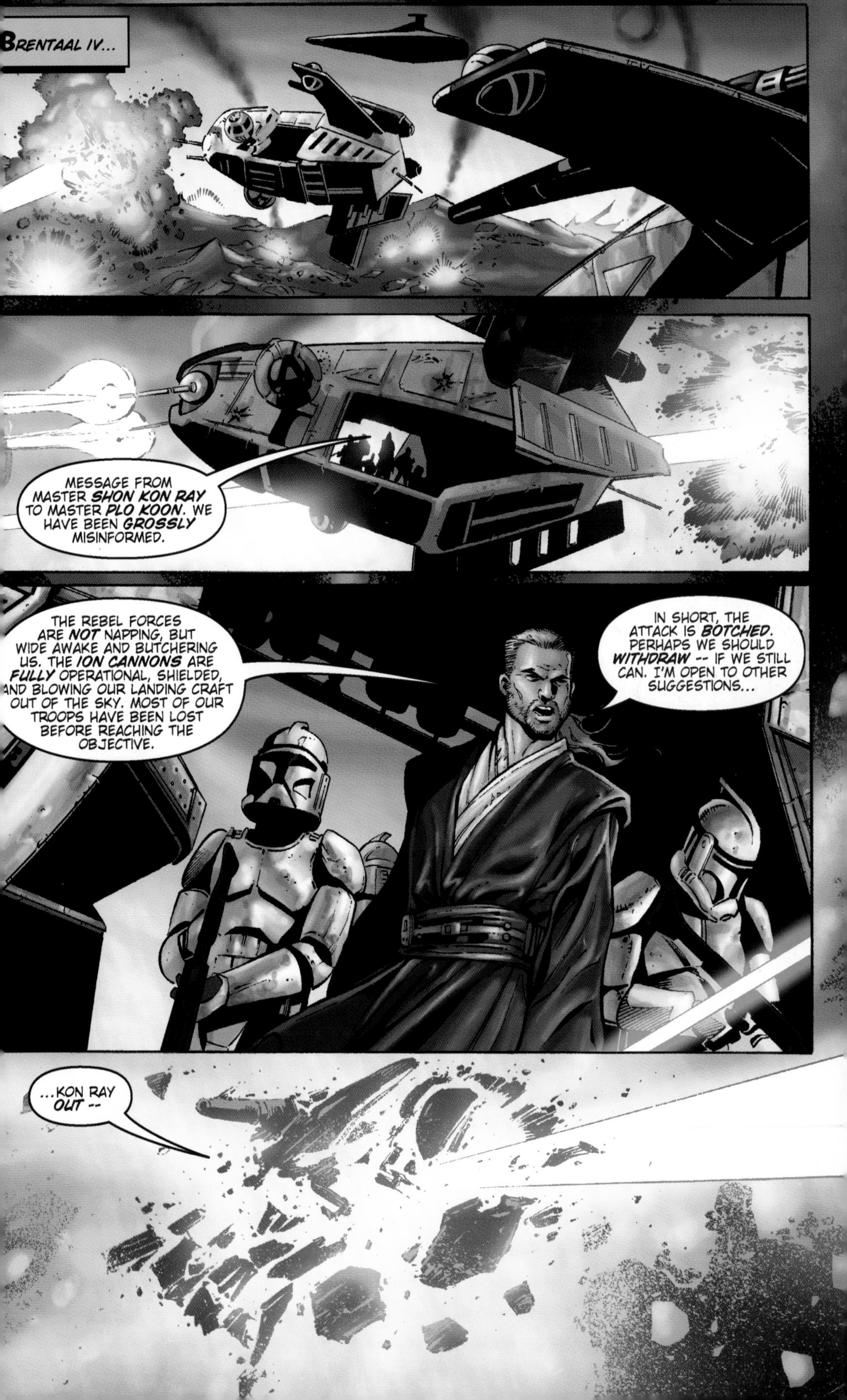
BRENTAAL IV...
MESSAGE FROM MASTER SHON KON RAY TO MASTER PLO KOON. WE HAVE BEEN GROSSLY MISINFORMED.
THE REBEL FORCES ARE NOT NAPPING, BUT WIDE AWAKE AND BUTCHERING US. THE ION CANNONS ARE FULLY OPERATIONAL, SHIELDED, AND BLOWING OUR LANDING CRAFT OUT OF THE SKY. MOST OF OUR TROOPS HAVE BEEN LOST BEFORE REACHING THE OBJECTIVE.
IN SHORT, THE ATTACK IS BOTCHED. PERHAPS WE SHOULD WITHDRAW -- IF WE STILL CAN. I'M OPEN TO OTHER SUGGESTIONS...
...KON RAY OUT --

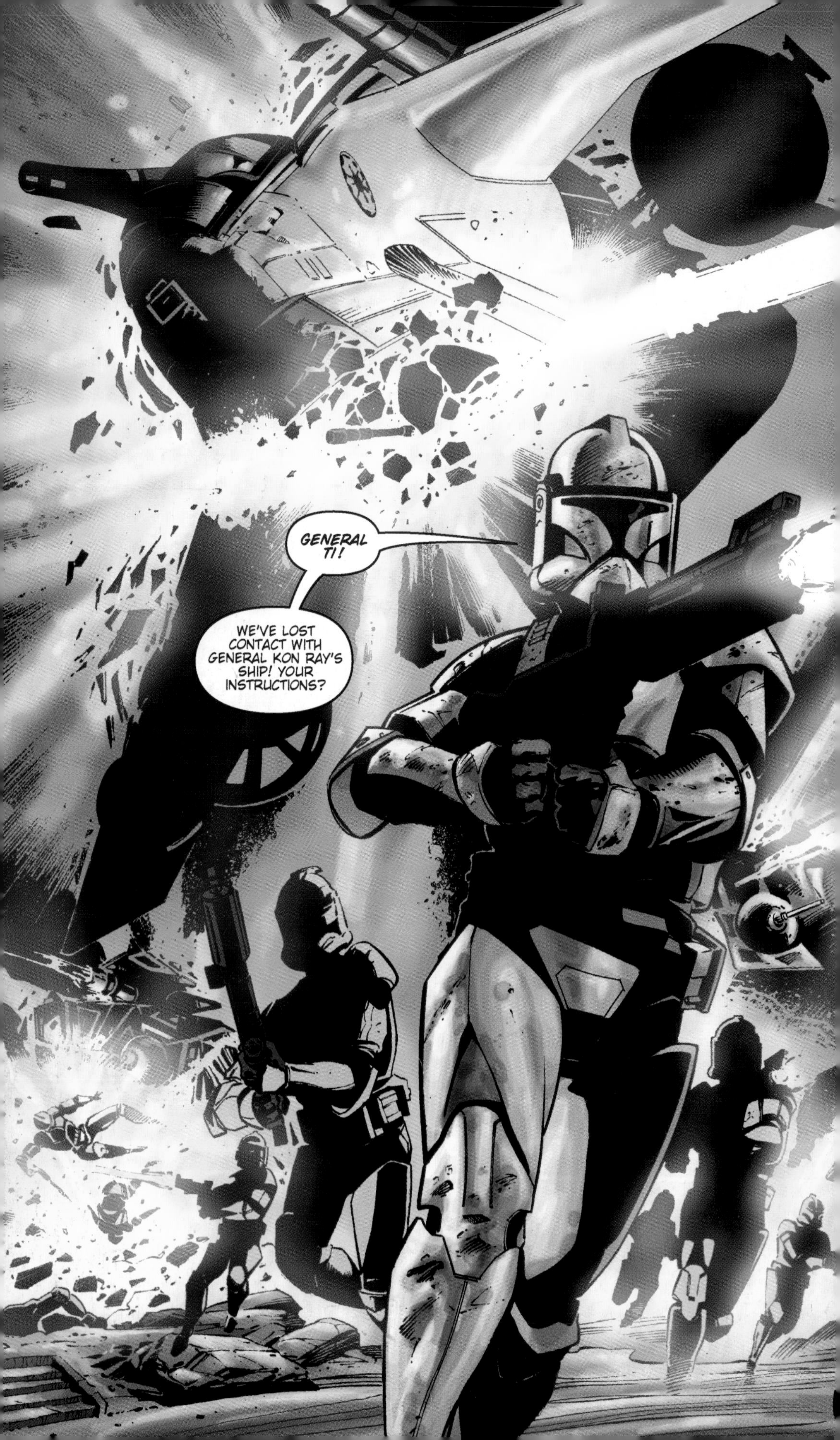
GENERAL TI!
WE'VE LOST CONTACT WITH GENERAL KON RAY'S SHIP! YOUR INSTRUCTIONS?

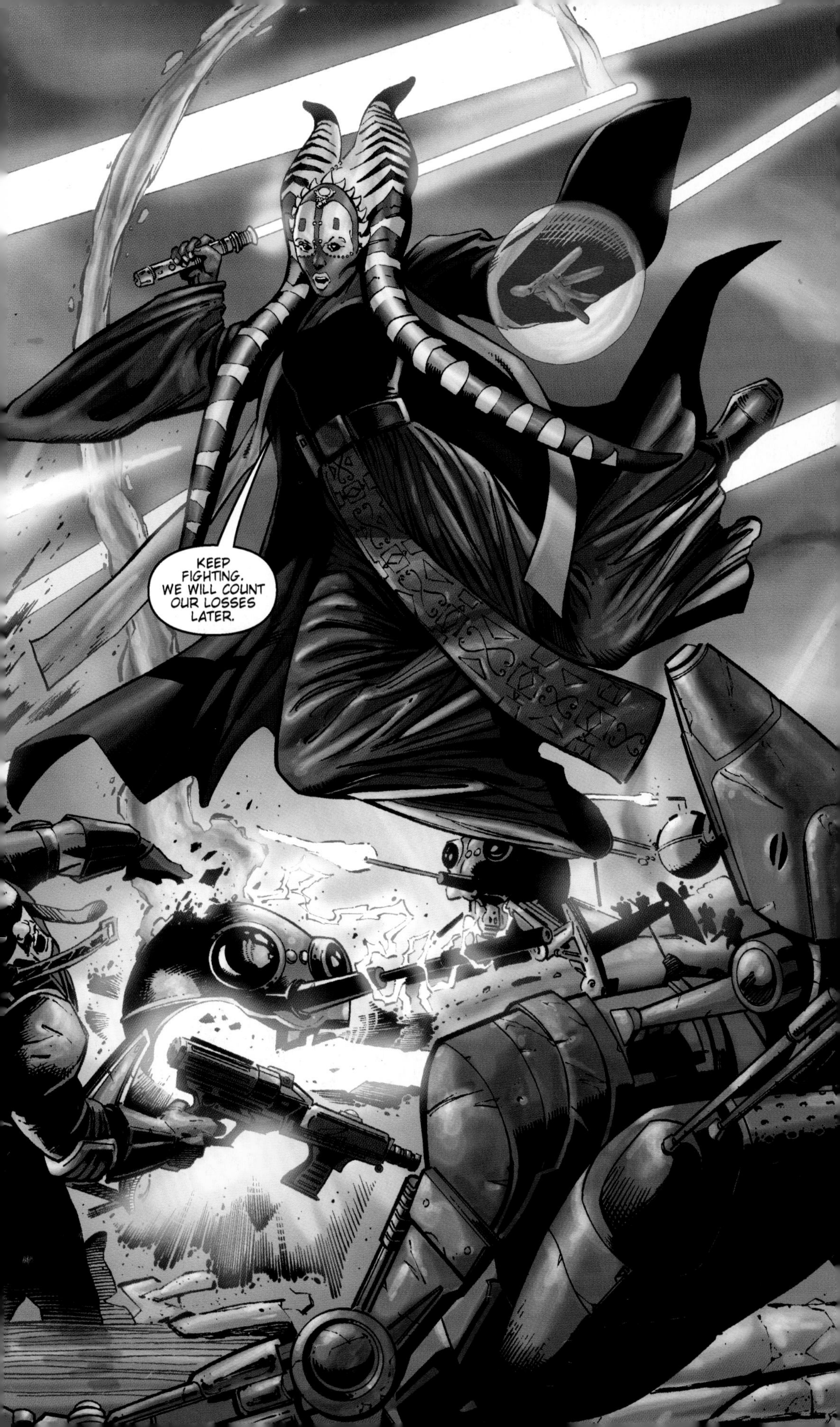
KEEP FIGHTING. WE WILL COUNT OUR LOSSES LATER.

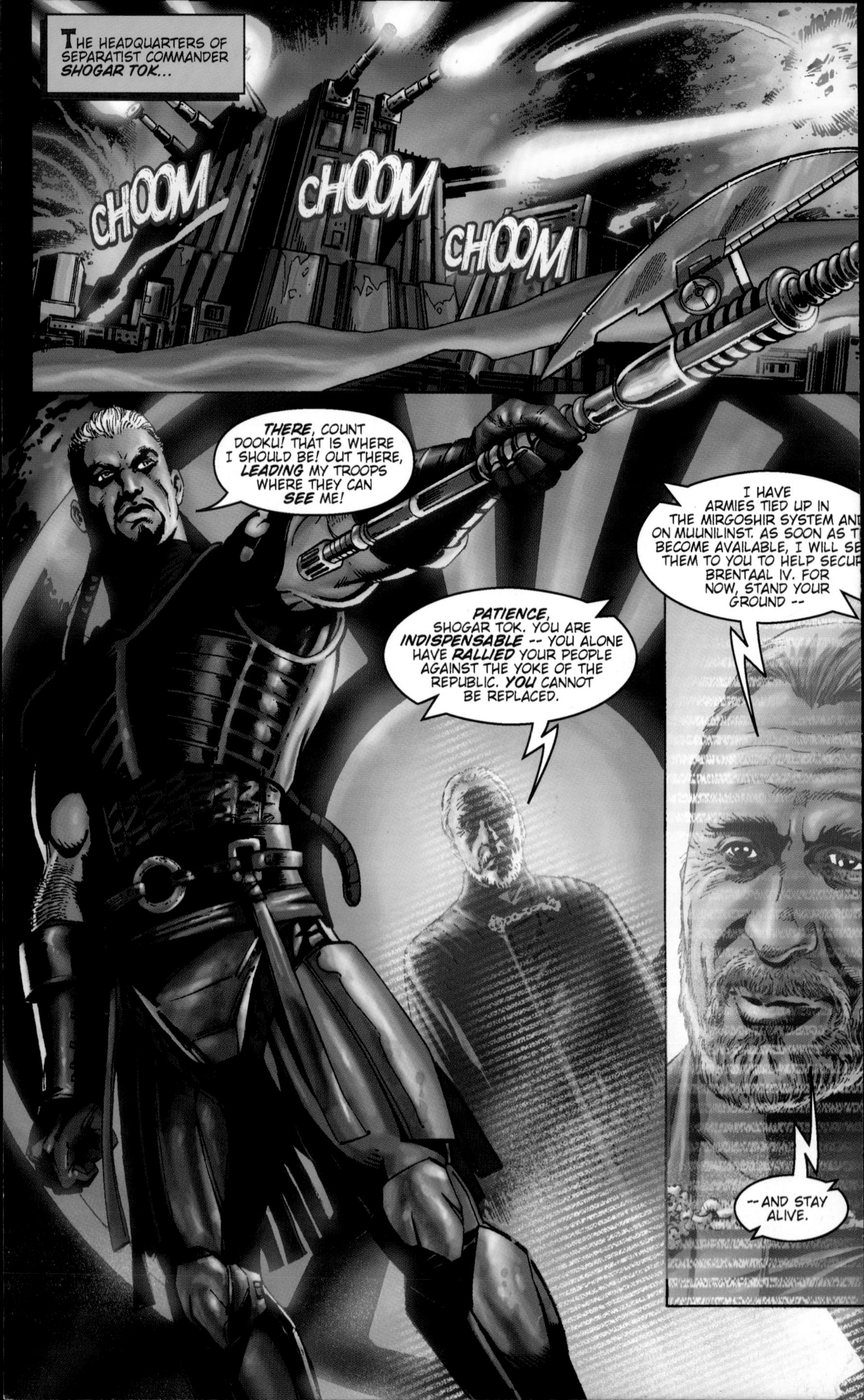
THE HEADQUARTERS OF SEPARATIST COMMANDER SHOGAR TOK...
CHOOM
CHOOM
CHOOM
THERE, COUNT DOOKU! THAT IS WHERE I SHOULD BE! OUT THERE, LEADING MY TROOPS WHERE THEY CAN SEE ME!
PATIENCE, SHOGAR TOK. YOU ARE INDISPENSABLE -- YOU ALONE HAVE RALLIED YOUR PEOPLE AGAINST THE YOKE OF THE REPUBLIC. YOU CANNOT BE REPLACED.
I HAVE ARMIES TIED UP IN THE MIRGOSHIR SYSTEM AN ON MUUNILINST. AS SOON AS T BECOME AVAILABLE, I WILL SE THEM TO YOU TO HELP SECUR BRENTAAL IV. FOR NOW, STAND YOUR GROUND --
-- AND STAY ALIVE.

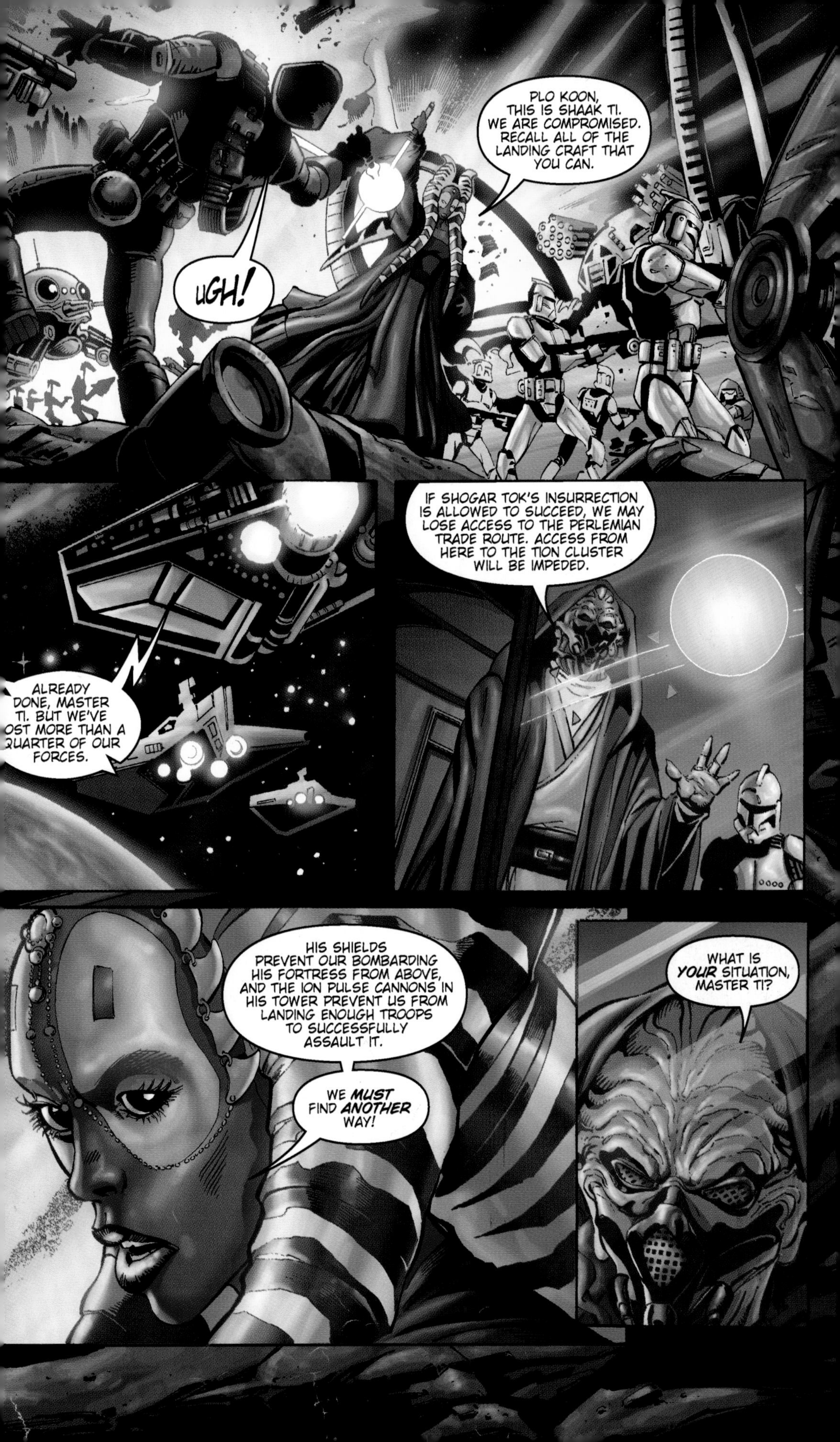

uGH!
PLO KOON, THIS IS SHAAK TI. WE ARE COMPROMISED. RECALL ALL OF THE LANDING CRAFT THAT YOU CAN.
ALREADY DONE, MASTER TI. BUT WE'VE OST MORE THAN A QUARTER OF OUR FORCES.
IF SHOGAR TOK'S INSURRECTION IS ALLOWED TO SUCCEED, WE MAY LOSE ACCESS TO THE PERLEMIAN TRADE ROUTE. ACCESS FROM HERE TO THE TION CLUSTER WILL BE IMPEDED.
WHAT IS YOUR SITUATION, MASTER TI?
HIS SHIELDS PREVENT OUR BOMBARDING HIS FORTRESS FROM ABOVE, AND THE ION PULSE CANNONS IN HIS TOWER PREVENT US FROM LANDING ENOUGH TROOPS TO SUCCESSFULLY ASSAULT IT.
WE MUST FIND ANOTHER WAY!

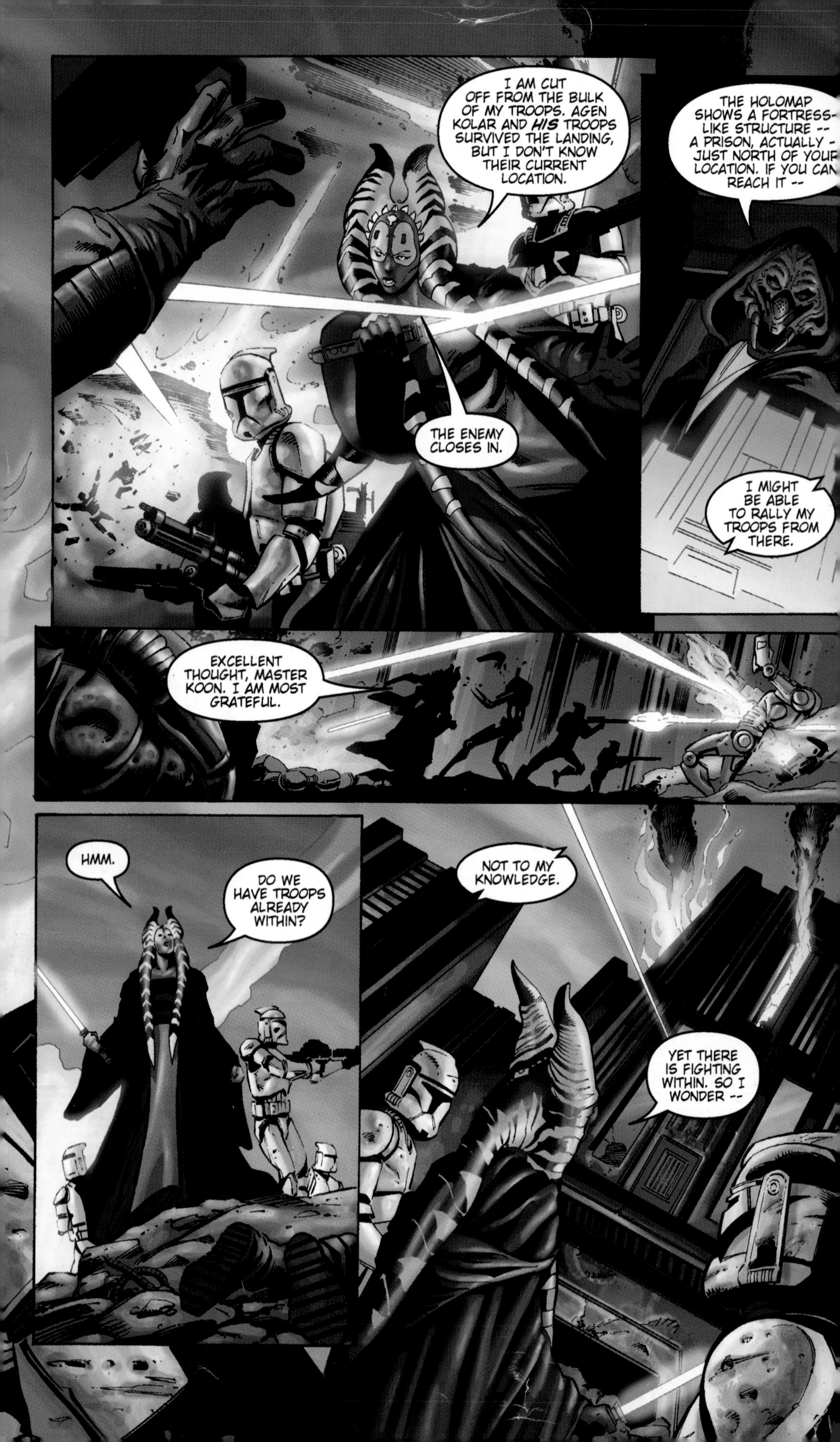

I AM CUT OFF FROM THE BULK OF MY TROOPS. AGEN KOLAR AND HIS TROOPS SURVIVED THE LANDING, BUT I DON'T KNOW THEIR CURRENT LOCATION.
THE ENEMY CLOSES IN.
THE HOLOMAP SHOWS A FORTRESS-LIKE STRUCTURE -- A PRISON, ACTUALLY -- JUST NORTH OF YOUR LOCATION. IF YOU CAN REACH IT --
I MIGHT BE ABLE TO RALLY MY TROOPS FROM THERE.
EXCELLENT THOUGHT, MASTER KOON. I AM MOST GRATEFUL.
HMM.
DO WE HAVE TROOPS ALREADY WITHIN?
NOT TO MY KNOWLEDGE.
YET THERE IS FIGHTING WITHIN. SO I WONDER --

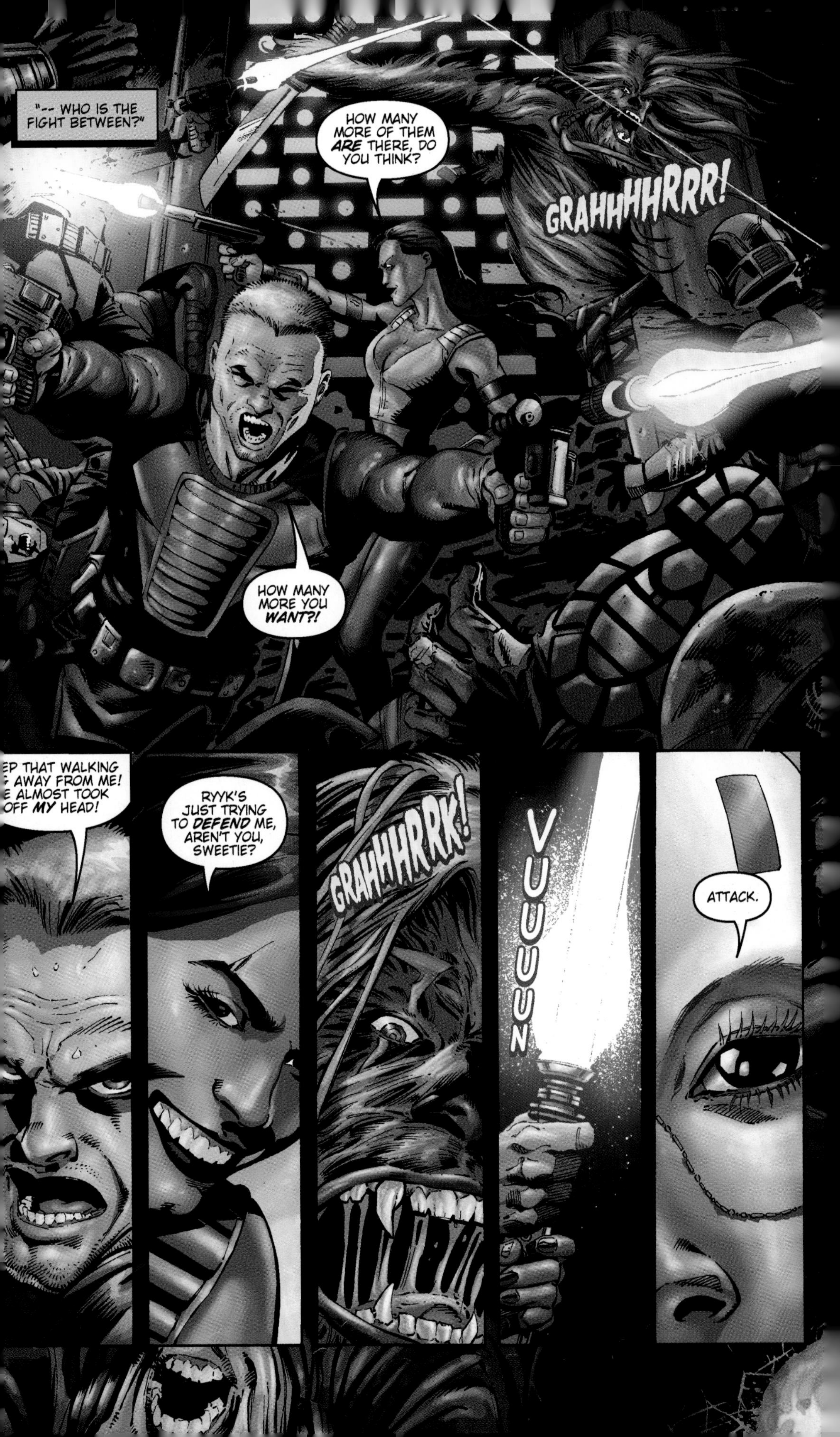
"-- WHO IS THE FIGHT BETWEEN?"
HOW MANY MORE OF THEM *ARE* THERE, DO YOU THINK?
GRAHHHHRRR!
HOW MANY MORE YOU *WANT?!*
EP THAT WALKING AWAY FROM ME! ALMOST TOOK OFF *MY* HEAD!
RYYK'S JUST TRYING TO *DEFEND* ME, AREN'T YOU, SWEETIE?
GRAHHHRRK!
VUUUUUN
ATTACK.

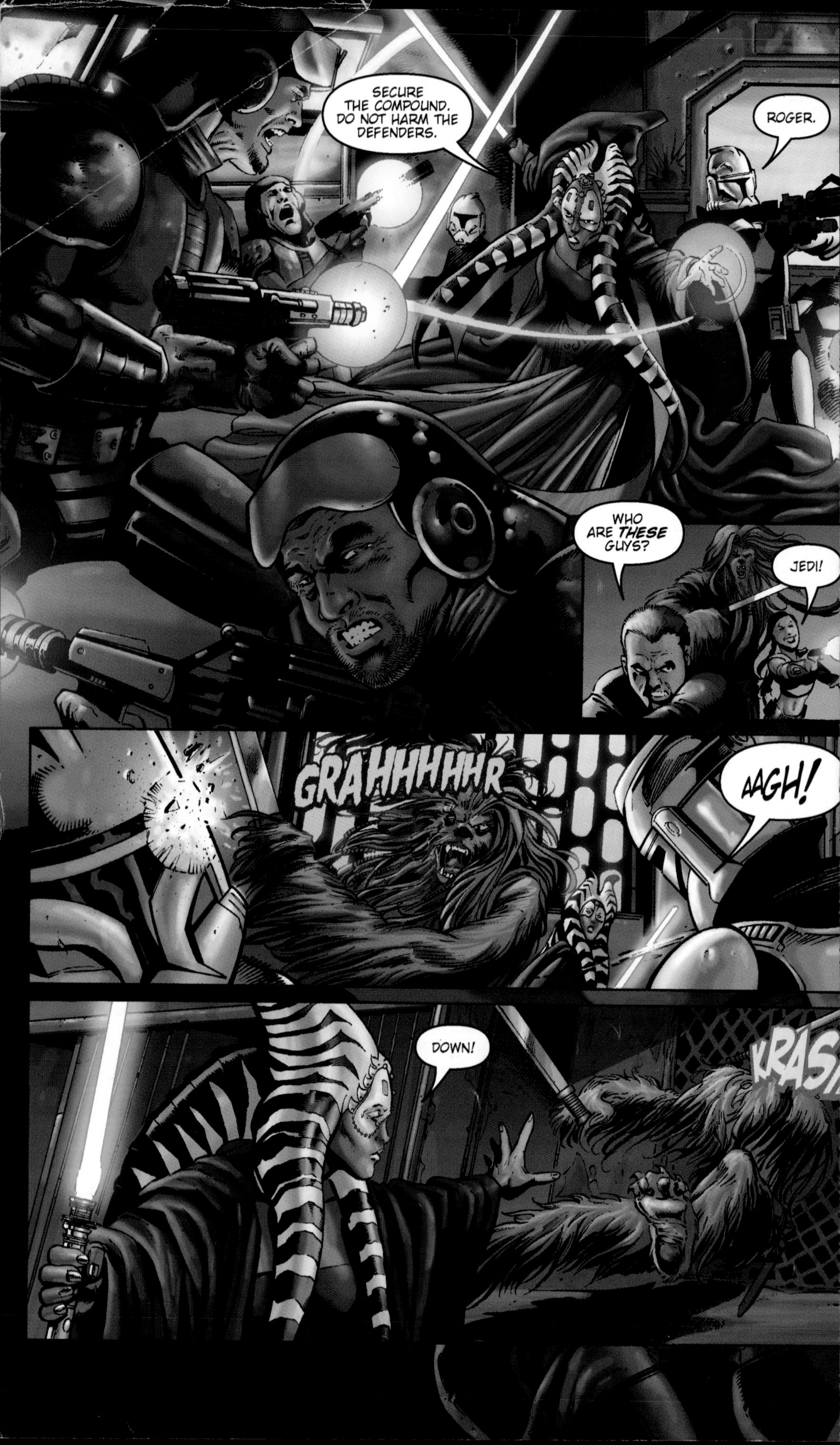
SECURE THE COMPOUND. DO NOT HARM THE DEFENDERS.
ROGER.
WHO ARE *THESE* GUYS?
JEDI!
GRAHHHHHR
AAGH!
DOWN!
KRASH

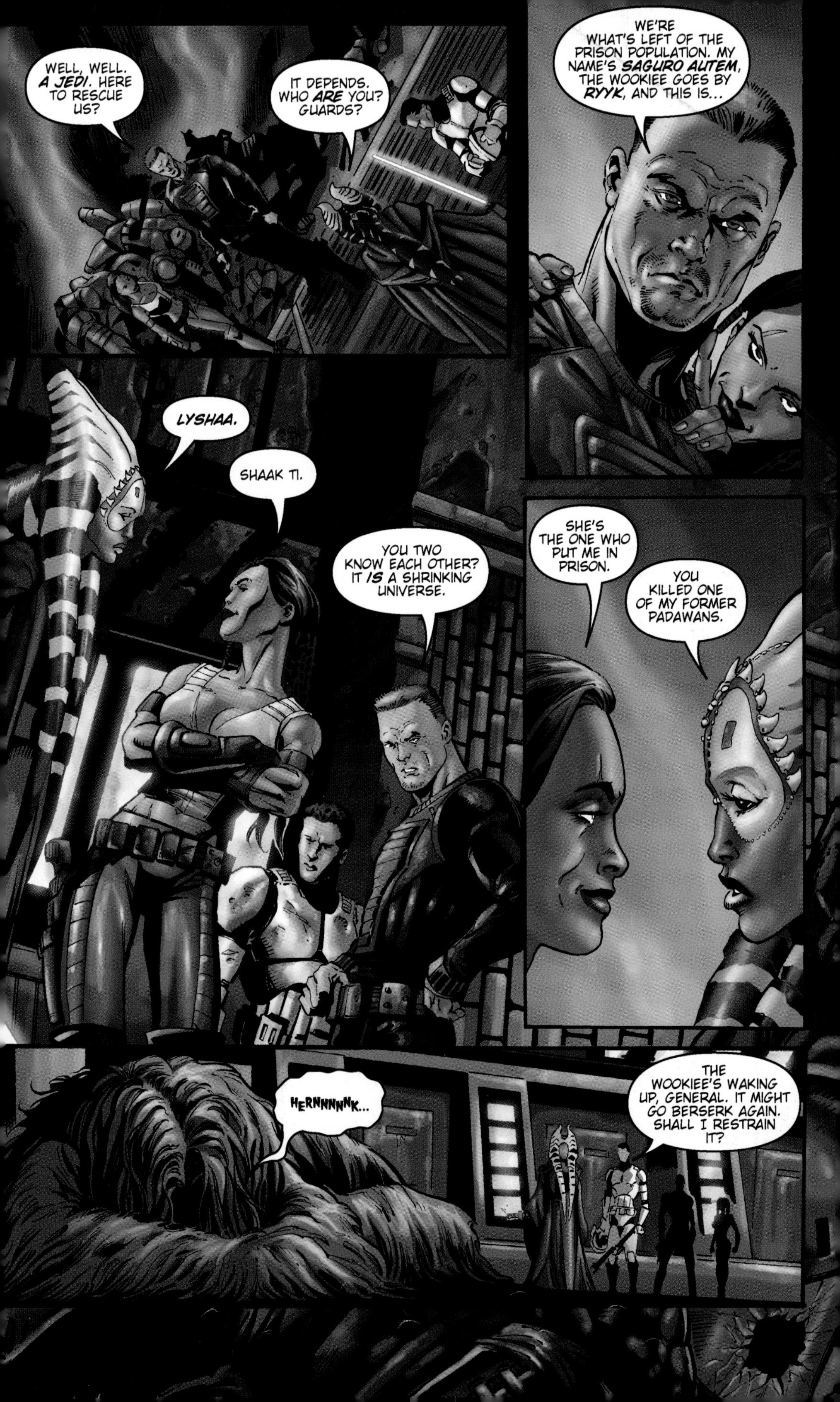
WELL, WELL. A JEDI. HERE TO RESCUE US?
IT DEPENDS. WHO ARE YOU? GUARDS?
WE'RE WHAT'S LEFT OF THE PRISON POPULATION. MY NAME'S SAGURO AUTEM, THE WOOKIEE GOES BY RYYK, AND THIS IS...
LYSHAA.
SHAAK TI.
YOU TWO KNOW EACH OTHER? IT IS A SHRINKING UNIVERSE.
SHE'S THE ONE WHO PUT ME IN PRISON.
YOU KILLED ONE OF MY FORMER PADAWANS.
HERNNNNNK...
THE WOOKIEE'S WAKING UP, GENERAL. IT MIGHT GO BERSERK AGAIN. SHALL I RESTRAIN IT?

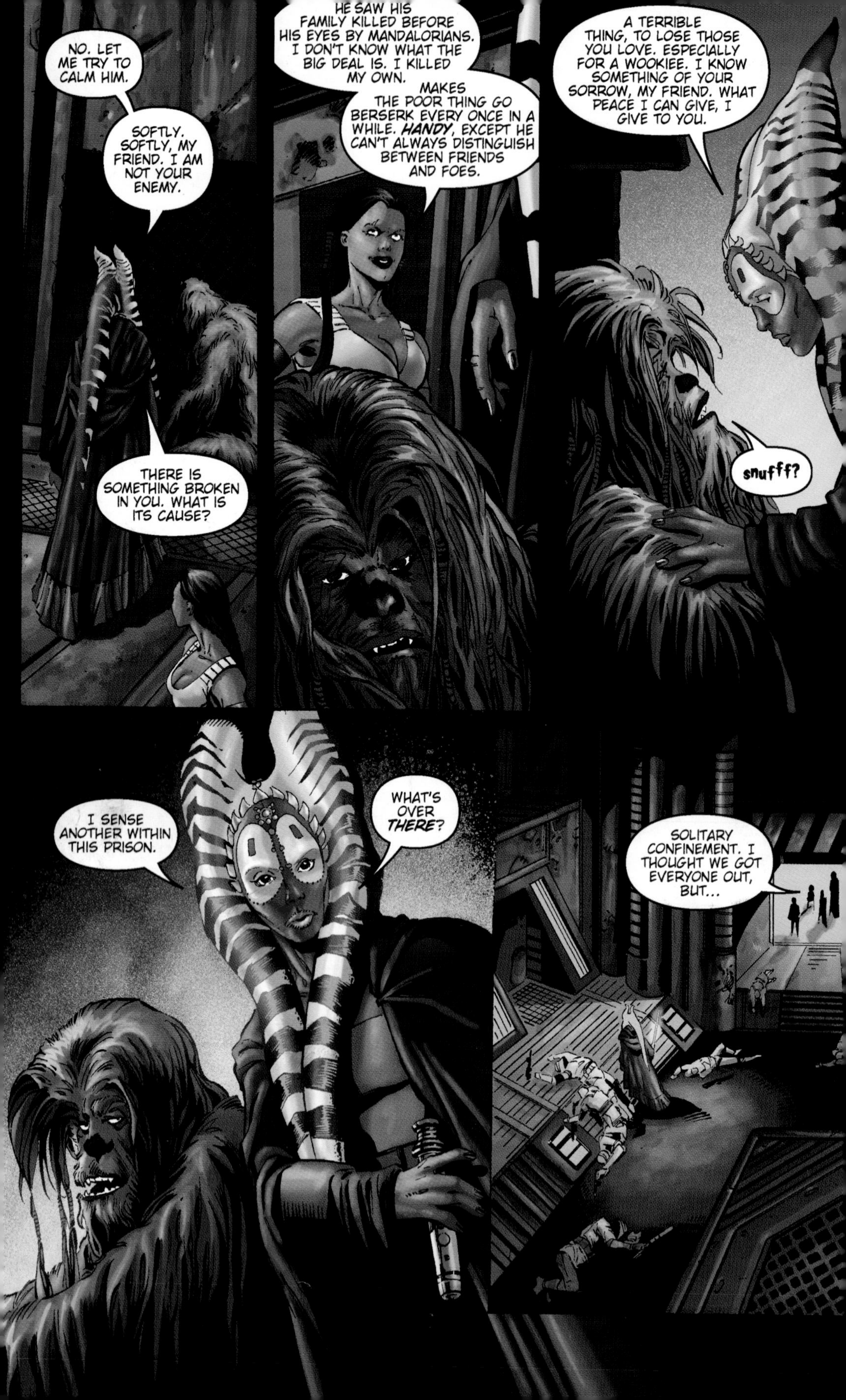
NO. LET ME TRY TO CALM HIM.
SOFTLY. SOFTLY, MY FRIEND. I AM NOT YOUR ENEMY.
THERE IS SOMETHING BROKEN IN YOU. WHAT IS ITS CAUSE?
HE SAW HIS FAMILY KILLED BEFORE HIS EYES BY MANDALORIANS. I DON'T KNOW WHAT THE BIG DEAL IS. I KILLED MY OWN.
MAKES THE POOR THING GO BERSERK EVERY ONCE IN A WHILE. HANDY, EXCEPT HE CAN'T ALWAYS DISTINGUISH BETWEEN FRIENDS AND FOES.
A TERRIBLE THING, TO LOSE THOSE YOU LOVE. ESPECIALLY FOR A WOOKIEE. I KNOW SOMETHING OF YOUR SORROW, MY FRIEND. WHAT PEACE I CAN GIVE, I GIVE TO YOU.
snufff?
I SENSE ANOTHER WITHIN THIS PRISON.
WHAT'S OVER THERE?
SOLITARY CONFINEMENT. I THOUGHT WE GOT EVERYONE OUT, BUT...

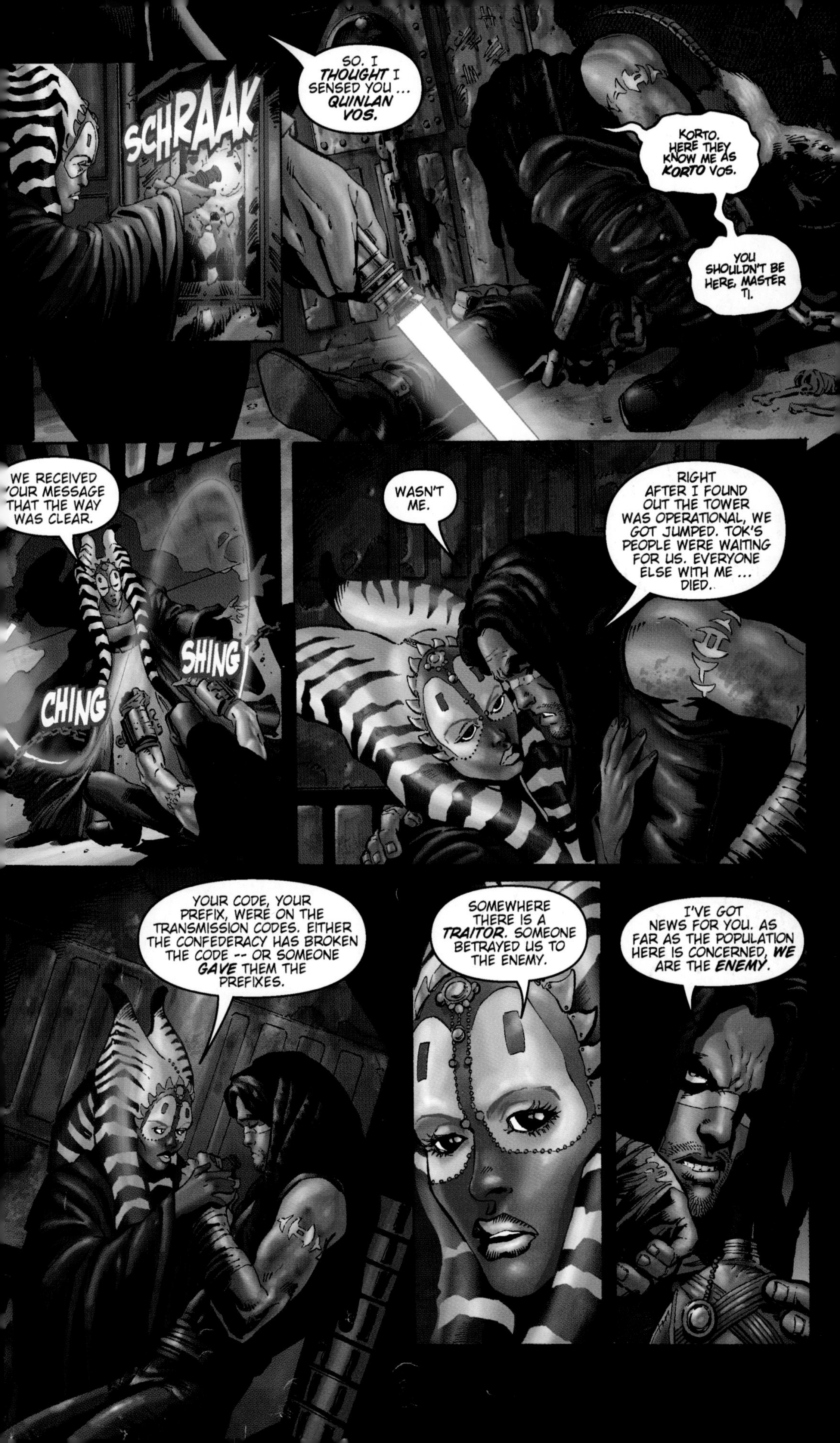
SCHRAAK
SO. I *THOUGHT* I SENSED YOU ... *QUINLAN VOS.*
KORTO. HERE THEY KNOW ME AS *KORTO* VOS.
YOU SHOULDN'T BE HERE, MASTER TI.
WE RECEIVED YOUR MESSAGE THAT THE WAY WAS CLEAR.
SHING
CHING
WASN'T ME.
RIGHT AFTER I FOUND OUT THE TOWER WAS OPERATIONAL, WE GOT JUMPED. TOK'S PEOPLE WERE WAITING FOR US. EVERYONE ELSE WITH ME ... DIED.
YOUR CODE, YOUR PREFIX, WERE ON THE TRANSMISSION CODES. EITHER THE CONFEDERACY HAS BROKEN THE CODE -- OR SOMEONE *GAVE* THEM THE PREFIXES.
SOMEWHERE THERE IS A *TRAITOR*. SOMEONE BETRAYED US TO THE ENEMY.
I'VE GOT NEWS FOR YOU. AS FAR AS THE POPULATION HERE IS CONCERNED, *WE* ARE THE *ENEMY*.

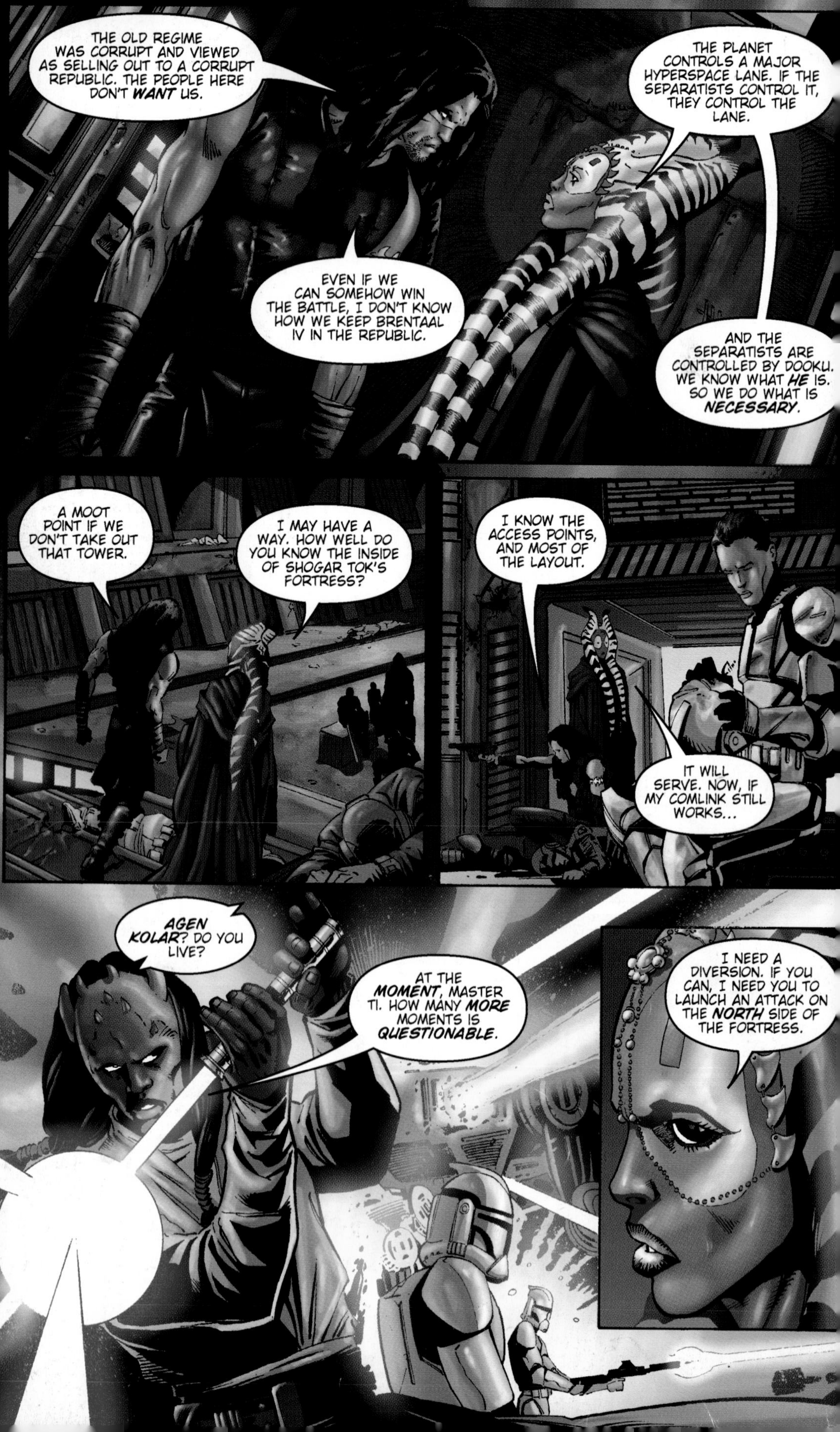
THE OLD REGIME WAS CORRUPT AND VIEWED AS SELLING OUT TO A CORRUPT REPUBLIC. THE PEOPLE HERE DON'T *WANT* US.
EVEN IF WE CAN SOMEHOW WIN THE BATTLE, I DON'T KNOW HOW WE KEEP BRENTAAL IV IN THE REPUBLIC.
THE PLANET CONTROLS A MAJOR HYPERSPACE LANE. IF THE SEPARATISTS CONTROL IT, THEY CONTROL THE LANE.
AND THE SEPARATISTS ARE CONTROLLED BY DOOKU. WE KNOW WHAT *HE* IS. SO WE DO WHAT IS *NECESSARY*.
A MOOT POINT IF WE DON'T TAKE OUT THAT TOWER.
I MAY HAVE A WAY. HOW WELL DO YOU KNOW THE INSIDE OF SHOGAR TOK'S FORTRESS?
I KNOW THE ACCESS POINTS, AND MOST OF THE LAYOUT.
IT WILL SERVE. NOW, IF MY COMLINK STILL WORKS...
AGEN KOLAR? DO YOU LIVE?
AT THE *MOMENT*, MASTER TI. HOW MANY *MORE* MOMENTS IS *QUESTIONABLE*.
I NEED A DIVERSION. IF YOU CAN, I NEED YOU TO LAUNCH AN ATTACK ON THE *NORTH* SIDE OF THE FORTRESS.

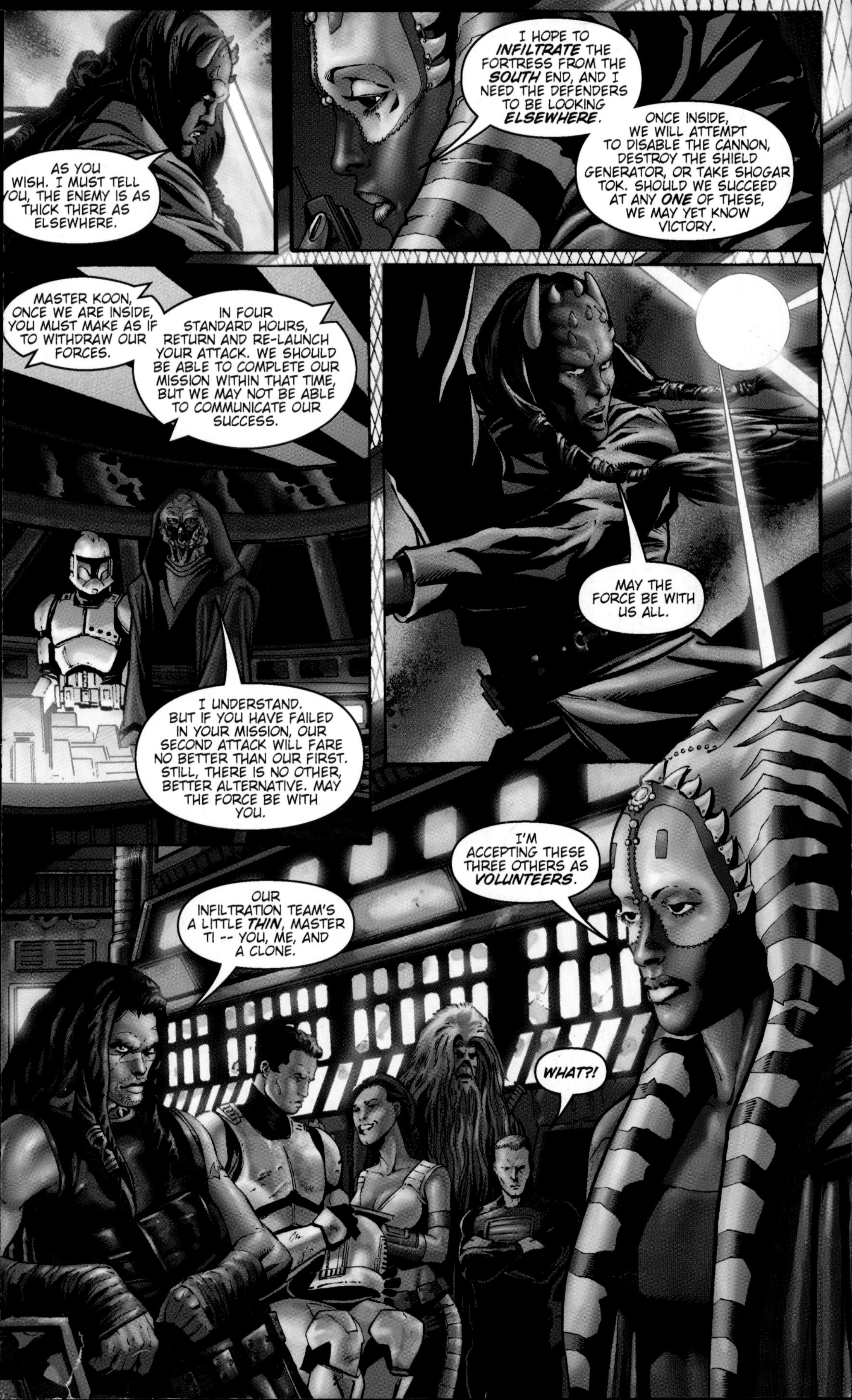
AS YOU WISH. I MUST TELL YOU, THE ENEMY IS AS THICK THERE AS ELSEWHERE.
I HOPE TO *INFILTRATE* THE FORTRESS FROM THE *SOUTH* END, AND I NEED THE DEFENDERS TO BE LOOKING *ELSEWHERE*.
ONCE INSIDE, WE WILL ATTEMPT TO DISABLE THE CANNON, DESTROY THE SHIELD GENERATOR, OR TAKE SHOGAR TOK. SHOULD WE SUCCEED AT ANY *ONE* OF THESE, WE MAY YET KNOW VICTORY.
MASTER KOON, ONCE WE ARE INSIDE, YOU MUST MAKE AS IF TO WITHDRAW OUR FORCES.
IN FOUR STANDARD HOURS, RETURN AND RE-LAUNCH YOUR ATTACK. WE SHOULD BE ABLE TO COMPLETE OUR MISSION WITHIN THAT TIME, BUT WE MAY NOT BE ABLE TO COMMUNICATE OUR SUCCESS.
I UNDERSTAND. BUT IF YOU HAVE FAILED IN YOUR MISSION, OUR SECOND ATTACK WILL FARE NO BETTER THAN OUR FIRST. STILL, THERE IS NO OTHER, BETTER ALTERNATIVE. MAY THE FORCE BE WITH YOU.
MAY THE FORCE BE WITH US ALL.
OUR INFILTRATION TEAM'S A LITTLE *THIN*, MASTER TI -- YOU, ME, AND A CLONE.
I'M ACCEPTING THESE THREE OTHERS AS *VOLUNTEERS*.
WHAT?!

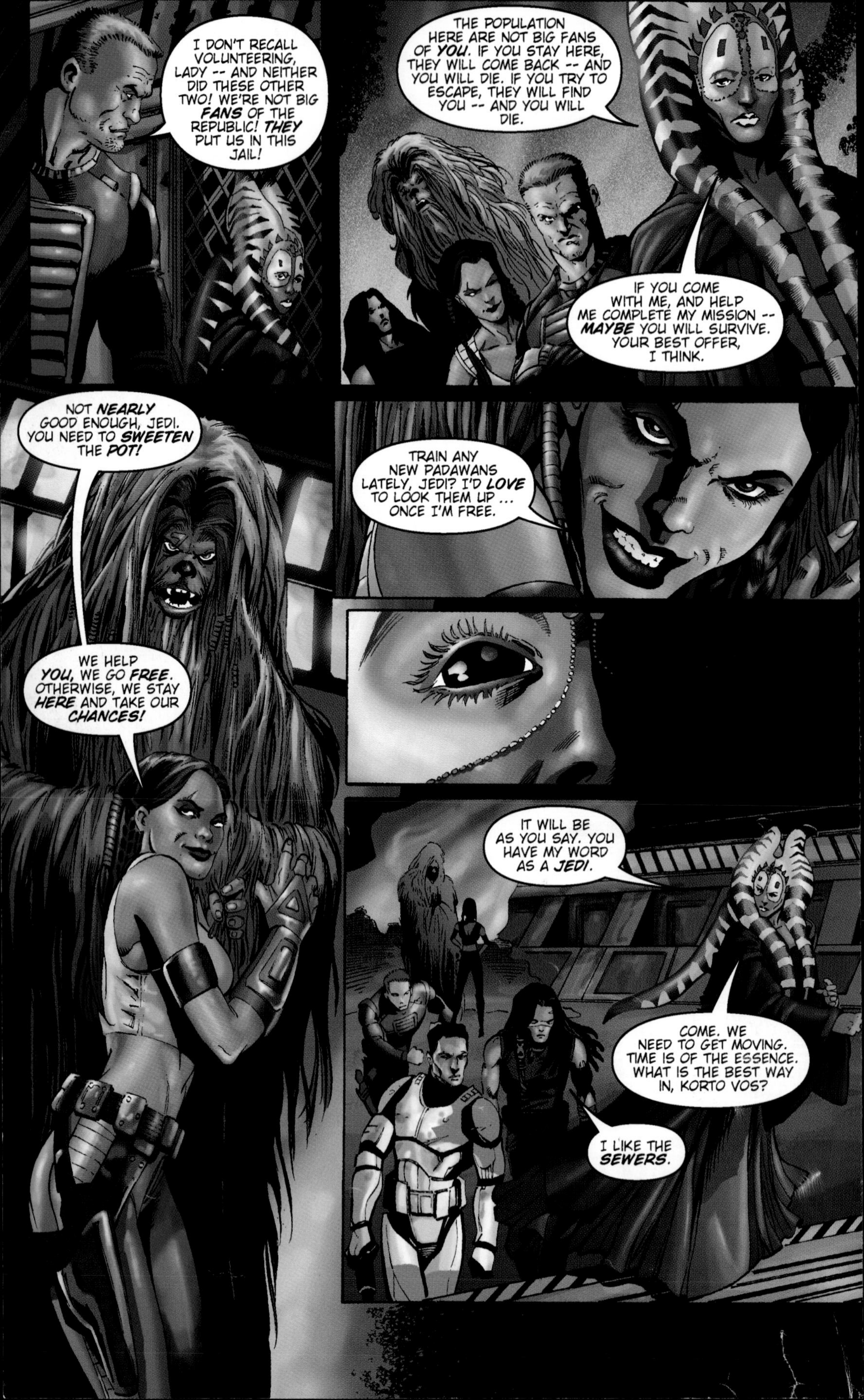
I DON'T RECALL VOLUNTEERING, LADY -- AND NEITHER DID THESE OTHER TWO! WE'RE NOT BIG FANS OF THE REPUBLIC! THEY PUT US IN THIS JAIL!
THE POPULATION HERE ARE NOT BIG FANS OF YOU. IF YOU STAY HERE, THEY WILL COME BACK -- AND YOU WILL DIE. IF YOU TRY TO ESCAPE, THEY WILL FIND YOU -- AND YOU WILL DIE.
IF YOU COME WITH ME, AND HELP ME COMPLETE MY MISSION -- MAYBE YOU WILL SURVIVE. YOUR BEST OFFER, I THINK.
NOT NEARLY GOOD ENOUGH, JEDI. YOU NEED TO SWEETEN THE POT!
WE HELP YOU, WE GO FREE. OTHERWISE, WE STAY HERE AND TAKE OUR CHANCES!
TRAIN ANY NEW PADAWANS LATELY, JEDI? I'D LOVE TO LOOK THEM UP ... ONCE I'M FREE.
IT WILL BE AS YOU SAY. YOU HAVE MY WORD AS A JEDI.
COME. WE NEED TO GET MOVING. TIME IS OF THE ESSENCE. WHAT IS THE BEST WAY IN, KORTO VOS?
I LIKE THE SEWERS.

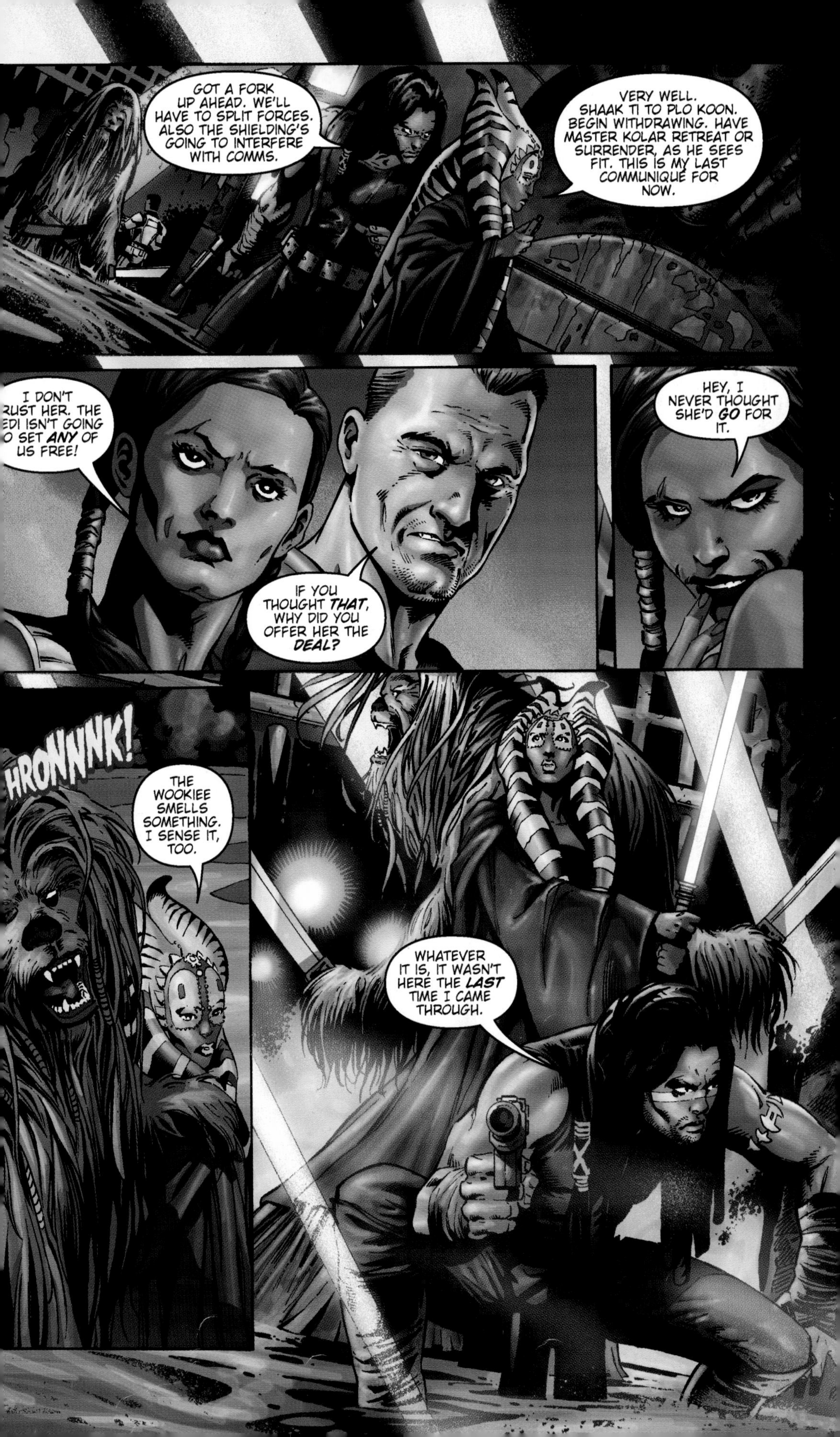
GOT A FORK UP AHEAD. WE'LL HAVE TO SPLIT FORCES. ALSO THE SHIELDING'S GOING TO INTERFERE WITH COMMS.
VERY WELL. SHAAK TI TO PLO KOON. BEGIN WITHDRAWING. HAVE MASTER KOLAR RETREAT OR SURRENDER, AS HE SEES FIT. THIS IS MY LAST COMMUNIQUE FOR NOW.
I DON'T RUST HER. THE EDI ISN'T GOING O SET ANY OF US FREE!
IF YOU THOUGHT THAT, WHY DID YOU OFFER HER THE DEAL?
HEY, I NEVER THOUGHT SHE'D GO FOR IT.
HRONNNK!
THE WOOKIEE SMELLS SOMETHING. I SENSE IT, TOO.
WHATEVER IT IS, IT WASN'T HERE THE LAST TIME I CAME THROUGH.

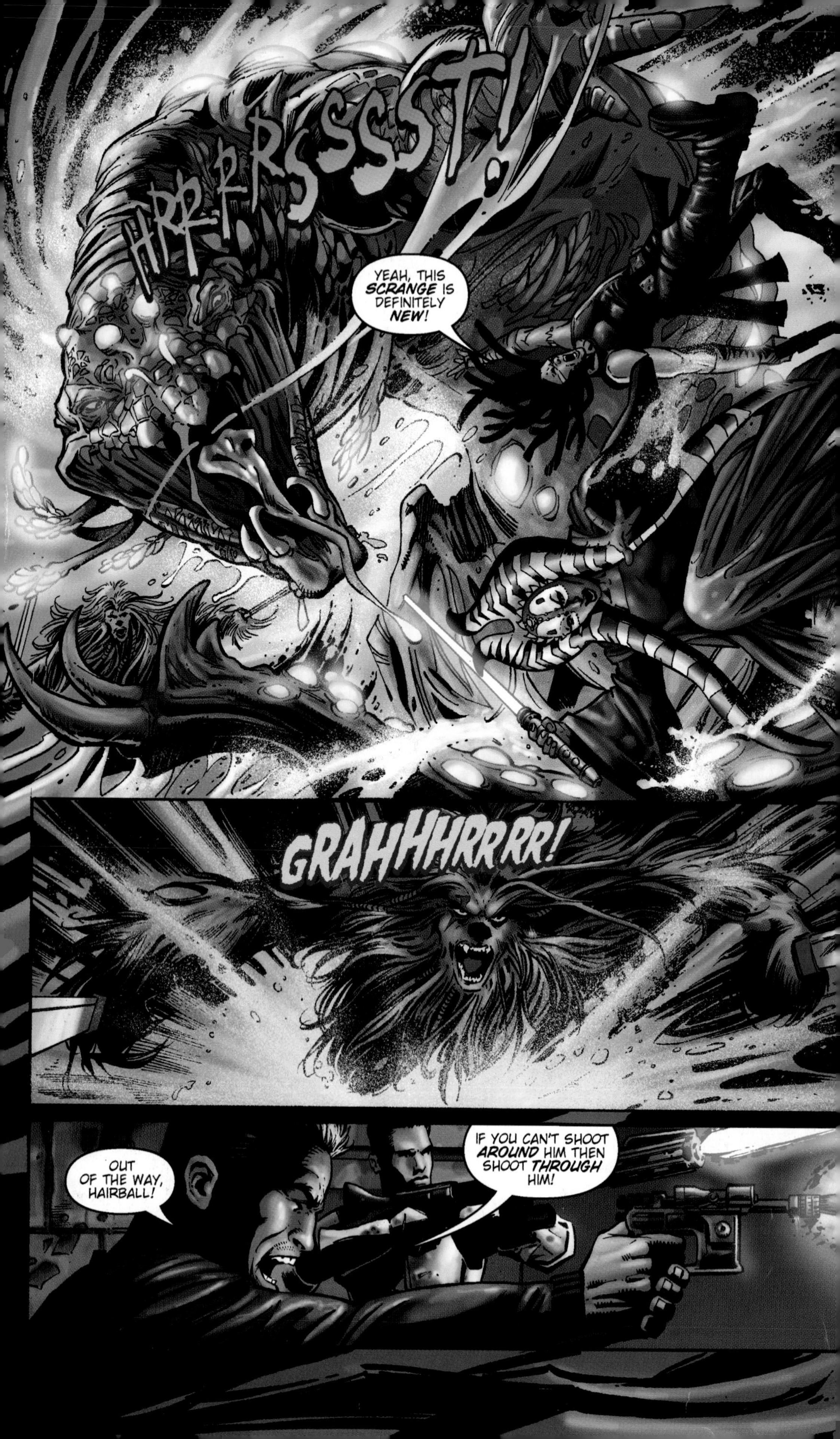
HRRRRSSSST!!
YEAH, THIS SCRANGE IS DEFINITELY NEW!
GRAHHHRRRRR!
OUT OF THE WAY, HAIRBALL!
IF YOU CAN'T SHOOT AROUND HIM THEN SHOOT THROUGH HIM!

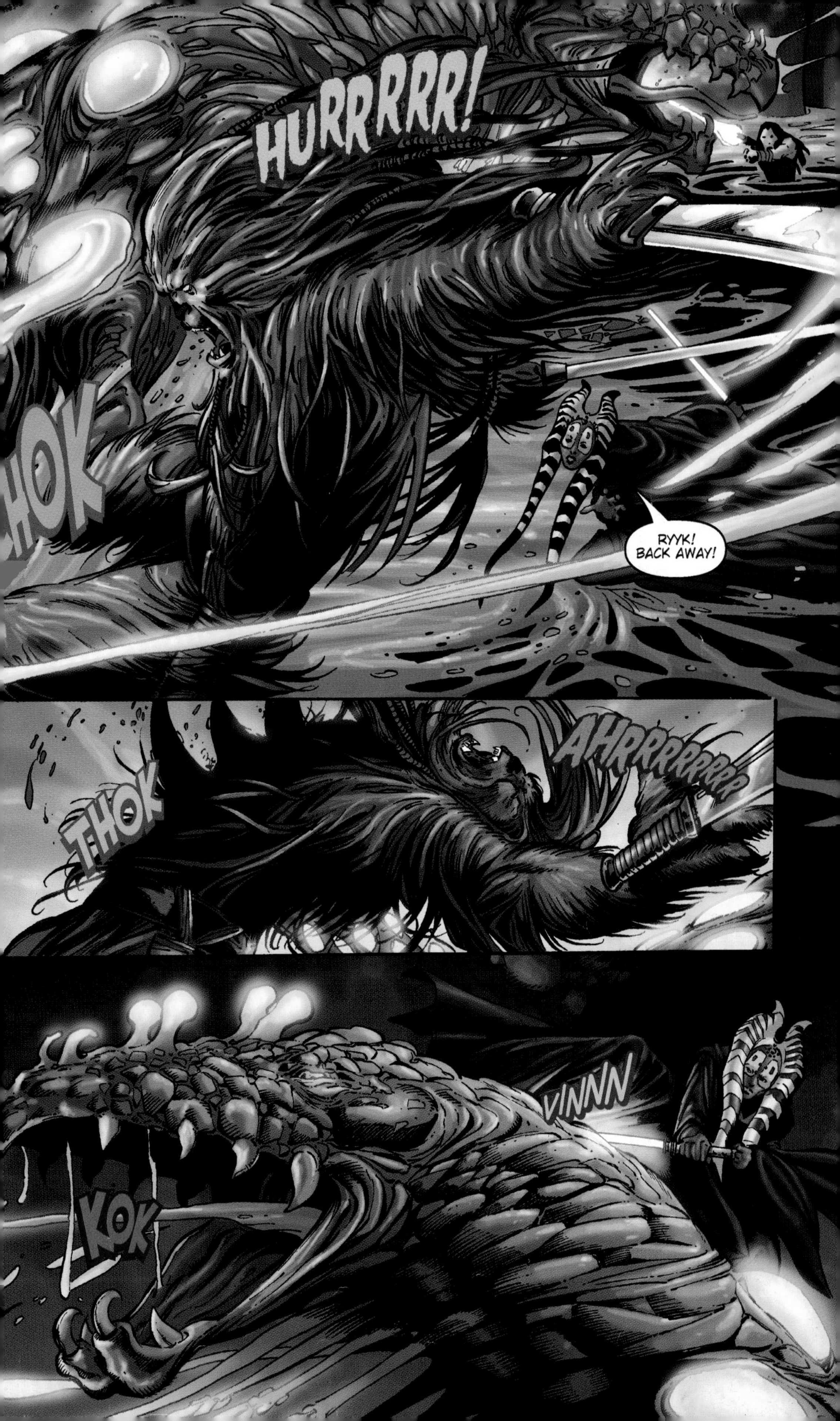
HURRRRR!
THOK
RYYK! BACK AWAY!
THOK
AHRRRRRRRR
VINNN
KOK

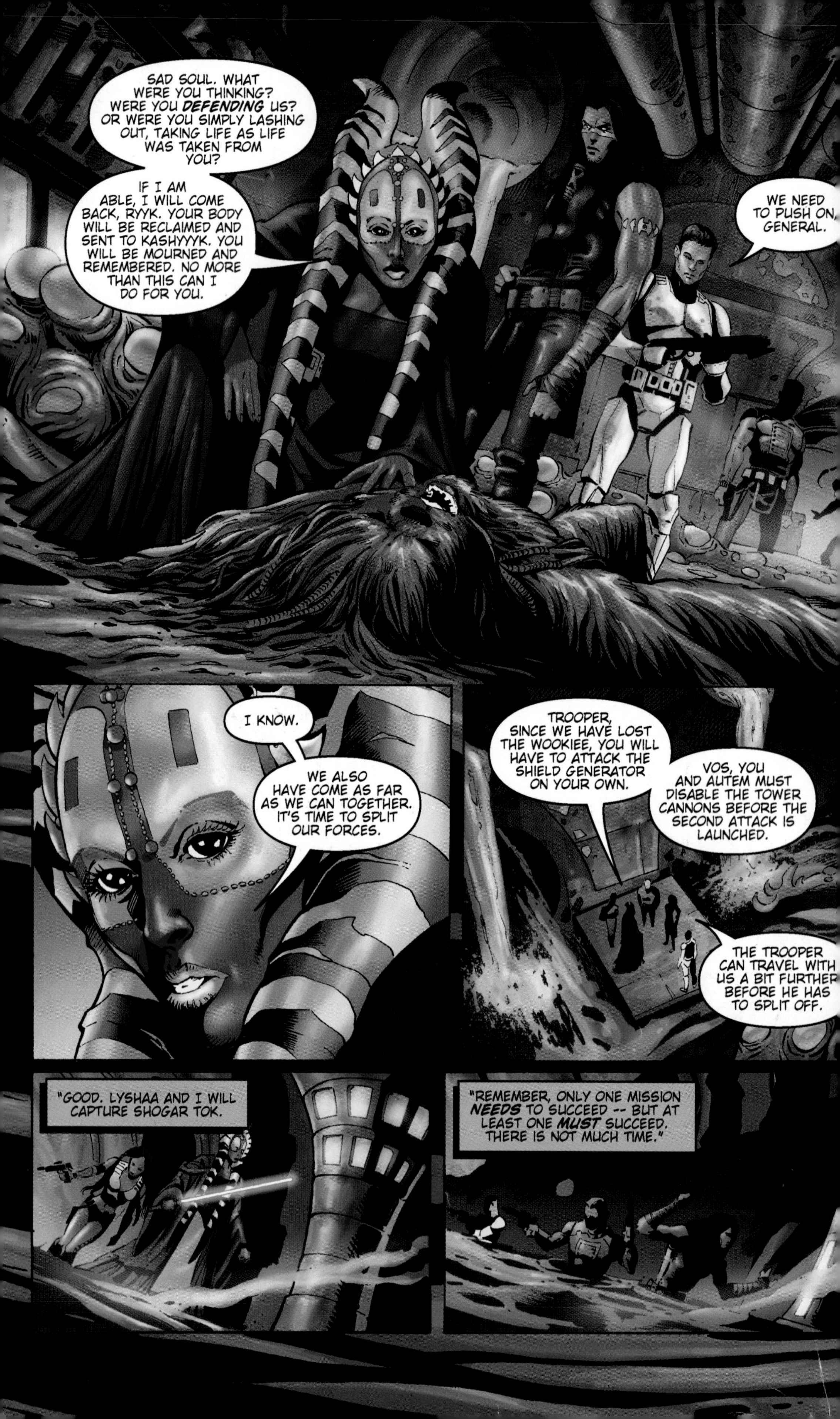
SAD SOUL. WHAT WERE YOU THINKING? WERE YOU DEFENDING US? OR WERE YOU SIMPLY LASHING OUT, TAKING LIFE AS LIFE WAS TAKEN FROM YOU?
IF I AM ABLE, I WILL COME BACK, RYYK. YOUR BODY WILL BE RECLAIMED AND SENT TO KASHYYYK. YOU WILL BE MOURNED AND REMEMBERED. NO MORE THAN THIS CAN I DO FOR YOU.
WE NEED TO PUSH ON, GENERAL.
I KNOW.
WE ALSO HAVE COME AS FAR AS WE CAN TOGETHER. IT'S TIME TO SPLIT OUR FORCES.
TROOPER, SINCE WE HAVE LOST THE WOOKIEE, YOU WILL HAVE TO ATTACK THE SHIELD GENERATOR ON YOUR OWN.
VOS, YOU AND AUTEM MUST DISABLE THE TOWER CANNONS BEFORE THE SECOND ATTACK IS LAUNCHED.
THE TROOPER CAN TRAVEL WITH US A BIT FURTHER BEFORE HE HAS TO SPLIT OFF.
"GOOD. LYSHAA AND I WILL CAPTURE SHOGAR TOK.
"REMEMBER, ONLY ONE MISSION NEEDS TO SUCCEED -- BUT AT LEAST ONE MUST SUCCEED. THERE IS NOT MUCH TIME."

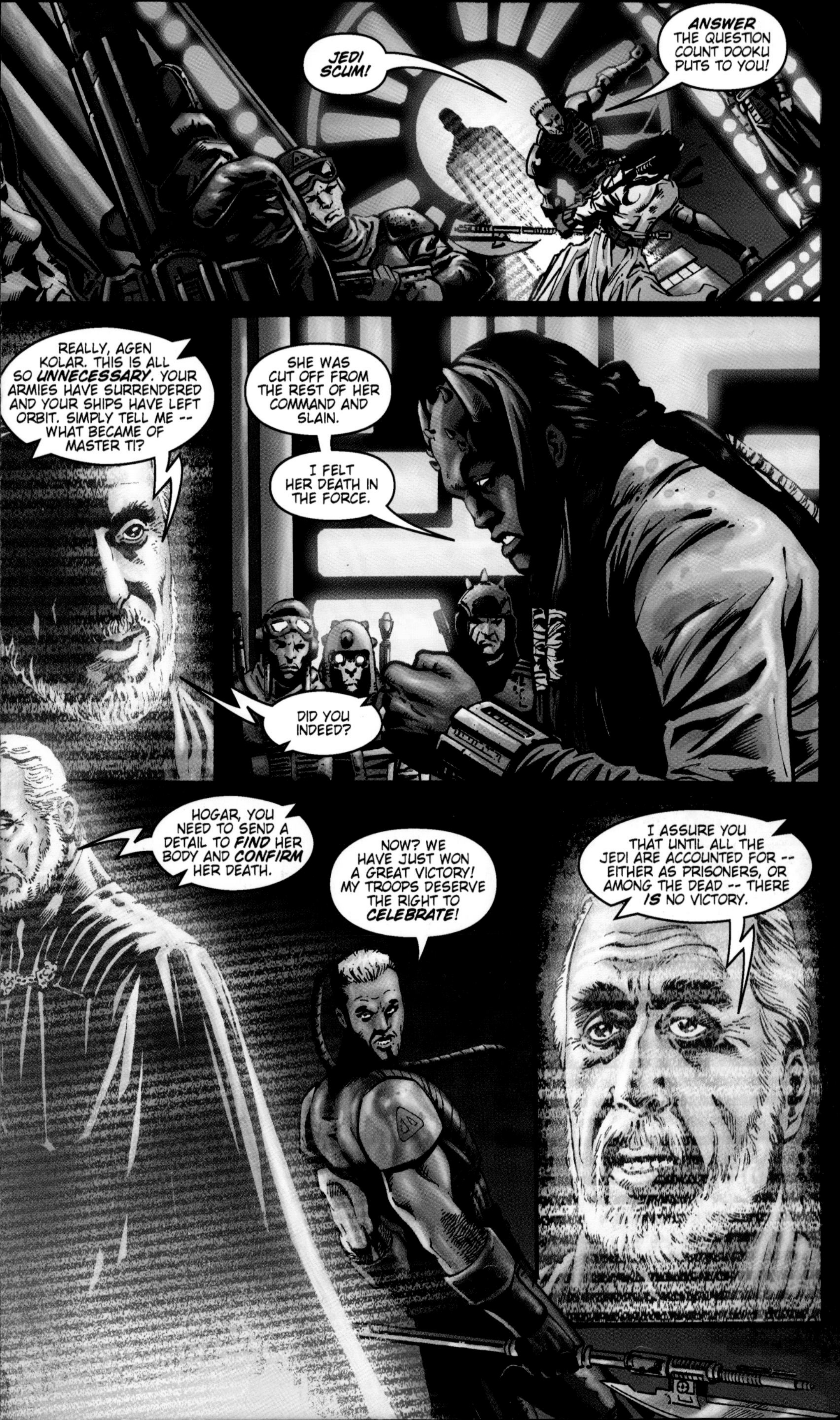

JEDI SCUM!
ANSWER THE QUESTION COUNT DOOKU PUTS TO YOU!
REALLY, AGEN KOLAR. THIS IS ALL SO UNNECESSARY. YOUR ARMIES HAVE SURRENDERED AND YOUR SHIPS HAVE LEFT ORBIT. SIMPLY TELL ME -- WHAT BECAME OF MASTER TI?
SHE WAS CUT OFF FROM THE REST OF HER COMMAND AND SLAIN.
I FELT HER DEATH IN THE FORCE.
DID YOU INDEED?
HOGAR, YOU NEED TO SEND A DETAIL TO FIND HER BODY AND CONFIRM HER DEATH.
NOW? WE HAVE JUST WON A GREAT VICTORY! MY TROOPS DESERVE THE RIGHT TO CELEBRATE!
I ASSURE YOU THAT UNTIL ALL THE JEDI ARE ACCOUNTED FOR -- EITHER AS PRISONERS, OR AMONG THE DEAD -- THERE IS NO VICTORY.

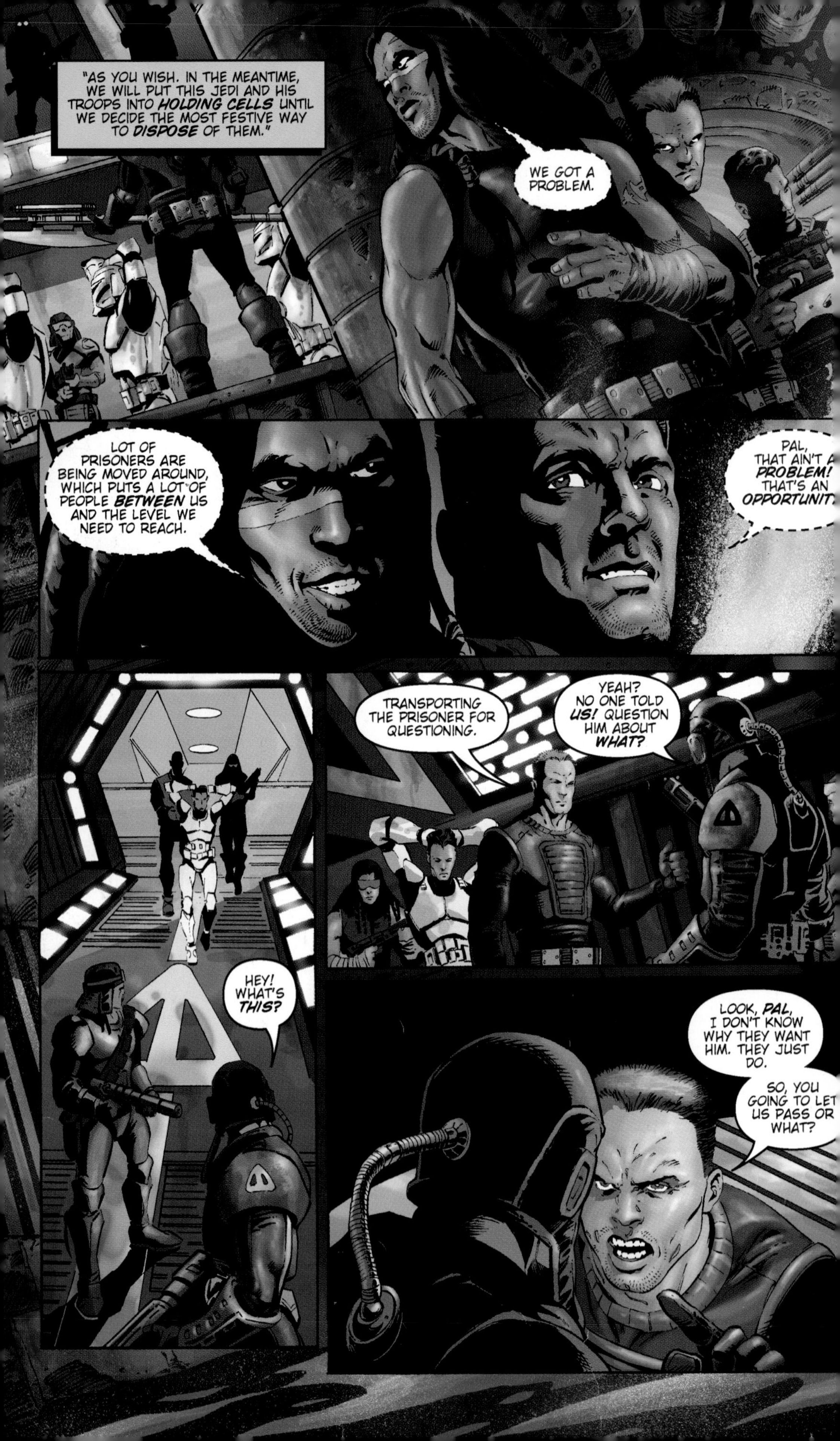
"AS YOU WISH. IN THE MEANTIME, WE WILL PUT THIS JEDI AND HIS TROOPS INTO HOLDING CELLS UNTIL WE DECIDE THE MOST FESTIVE WAY TO DISPOSE OF THEM."
WE GOT A PROBLEM.
LOT OF PRISONERS ARE BEING MOVED AROUND, WHICH PUTS A LOT OF PEOPLE BETWEEN US AND THE LEVEL WE NEED TO REACH.
PAL, THAT AIN'T A PROBLEM! THAT'S AN OPPORTUNIT
HEY! WHAT'S THIS?
TRANSPORTING THE PRISONER FOR QUESTIONING.
YEAH? NO ONE TOLD US! QUESTION HIM ABOUT WHAT?
LOOK, PAL, I DON'T KNOW WHY THEY WANT HIM. THEY JUST DO.
SO, YOU GOING TO LET US PASS OR WHAT?

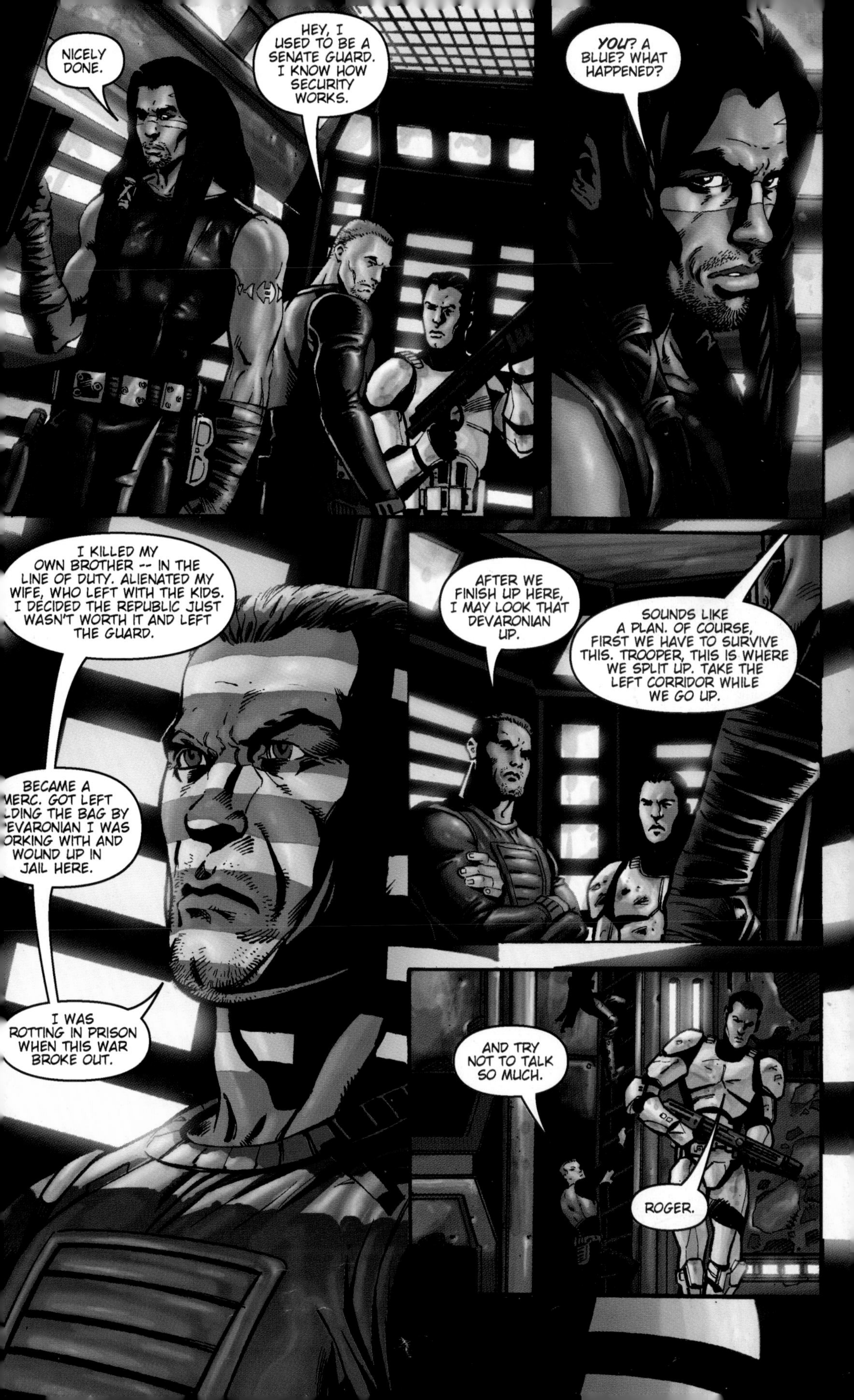
NICELY DONE.
HEY, I USED TO BE A SENATE GUARD. I KNOW HOW SECURITY WORKS.
YOU? A BLUE? WHAT HAPPENED?
I KILLED MY OWN BROTHER -- IN THE LINE OF DUTY. ALIENATED MY WIFE, WHO LEFT WITH THE KIDS. I DECIDED THE REPUBLIC JUST WASN'T WORTH IT AND LEFT THE GUARD.
BECAME A MERC. GOT LEFT LDING THE BAG BY EVARONIAN I WAS ORKING WITH AND WOUND UP IN JAIL HERE.
I WAS ROTTING IN PRISON WHEN THIS WAR BROKE OUT.
AFTER WE FINISH UP HERE, I MAY LOOK THAT DEVARONIAN UP.
SOUNDS LIKE A PLAN. OF COURSE, FIRST WE HAVE TO SURVIVE THIS. TROOPER, THIS IS WHERE WE SPLIT UP. TAKE THE LEFT CORRIDOR WHILE WE GO UP.
AND TRY NOT TO TALK SO MUCH.
ROGER.

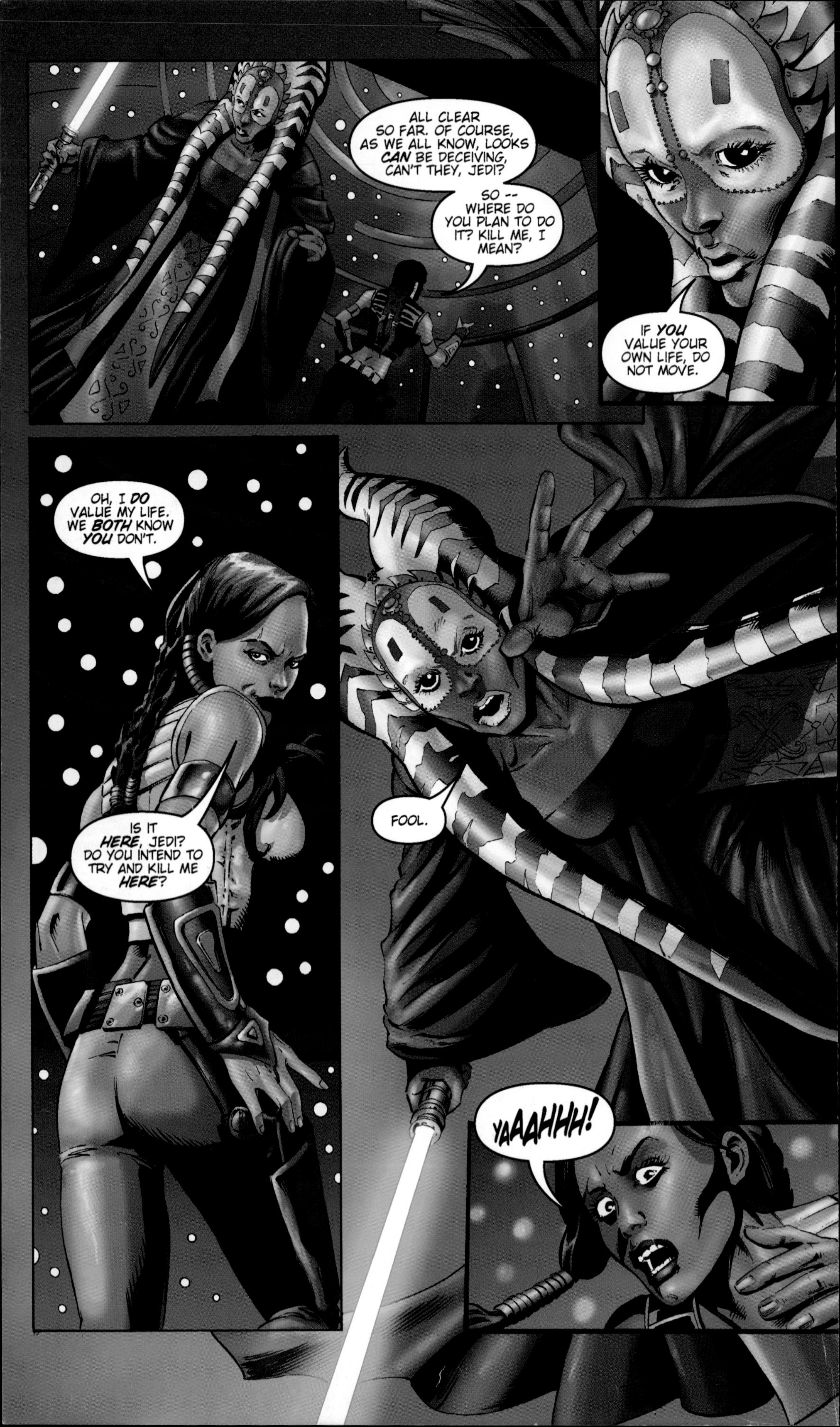
ALL CLEAR SO FAR. OF COURSE, AS WE ALL KNOW, LOOKS CAN BE DECEIVING, CAN'T THEY, JEDI?
SO -- WHERE DO YOU PLAN TO DO IT? KILL ME, I MEAN?
IF YOU VALUE YOUR OWN LIFE, DO NOT MOVE.
OH, I DO VALUE MY LIFE. WE BOTH KNOW YOU DON'T.
IS IT HERE, JEDI? DO YOU INTEND TO TRY AND KILL ME HERE?
FOOL.
YAAAHHH!

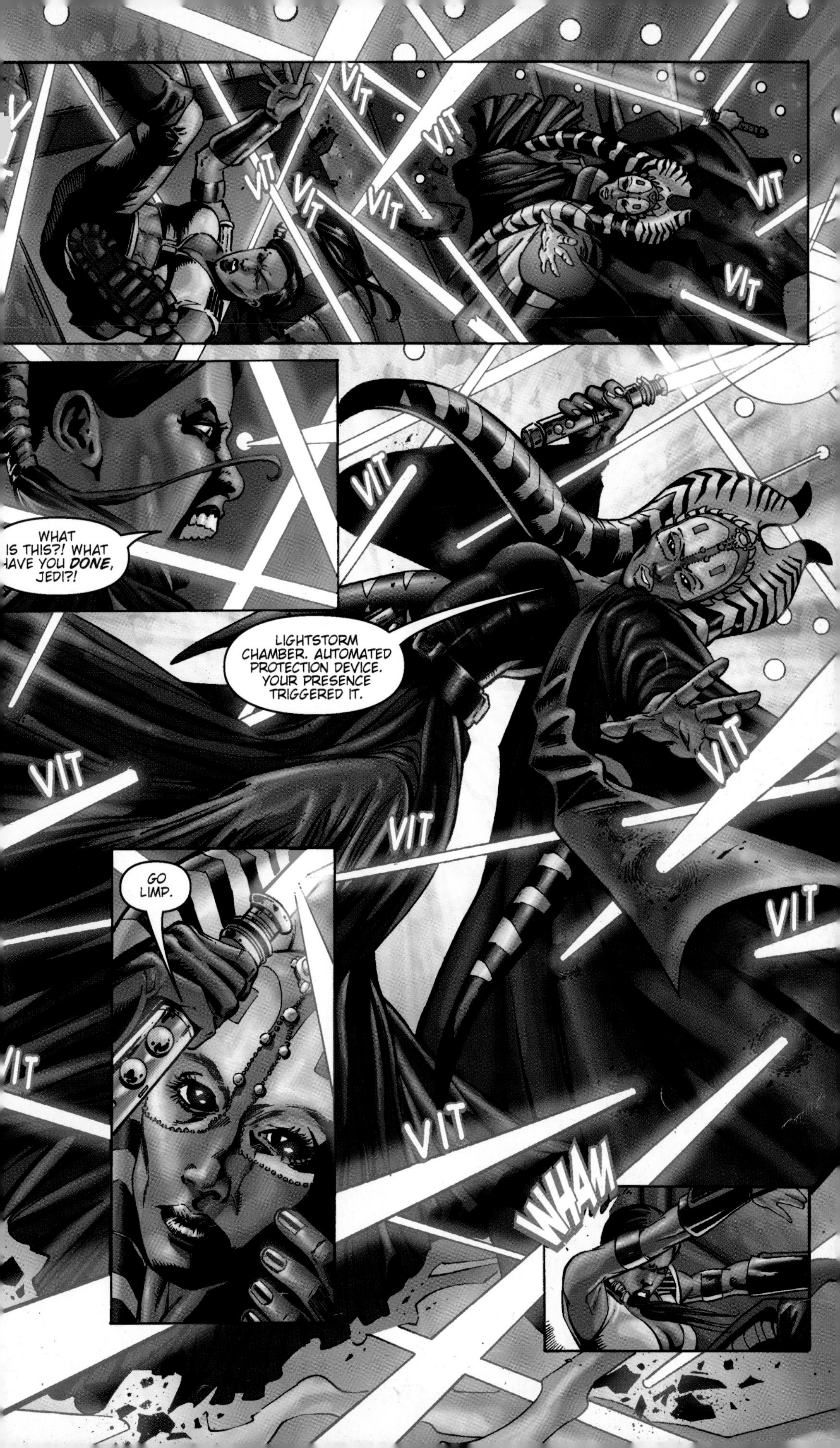
VIT
VIT
VIT
VIT
VIT
VIT
VIT
VIT
WHAT IS THIS?! WHAT HAVE YOU DONE, JEDI?!
VIT
LIGHTSTORM CHAMBER. AUTOMATED PROTECTION DEVICE. YOUR PRESENCE TRIGGERED IT.
VIT
VIT
VIT
GO LIMP.
VIT
VIT
VIT
WHAM

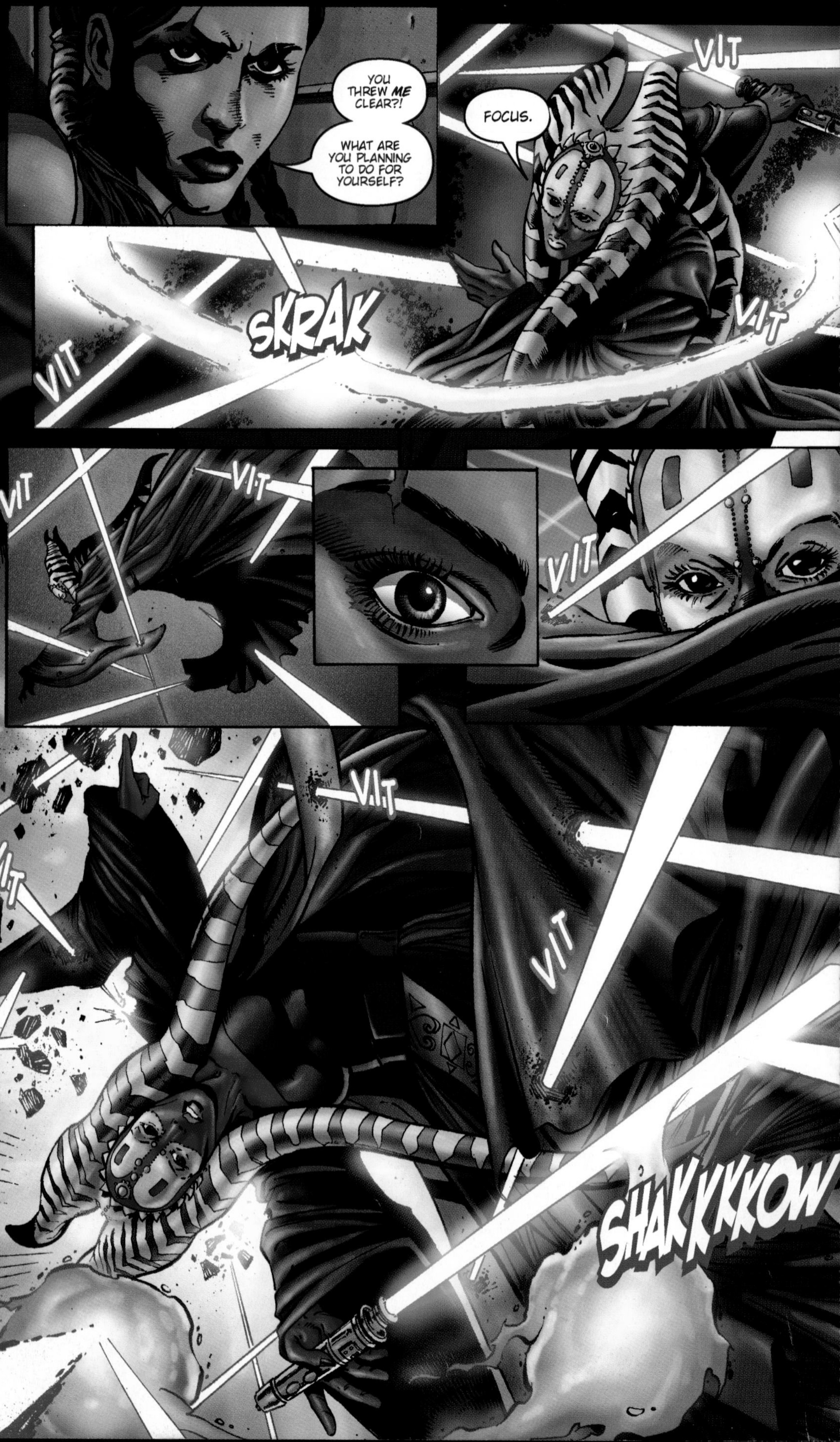

YOU THREW ME CLEAR?!
WHAT ARE YOU PLANNING TO DO FOR YOURSELF?
VIT
FOCUS.
SKRAK
VIT
VIT
VIT
VIT
VIT
VIT
VIT
VIT
SHAKKKOW

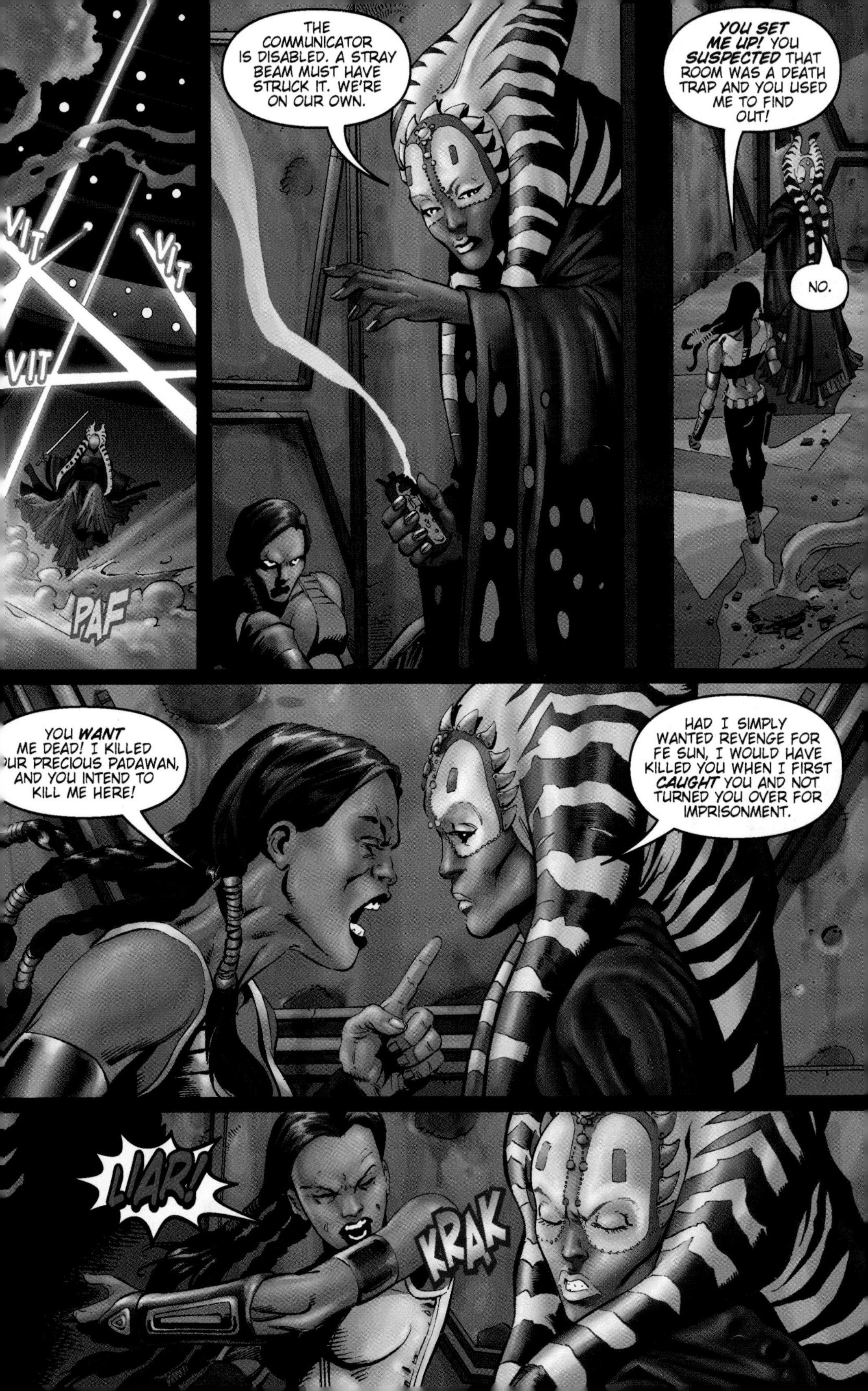
VIT
VIT
VIT
PAF
THE COMMUNICATOR IS DISABLED. A STRAY BEAM MUST HAVE STRUCK IT. WE'RE ON OUR OWN.
YOU SET ME UP! YOU SUSPECTED THAT ROOM WAS A DEATH TRAP AND YOU USED ME TO FIND OUT!
NO.
YOU WANT ME DEAD! I KILLED OUR PRECIOUS PADAWAN, AND YOU INTEND TO KILL ME HERE!
HAD I SIMPLY WANTED REVENGE FOR FE SUN, I WOULD HAVE KILLED YOU WHEN I FIRST CAUGHT YOU AND NOT TURNED YOU OVER FOR IMPRISONMENT.
LIAR!
KRAK

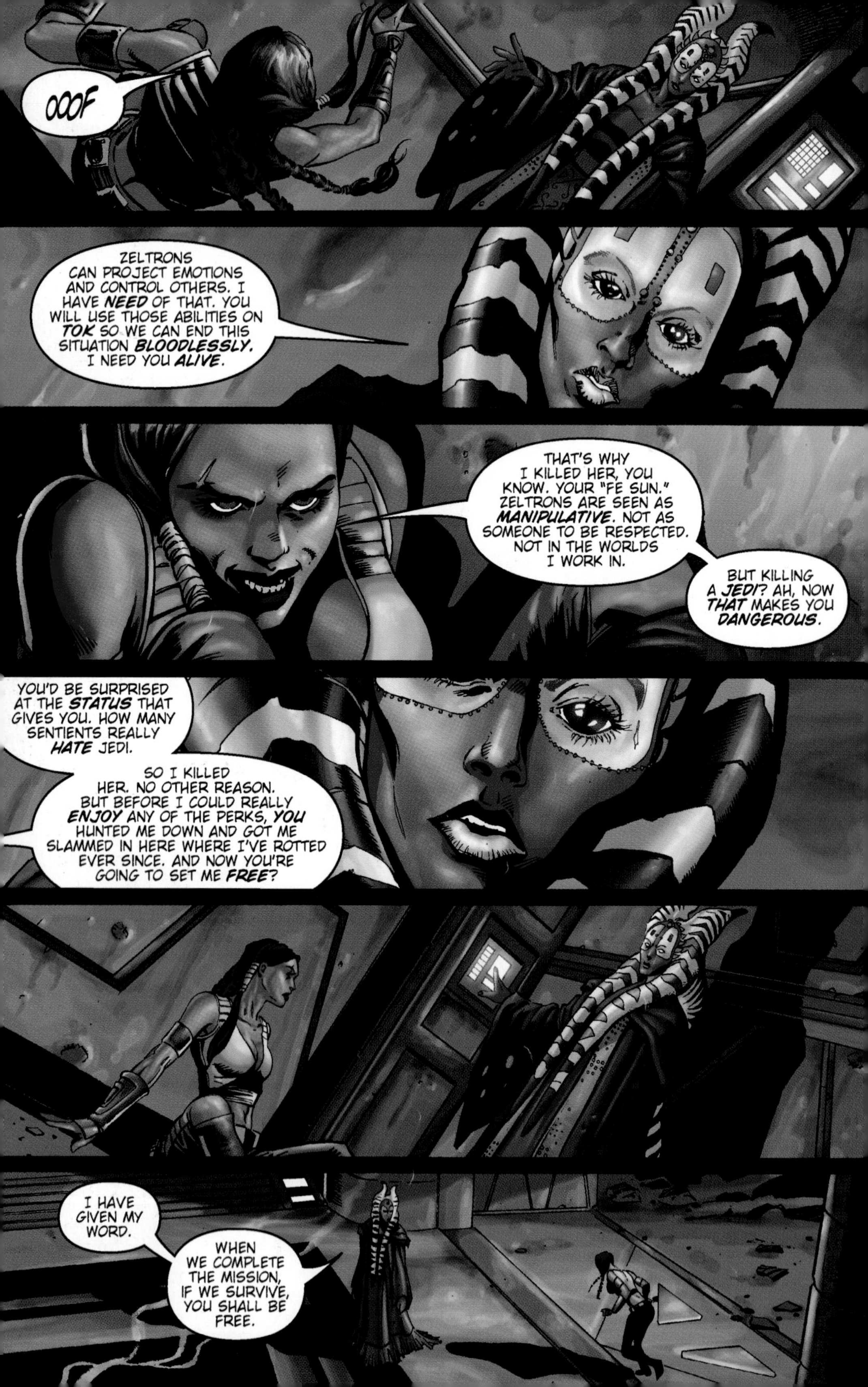
OOOF
ZELTRONS CAN PROJECT EMOTIONS AND CONTROL OTHERS. I HAVE NEED OF THAT. YOU WILL USE THOSE ABILITIES ON TOK SO WE CAN END THIS SITUATION BLOODLESSLY. I NEED YOU ALIVE.
THAT'S WHY I KILLED HER, YOU KNOW. YOUR "FE SUN." ZELTRONS ARE SEEN AS MANIPULATIVE. NOT AS SOMEONE TO BE RESPECTED. NOT IN THE WORLDS I WORK IN.
BUT KILLING A JEDI? AH, NOW THAT MAKES YOU DANGEROUS.
YOU'D BE SURPRISED AT THE STATUS THAT GIVES YOU. HOW MANY SENTIENTS REALLY HATE JEDI.
SO I KILLED HER. NO OTHER REASON. BUT BEFORE I COULD REALLY ENJOY ANY OF THE PERKS, YOU HUNTED ME DOWN AND GOT ME SLAMMED IN HERE WHERE I'VE ROTTED EVER SINCE. AND NOW YOU'RE GOING TO SET ME FREE?
I HAVE GIVEN MY WORD.
WHEN WE COMPLETE THE MISSION, IF WE SURVIVE, YOU SHALL BE FREE.

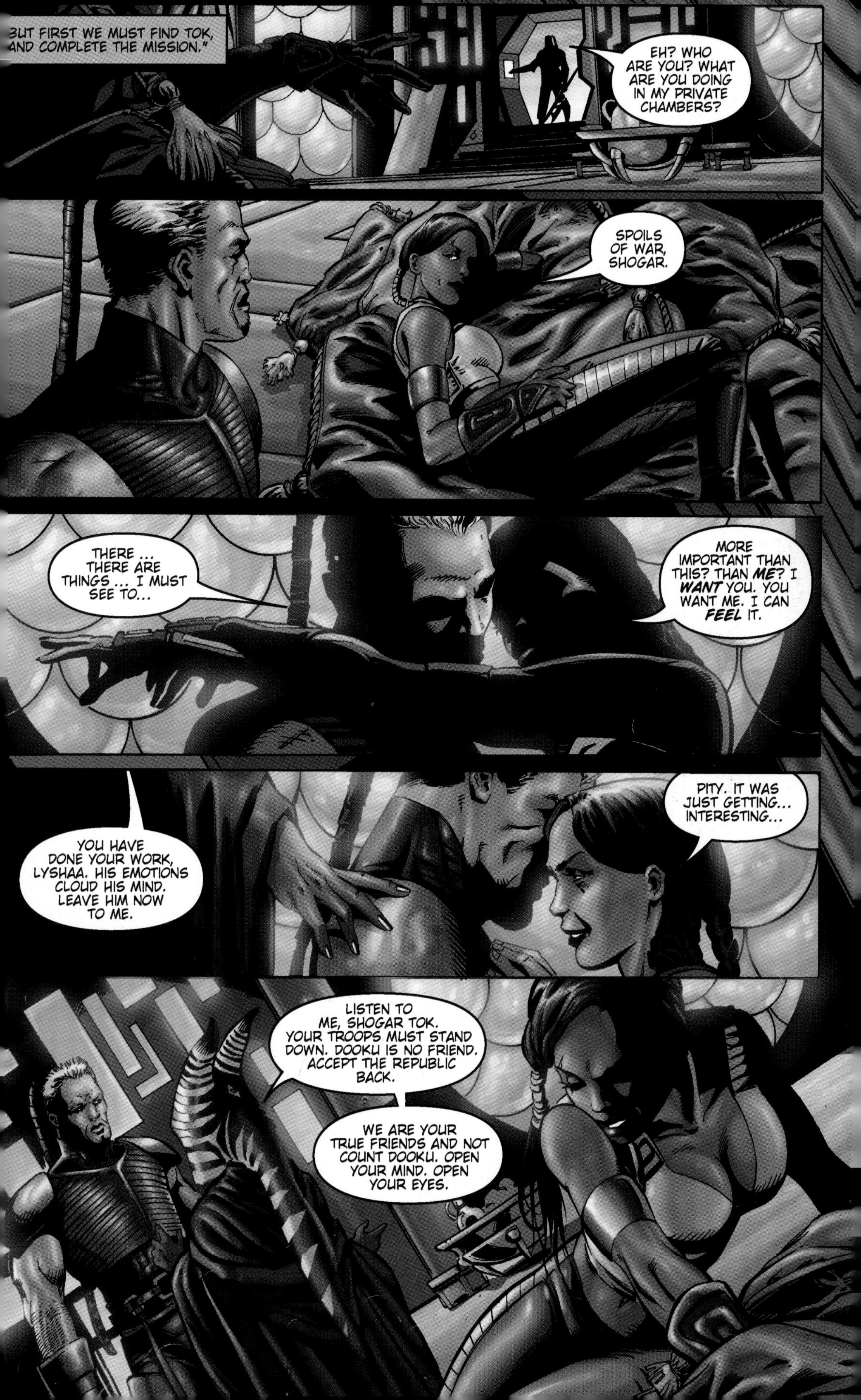
BUT FIRST WE MUST FIND TOK, AND COMPLETE THE MISSION."
EH? WHO ARE YOU? WHAT ARE YOU DOING IN MY PRIVATE CHAMBERS?
SPOILS OF WAR, SHOGAR.
THERE ... THERE ARE THINGS ... I MUST SEE TO...
MORE IMPORTANT THAN THIS? THAN ME? I WANT YOU. YOU WANT ME. I CAN FEEL IT.
PITY. IT WAS JUST GETTING... INTERESTING...
YOU HAVE DONE YOUR WORK, LYSHAA. HIS EMOTIONS CLOUD HIS MIND. LEAVE HIM NOW TO ME.
LISTEN TO ME, SHOGAR TOK. YOUR TROOPS MUST STAND DOWN. DOOKU IS NO FRIEND. ACCEPT THE REPUBLIC BACK.
WE ARE YOUR TRUE FRIENDS AND NOT COUNT DOOKU. OPEN YOUR MIND. OPEN YOUR EYES.

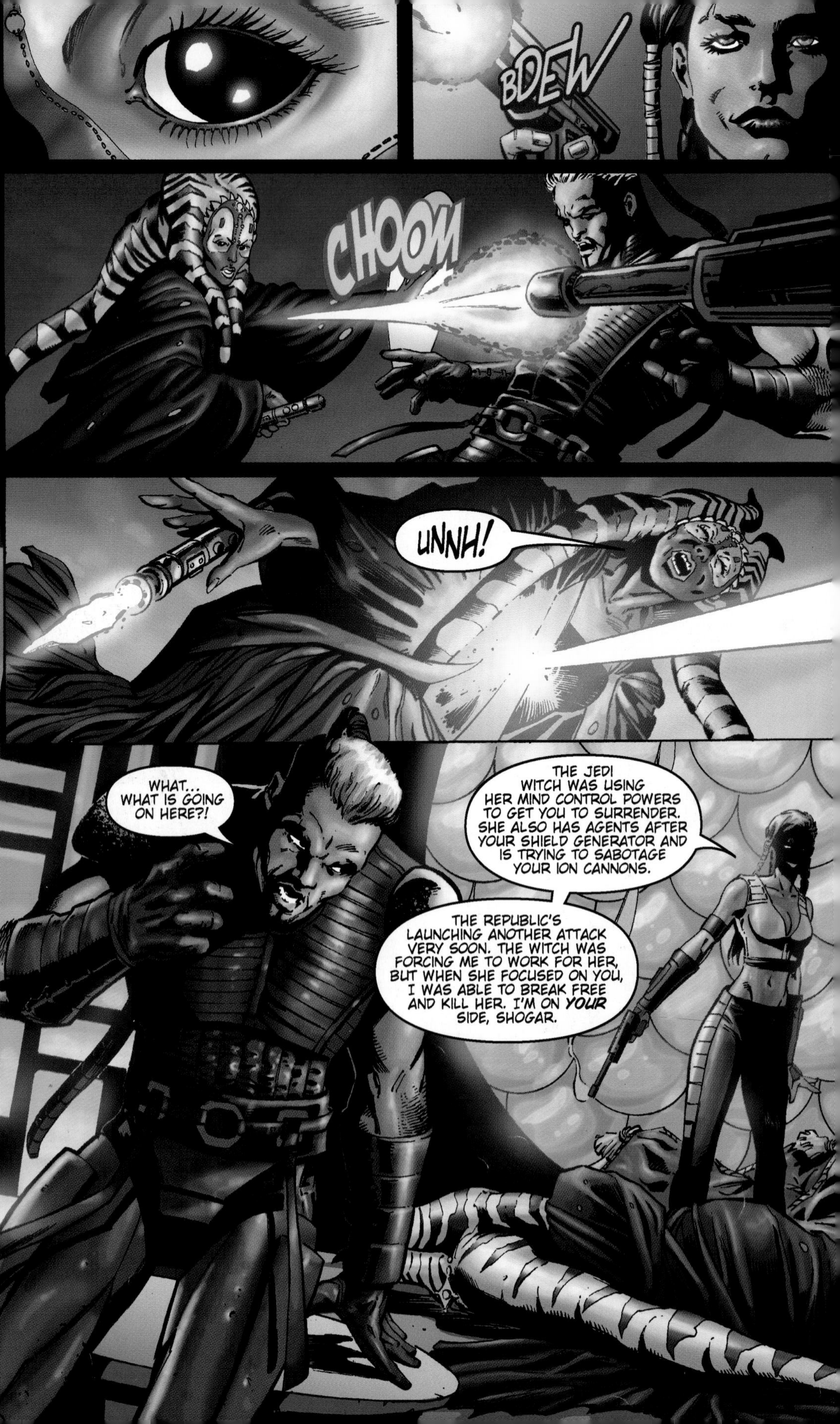
BDEW
CHOOM
UNNH!
WHAT... WHAT IS GOING ON HERE?!
THE JEDI WITCH WAS USING HER MIND CONTROL POWERS TO GET YOU TO SURRENDER. SHE ALSO HAS AGENTS AFTER YOUR SHIELD GENERATOR AND IS TRYING TO SABOTAGE YOUR ION CANNONS.
THE REPUBLIC'S LAUNCHING ANOTHER ATTACK VERY SOON. THE WITCH WAS FORCING ME TO WORK FOR HER, BUT WHEN SHE FOCUSED ON YOU, I WAS ABLE TO BREAK FREE AND KILL HER. I'M ON YOUR SIDE, SHOGAR.

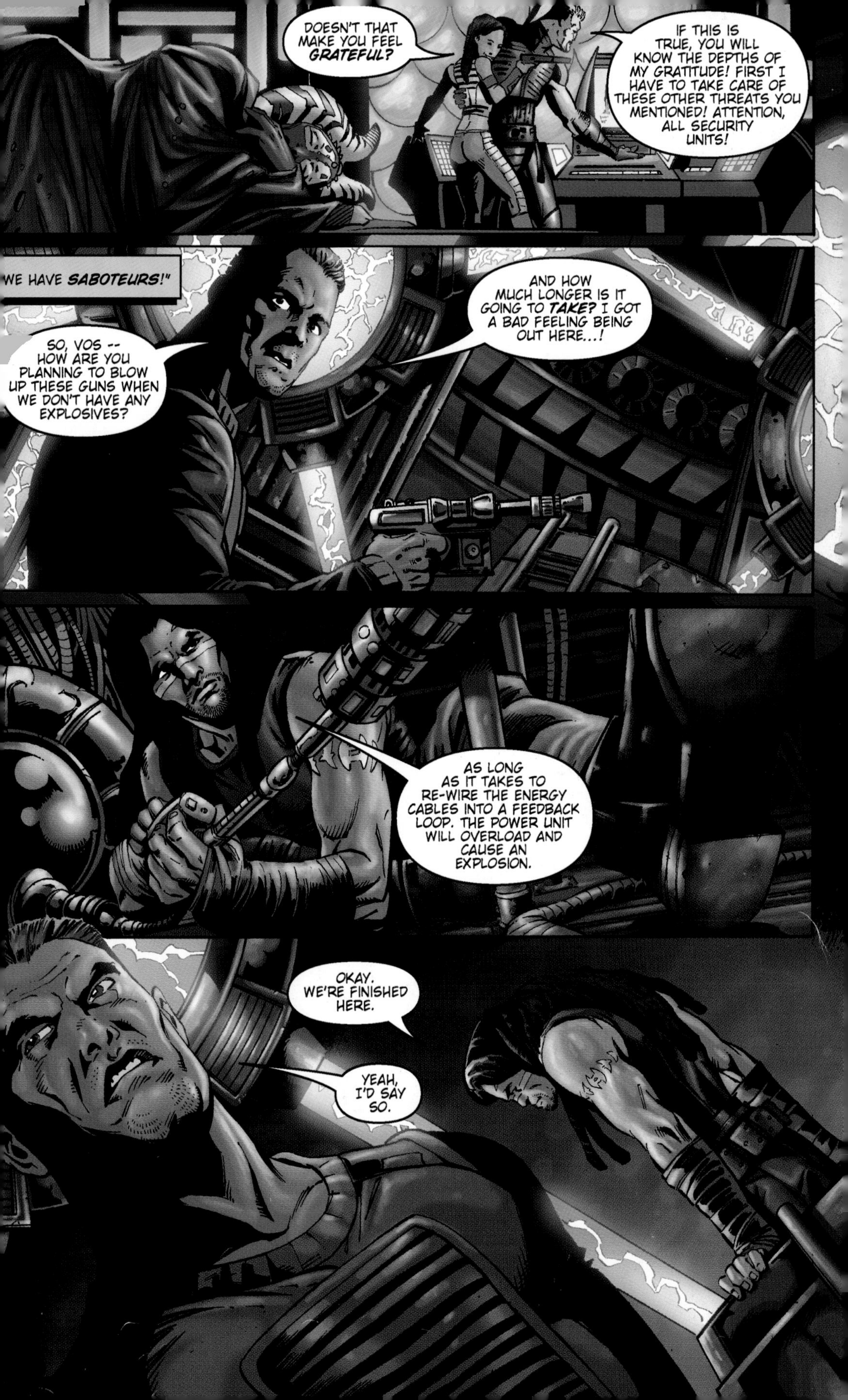
DOESN'T THAT MAKE YOU FEEL GRATEFUL?
IF THIS IS TRUE, YOU WILL KNOW THE DEPTHS OF MY GRATITUDE! FIRST I HAVE TO TAKE CARE OF THESE OTHER THREATS YOU MENTIONED! ATTENTION, ALL SECURITY UNITS!
WE HAVE SABOTEURS!"
SO, VOS -- HOW ARE YOU PLANNING TO BLOW UP THESE GUNS WHEN WE DON'T HAVE ANY EXPLOSIVES?
AND HOW MUCH LONGER IS IT GOING TO TAKE? I GOT A BAD FEELING BEING OUT HERE...!
AS LONG AS IT TAKES TO RE-WIRE THE ENERGY CABLES INTO A FEEDBACK LOOP. THE POWER UNIT WILL OVERLOAD AND CAUSE AN EXPLOSION.
OKAY. WE'RE FINISHED HERE.
YEAH, I'D SAY SO.

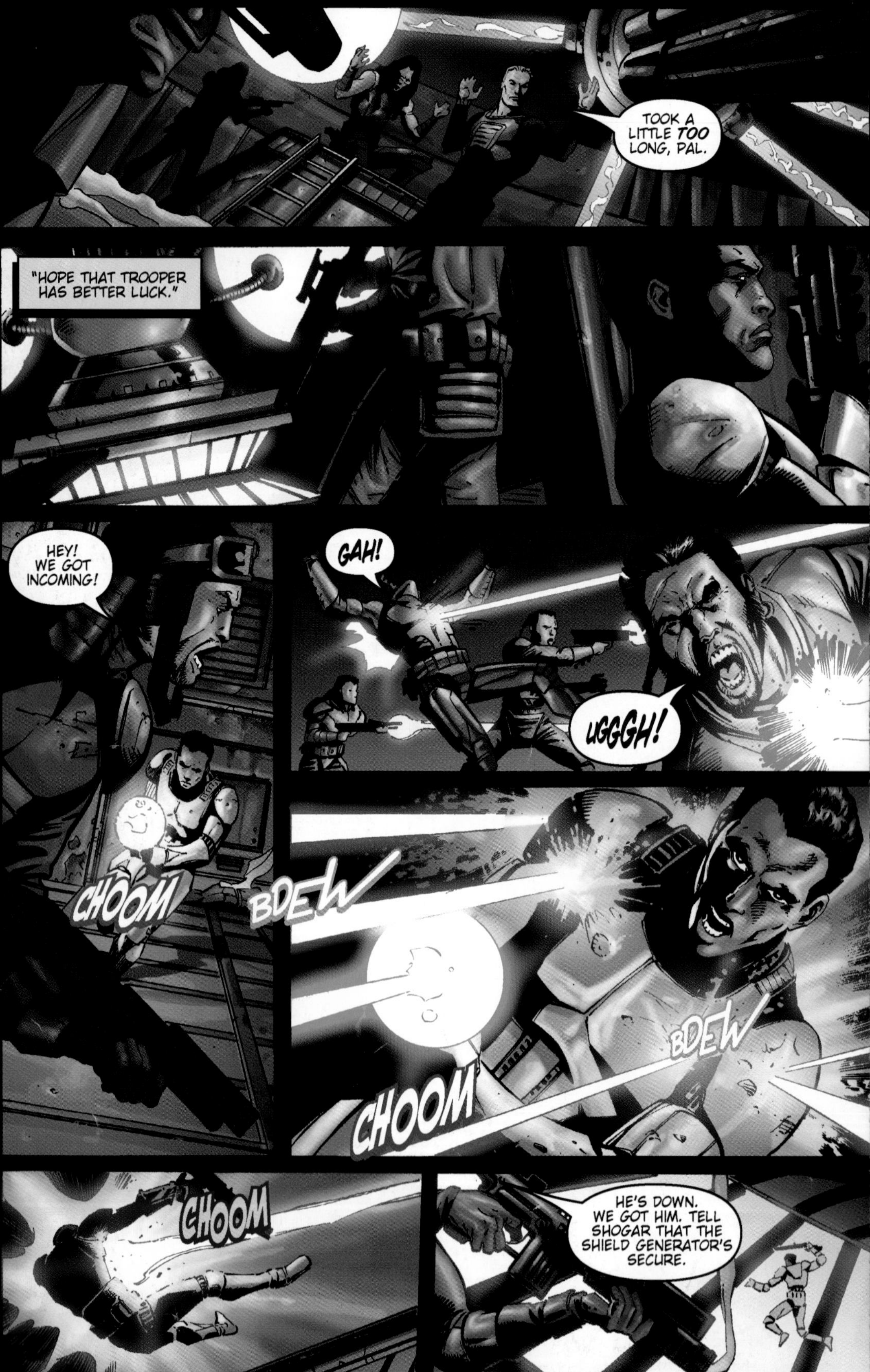
TOOK A LITTLE *TOO* LONG, PAL.
"HOPE THAT TROOPER HAS BETTER LUCK."
HEY! WE GOT INCOMING!
GAH!
UGGGH!
CHOOM
BDEW
BDEW
CHOOM
CHOOM
HE'S DOWN. WE GOT HIM. TELL SHOGAR THAT THE SHIELD GENERATOR'S SECURE.

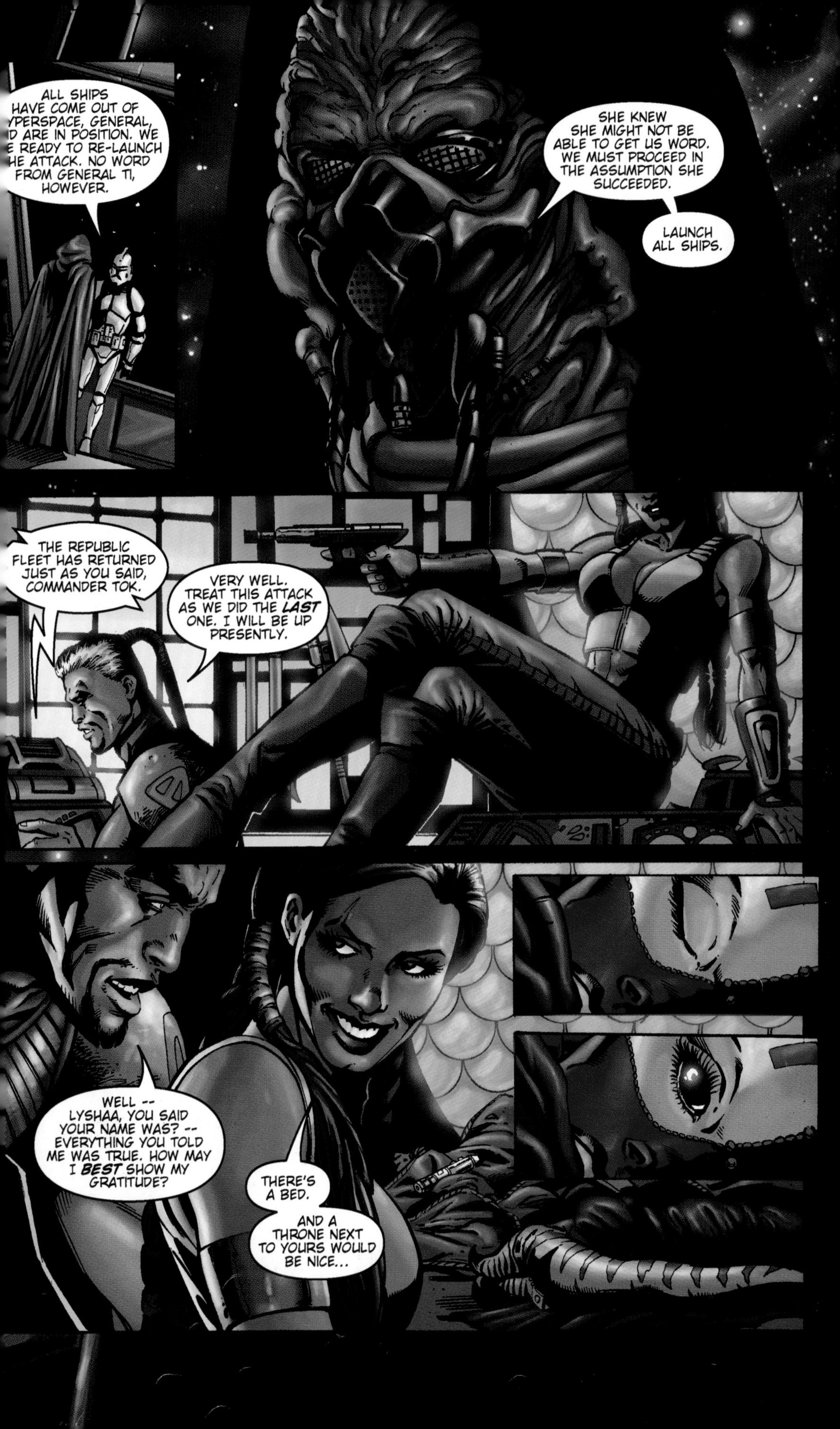
ALL SHIPS HAVE COME OUT OF YPERSPACE, GENERAL, D ARE IN POSITION. WE E READY TO RE-LAUNCH HE ATTACK. NO WORD FROM GENERAL TI, HOWEVER.
SHE KNEW SHE MIGHT NOT BE ABLE TO GET US WORD. WE MUST PROCEED IN THE ASSUMPTION SHE SUCCEEDED.
LAUNCH ALL SHIPS.
THE REPUBLIC FLEET HAS RETURNED JUST AS YOU SAID, COMMANDER TOK.
VERY WELL. TREAT THIS ATTACK AS WE DID THE *LAST* ONE. I WILL BE UP PRESENTLY.
WELL -- LYSHAA, YOU SAID YOUR NAME WAS? -- EVERYTHING YOU TOLD ME WAS TRUE. HOW MAY I *BEST* SHOW MY GRATITUDE?
THERE'S A BED.
AND A THRONE NEXT TO YOURS WOULD BE NICE...

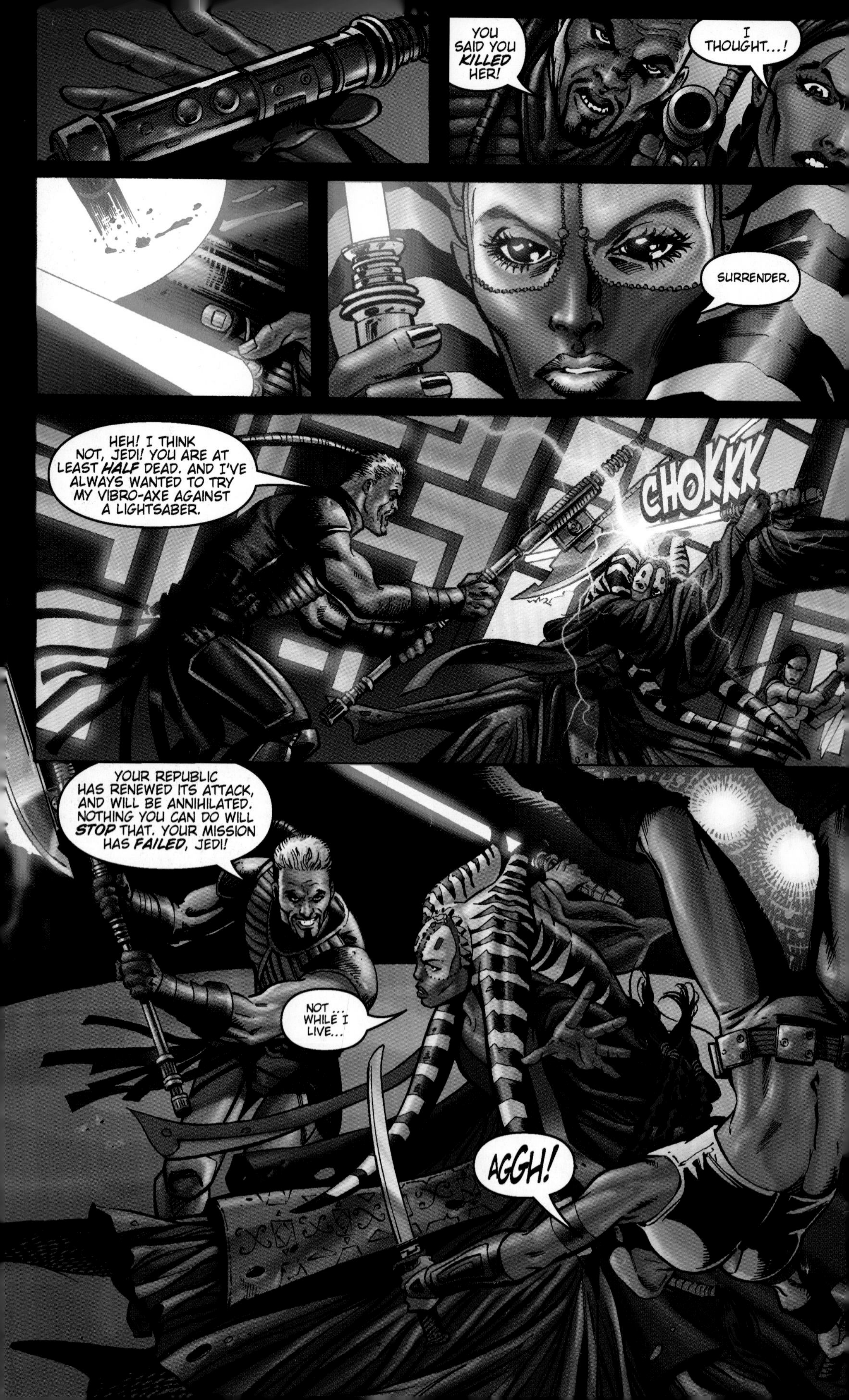
YOU SAID YOU KILLED HER!
I THOUGHT...!
SURRENDER.
HEH! I THINK NOT, JEDI! YOU ARE AT LEAST HALF DEAD. AND I'VE ALWAYS WANTED TO TRY MY VIBRO-AXE AGAINST A LIGHTSABER.
CHOKKK
YOUR REPUBLIC HAS RENEWED ITS ATTACK, AND WILL BE ANNIHILATED. NOTHING YOU CAN DO WILL STOP THAT. YOUR MISSION HAS FAILED, JEDI!
NOT... WHILE I LIVE...
AGGH!

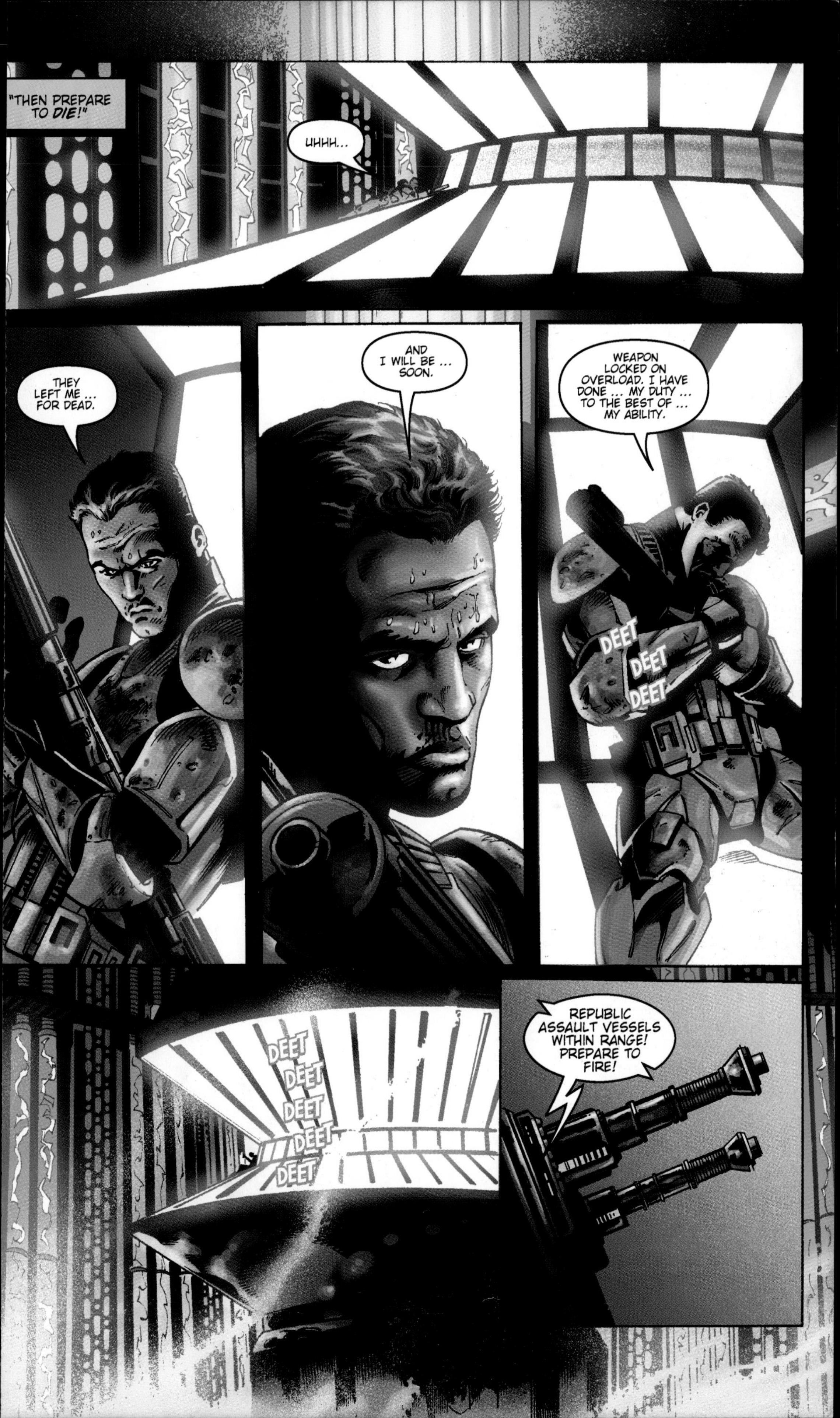
"THEN PREPARE TO *DIE!*"
UHHH...
THEY LEFT ME ... FOR DEAD.
AND I WILL BE ... SOON.
WEAPON LOCKED ON OVERLOAD. I HAVE DONE ... MY DUTY ... TO THE BEST OF ... MY ABILITY.
DEET DEET DEET
DEET DEET DEET DEET DEET
REPUBLIC ASSAULT VESSELS WITHIN RANGE! PREPARE TO FIRE!

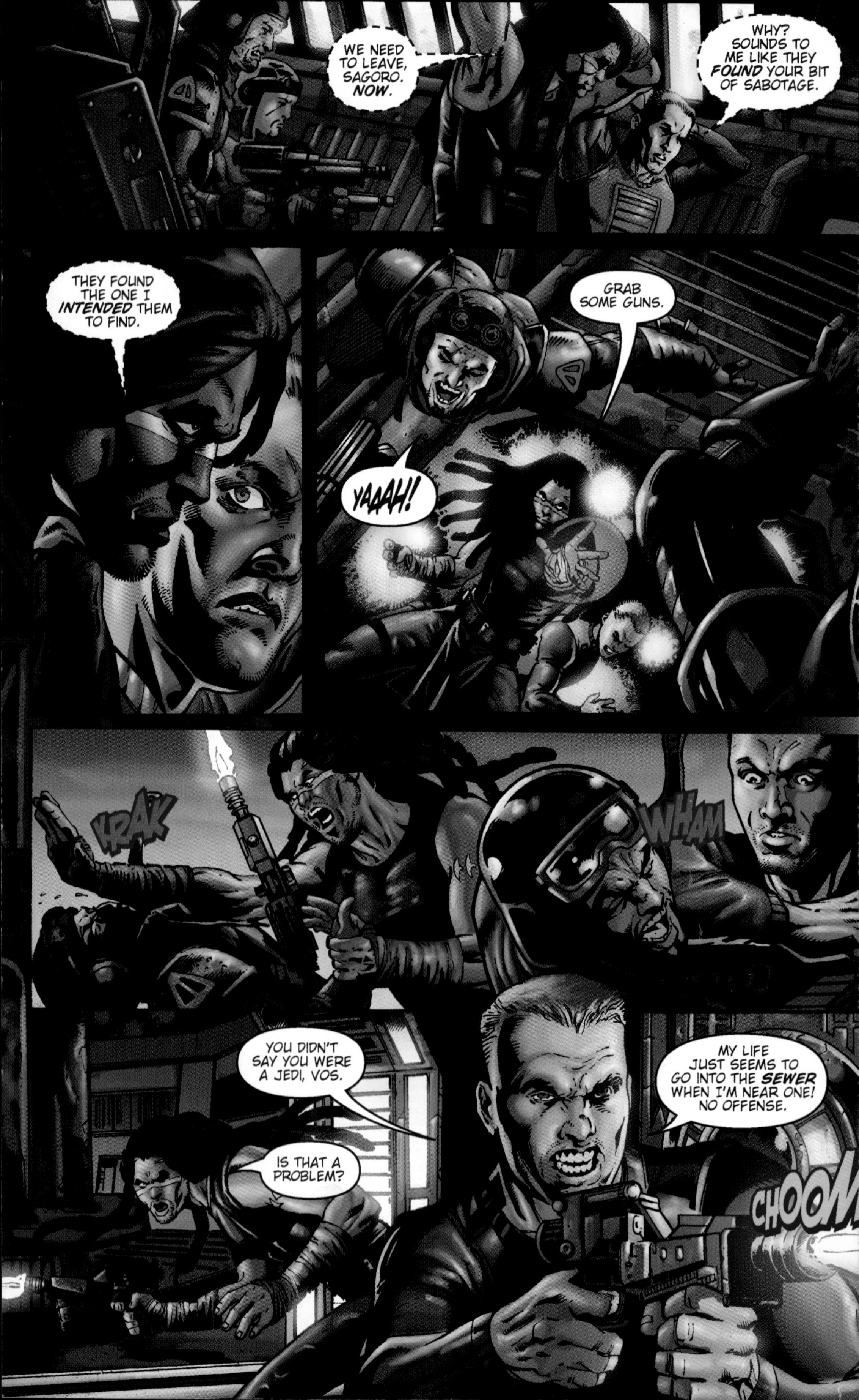
WE NEED TO LEAVE, SAGORO. NOW.
WHY? SOUNDS TO ME LIKE THEY FOUND YOUR BIT OF SABOTAGE.
THEY FOUND THE ONE I INTENDED THEM TO FIND.
GRAB SOME GUNS.
YAAAH!
KRAK
WHAM
YOU DIDN'T SAY YOU WERE A JEDI, VOS.
IS THAT A PROBLEM?
MY LIFE JUST SEEMS TO GO INTO THE SEWER WHEN I'M NEAR ONE! NO OFFENSE.
CHOOM

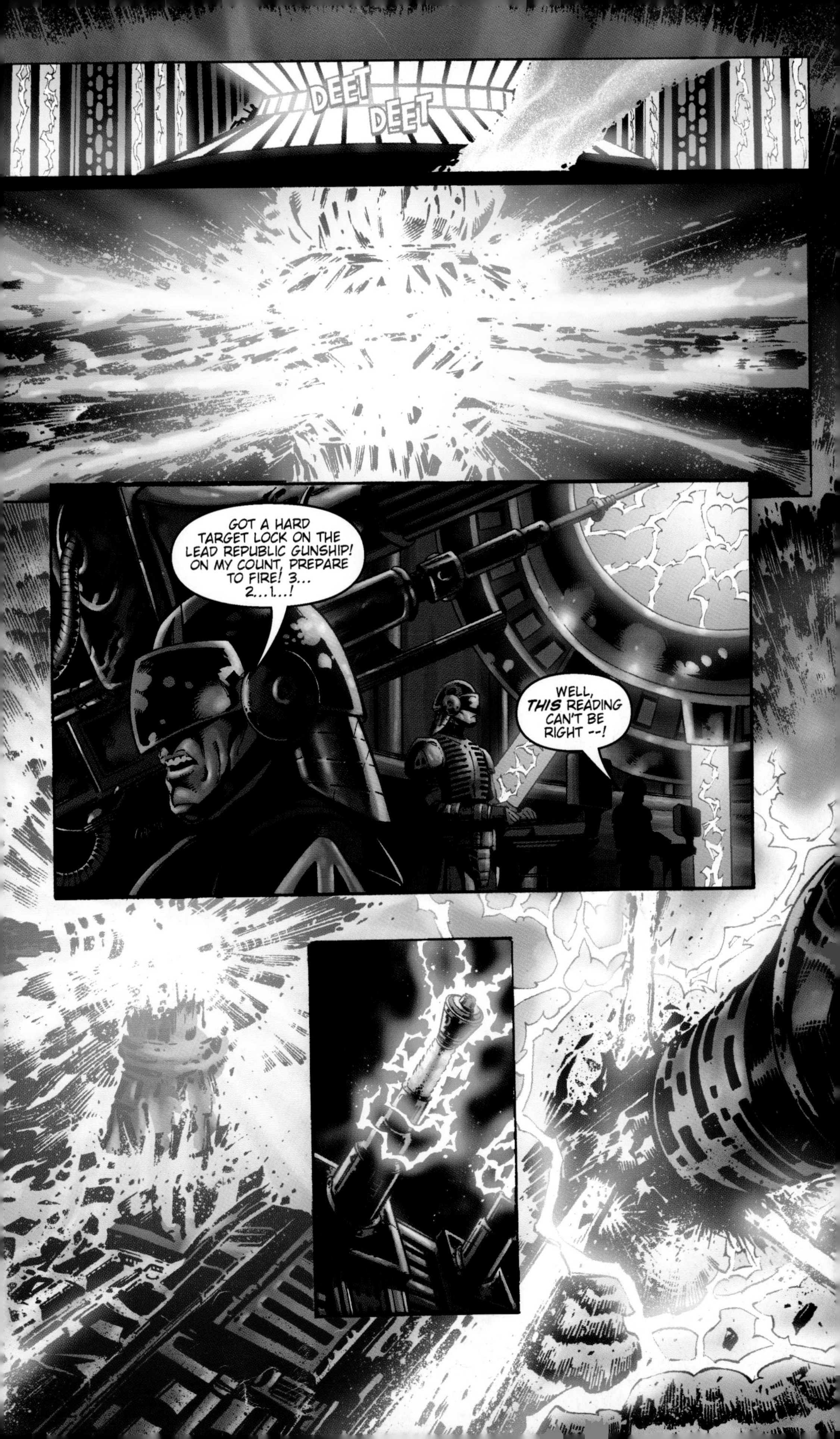
DEET DEET
GOT A HARD TARGET LOCK ON THE LEAD REPUBLIC GUNSHIP! ON MY COUNT, PREPARE TO FIRE! 3... 2...1...!
WELL, THIS READING CAN'T BE RIGHT --!

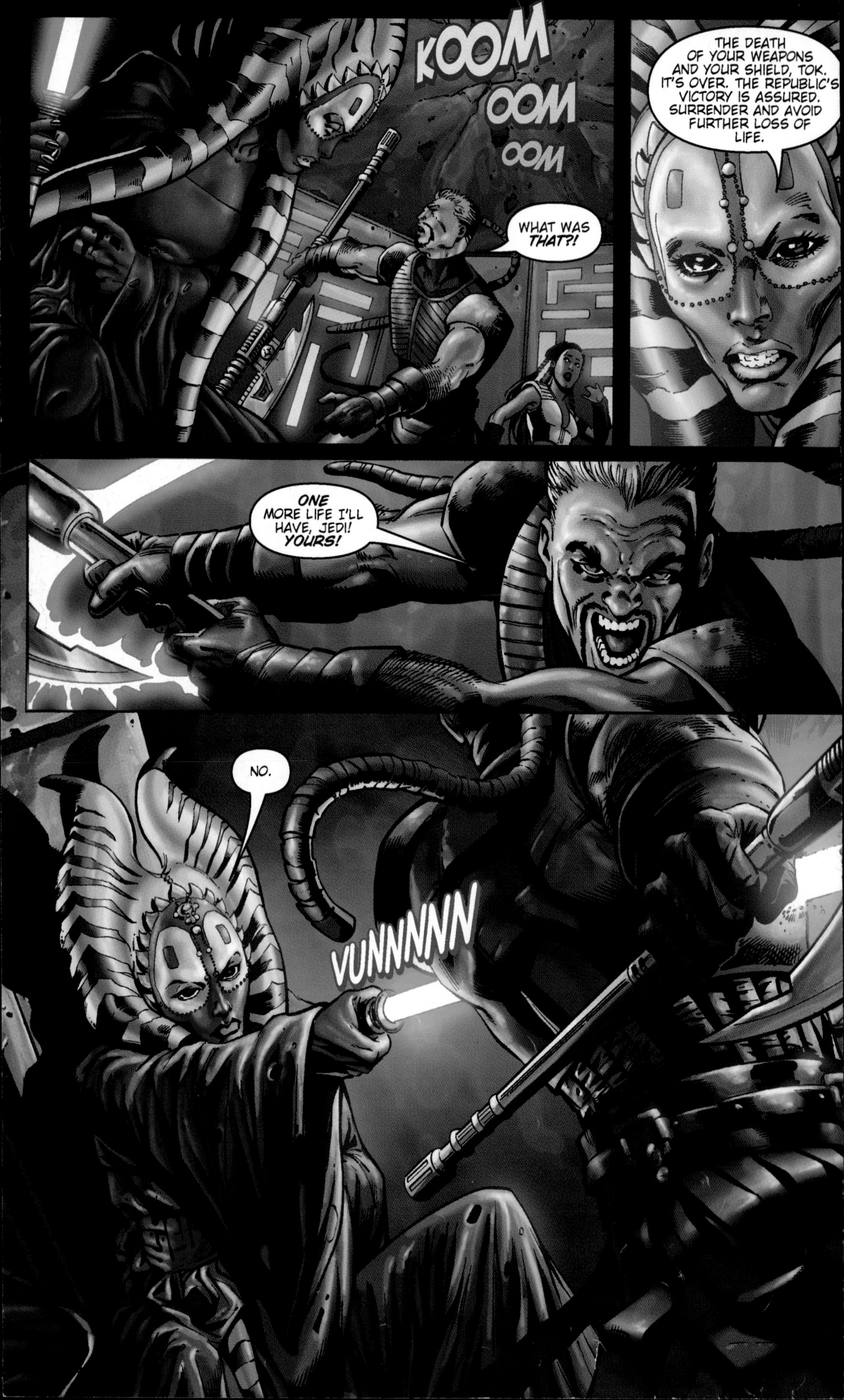
KOOM
OOM
OOM
WHAT WAS *THAT?!*
THE DEATH OF YOUR WEAPONS AND YOUR SHIELD, TOK. IT'S OVER. THE REPUBLIC'S VICTORY IS ASSURED. SURRENDER AND AVOID FURTHER LOSS OF LIFE.
ONE MORE LIFE I'LL HAVE, JEDI! *YOURS!*
NO.
VUNNNNN

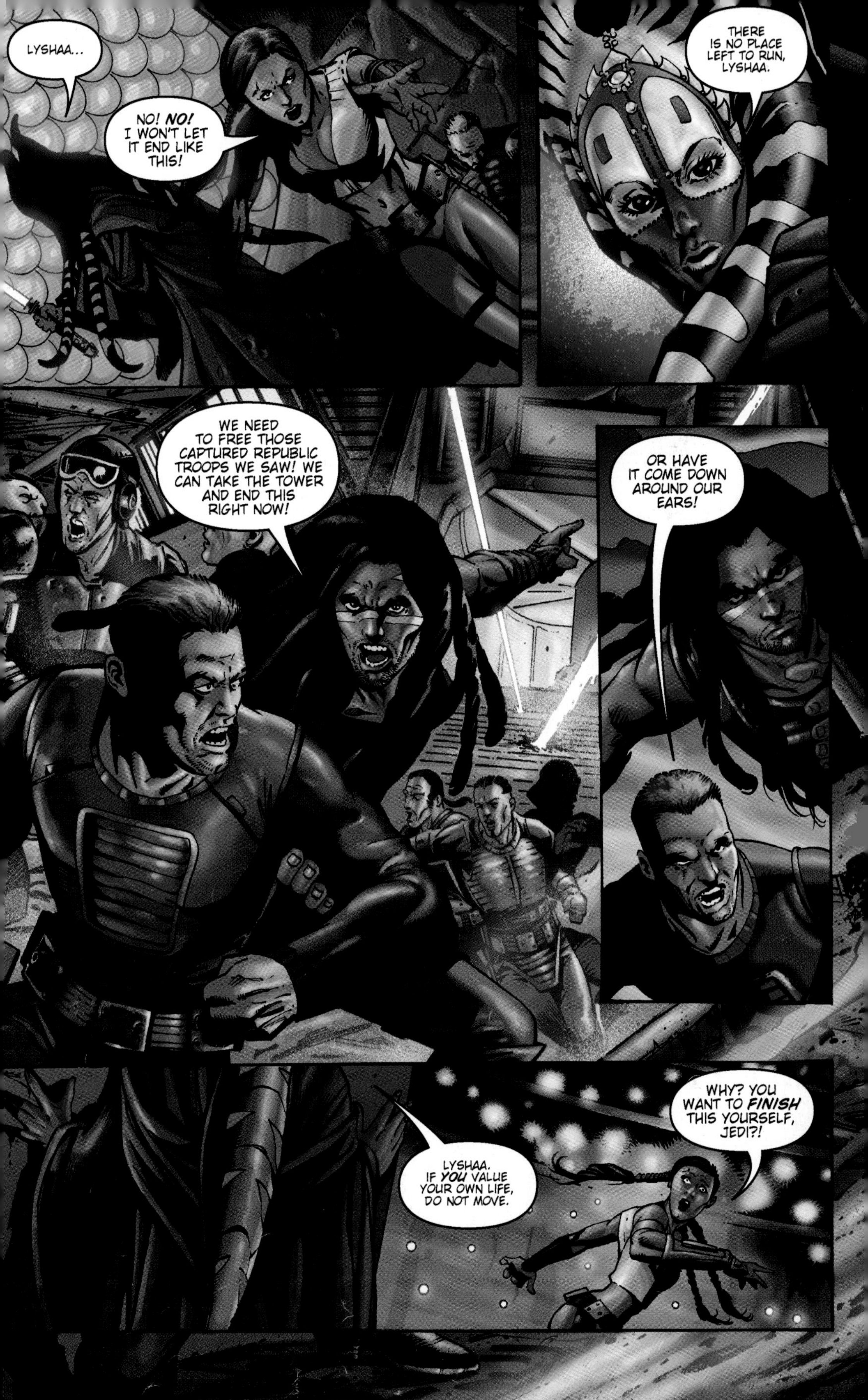
LYSHAA...
NO! *NO!* I WON'T LET IT END LIKE THIS!
THERE IS NO PLACE LEFT TO RUN, LYSHAA.
WE NEED TO FREE THOSE CAPTURED REPUBLIC TROOPS WE SAW! WE CAN TAKE THE TOWER AND END THIS RIGHT NOW!
OR HAVE IT COME DOWN AROUND OUR EARS!
LYSHAA. IF *YOU* VALUE YOUR OWN LIFE, DO NOT MOVE.
WHY? YOU WANT TO *FINISH* THIS YOURSELF, JEDI?!

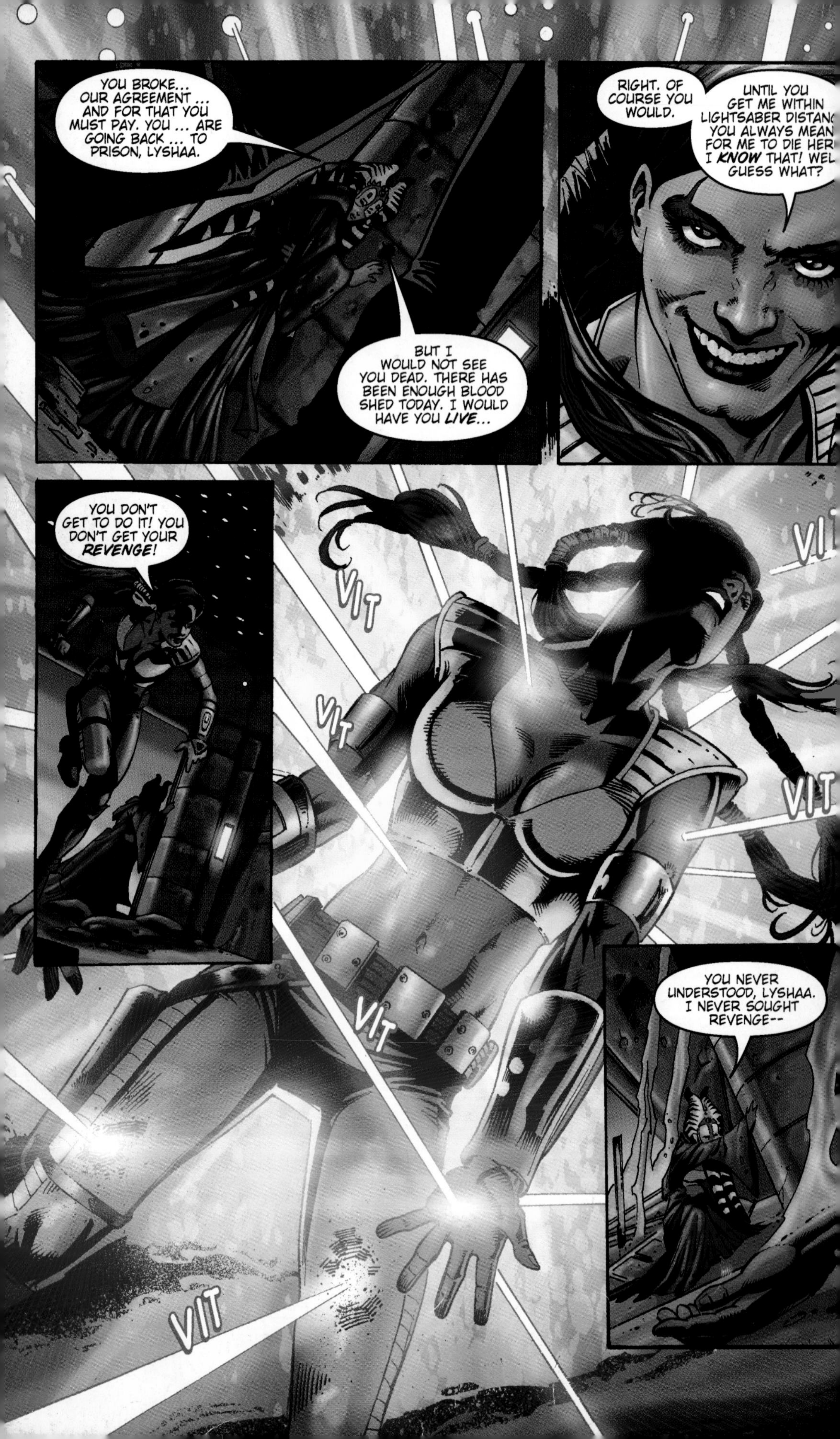
YOU BROKE... OUR AGREEMENT ... AND FOR THAT YOU MUST PAY. YOU ... ARE GOING BACK ... TO PRISON, LYSHAA.
BUT I WOULD NOT SEE YOU DEAD. THERE HAS BEEN ENOUGH BLOOD SHED TODAY. I WOULD HAVE YOU *LIVE*...
RIGHT. OF COURSE YOU WOULD.
UNTIL YOU GET ME WITHIN LIGHTSABER DISTAN YOU ALWAYS MEAN FOR ME TO DIE HER I *KNOW* THAT! WEL GUESS WHAT?
YOU DON'T GET TO DO IT! YOU DON'T GET YOUR *REVENGE*!
VIT
VIT
VIT
VIT
VIT
VIT
YOU NEVER UNDERSTOOD, LYSHAA. I NEVER SOUGHT REVENGE--

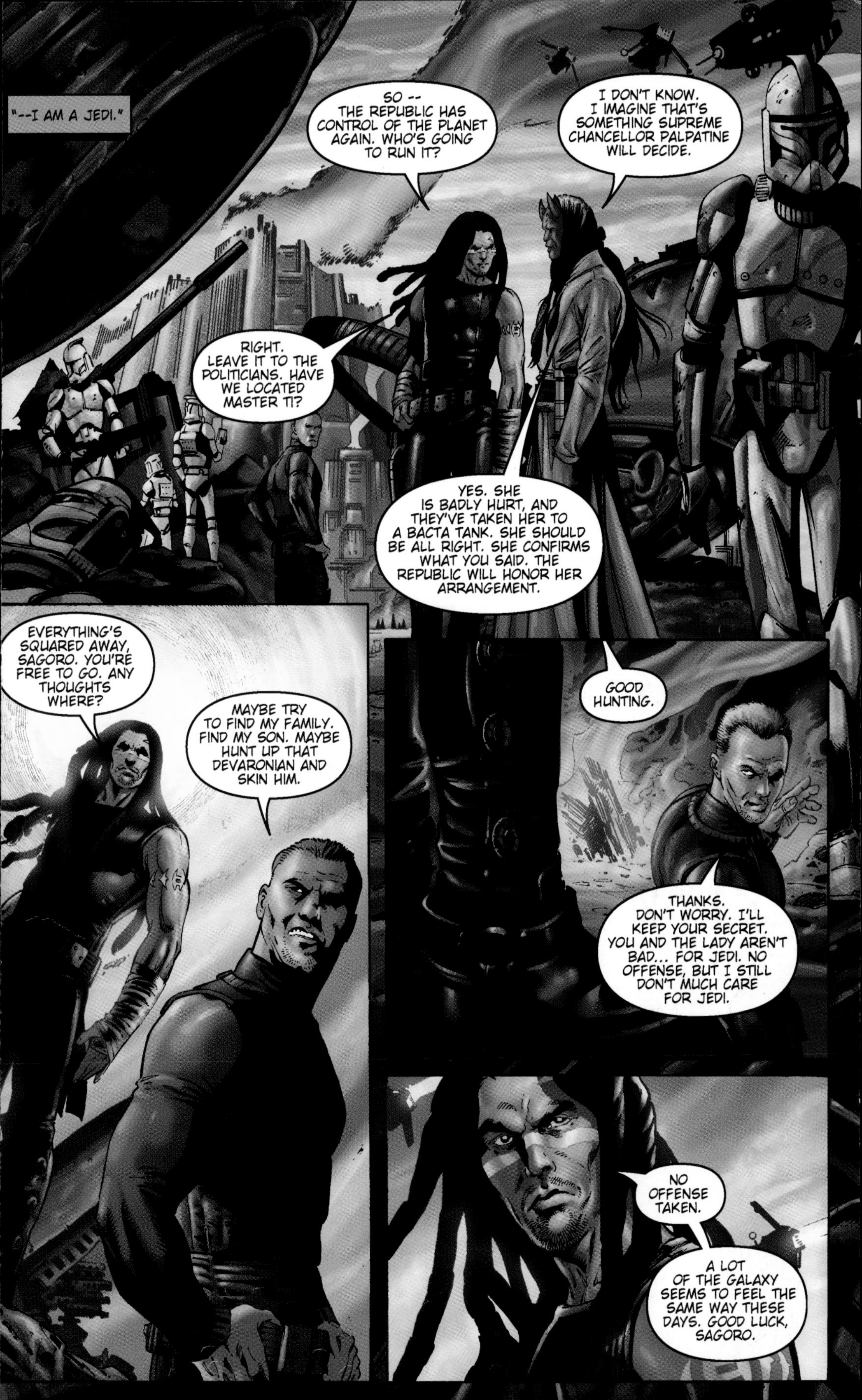
"--I AM A JEDI."
SO -- THE REPUBLIC HAS CONTROL OF THE PLANET AGAIN. WHO'S GOING TO RUN IT?
I DON'T KNOW. I IMAGINE THAT'S SOMETHING SUPREME CHANCELLOR PALPATINE WILL DECIDE.
RIGHT. LEAVE IT TO THE POLITICIANS. HAVE WE LOCATED MASTER TI?
YES. SHE IS BADLY HURT, AND THEY'VE TAKEN HER TO A BACTA TANK. SHE SHOULD BE ALL RIGHT. SHE CONFIRMS WHAT YOU SAID. THE REPUBLIC WILL HONOR HER ARRANGEMENT.
EVERYTHING'S SQUARED AWAY, SAGORO. YOU'RE FREE TO GO. ANY THOUGHTS WHERE?
MAYBE TRY TO FIND MY FAMILY. FIND MY SON. MAYBE HUNT UP THAT DEVARONIAN AND SKIN HIM.
GOOD HUNTING.
THANKS. DON'T WORRY. I'LL KEEP YOUR SECRET. YOU AND THE LADY AREN'T BAD... FOR JEDI. NO OFFENSE, BUT I STILL DON'T MUCH CARE FOR JEDI.
NO OFFENSE TAKEN.
A LOT OF THE GALAXY SEEMS TO FEEL THE SAME WAY THESE DAYS. GOOD LUCK, SAGORO.

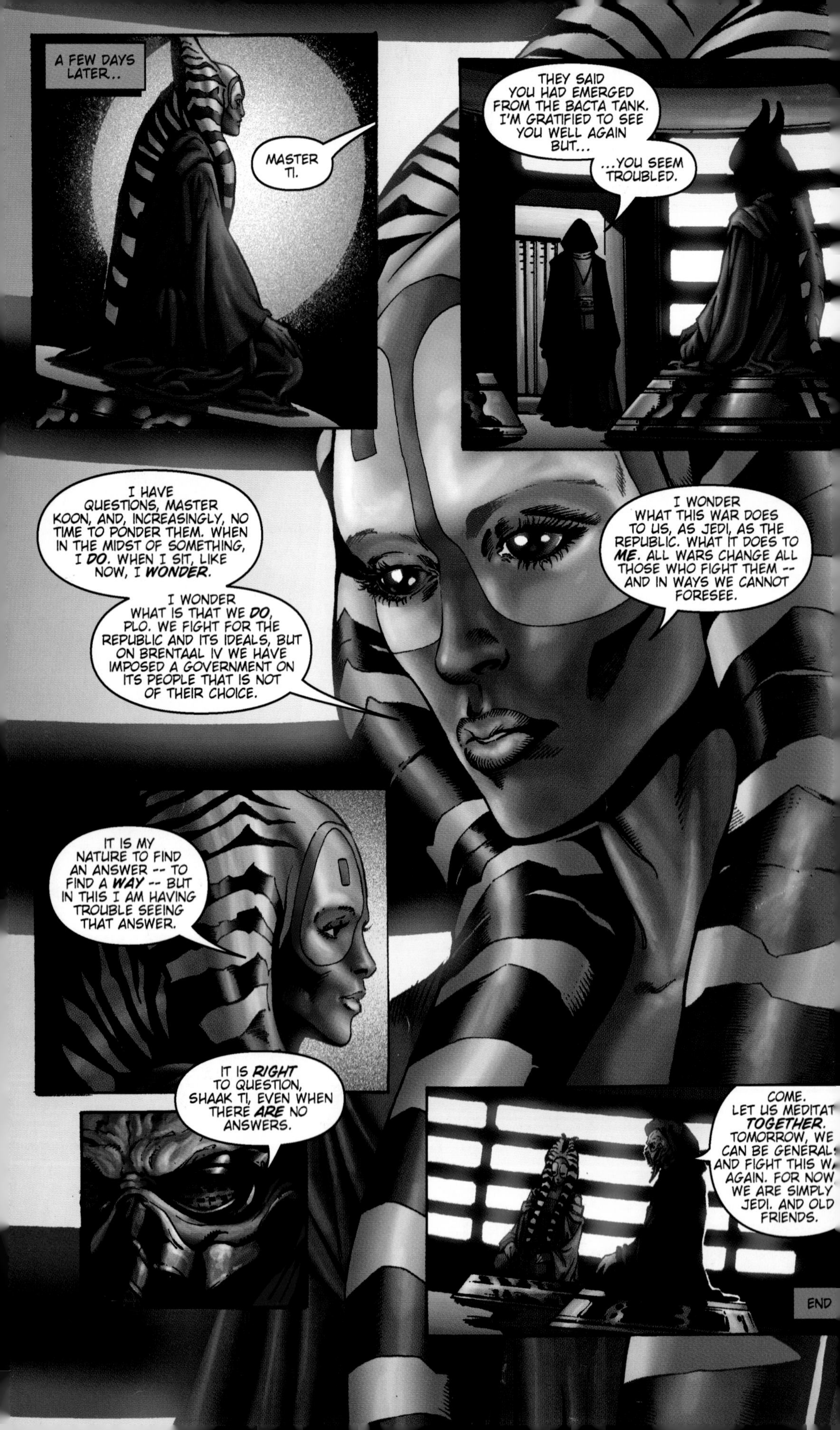
A FEW DAYS LATER...
MASTER TI.
THEY SAID YOU HAD EMERGED FROM THE BACTA TANK. I'M GRATIFIED TO SEE YOU WELL AGAIN BUT...
...YOU SEEM TROUBLED.
I HAVE QUESTIONS, MASTER KOON, AND, INCREASINGLY, NO TIME TO PONDER THEM. WHEN IN THE MIDST OF SOMETHING, I DO. WHEN I SIT, LIKE NOW, I WONDER.
I WONDER WHAT IS THAT WE DO, PLO. WE FIGHT FOR THE REPUBLIC AND ITS IDEALS, BUT ON BRENTAAL IV WE HAVE IMPOSED A GOVERNMENT ON ITS PEOPLE THAT IS NOT OF THEIR CHOICE.
I WONDER WHAT THIS WAR DOES TO US, AS JEDI, AS THE REPUBLIC. WHAT IT DOES TO ME. ALL WARS CHANGE ALL THOSE WHO FIGHT THEM -- AND IN WAYS WE CANNOT FORESEE.
IT IS MY NATURE TO FIND AN ANSWER -- TO FIND A WAY -- BUT IN THIS I AM HAVING TROUBLE SEEING THAT ANSWER.
IT IS RIGHT TO QUESTION, SHAAK TI, EVEN WHEN THERE ARE NO ANSWERS.
COME. LET US MEDITAT TOGETHER. TOMORROW, WE CAN BE GENERAL AND FIGHT THIS W AGAIN. FOR NOW WE ARE SIMPLY JEDI. AND OLD FRIENDS.
END

CLONE WARS
TIMELINE

MONTHS
(AFTER ATTACK OF THE CLONES)

0	**THE BATTLE OF GEONOSIS** *Star Wars:* Episode II — *Attack of the Clones* (LF, May '02)
0	**THE SEARCH FOR COUNT DOOKU** Boba Fett #1: *The Fight to Survive* (SB, April '02)
+1	**THE BATTLE OF RAXUS PRIME** Boba Fett #2: *Crossfire* (SB, November '02)
+1	**THE DARK REAPER PROJECT** The Clone Wars (LA, May '03)
+1.5	**CONSPIRACY ON AARGAU** Boba Fett #3: *Maze of Deception* (SB, April '03)
+2	**THE BATTLE OF KAMINO** Clone Wars I: *The Defense of Kamino* (DH, June '03)
+2	**DURGE VS BOBA FETT** Boba Fett #4: *Hunted* (SB, October '03)
+3	**THE DEFENSE OF NABOO** Clone Wars II: *Victories and Sacrifices* (DH, September '03)
+6	**THE DEVARON RUSE** Clone Wars IV: *Light and Dark* (DH, May '04)
+6	**THE HARUUN KAL CRISIS** *Shatterpoint* (DR, June '03)
+12	**THE BIO-DROID THREAT** *The Cestus Deception* (DR, June '04)
+15	**THE BATTLE OF JABIIM** Clone Wars III: *Last Stand on Jabiim* (DH, February '04)
+24	**THE CASUALTIES OF DRONGAR** **MEDSTAR DUOLOGY** *Battle Surgeons* (DR, July '04) *Jedi Healer* (DR, October '04)
+30	**THE PRAESITLYN CONQUEST** *Jedi Trial* (DR, November '04)

ABBREVIATION KEY

DH = Dark Horse Comics, graphic novels *www.darkhorse.com*
DR = Del Rey, hardcover and paperback novels *www.delreydigital.com*
LA = LucasArts Games, games for XBox, Game Cube, PS2, and PC platforms
www.lucasarts.com
LF = Lucasfilm Ltd., motion pictures *www.starwars.com*
SB = Scholastic Books, juvenile fiction *www.scholastic.com/starwars*

STAR WARS *TIMELINE*

GRAPHIC NOVELS AND TRADE PAPERBACKS FROM DARK HORSE COMICS

For more information go to www.darkhorse.com

TALES OF THE SITH ERA 25,000-1000 YEARS BEFORE STAR WARS: A NEW HOPE

TALES OF THE JEDI
THE GOLDEN AGE OF THE SITH
Anderson • Carrasco, Jr. • Gossett
ISBN: 1-56971-229-8 $16.95
FALL OF THE SITH EMPIRE
Anderson • Heike • Carrasco, Jr.
ISBN: 1-56971-320-0 $14 .95
KNIGHTS OF THE OLD REPUBLIC
Veitch • Gossett
ISBN: 1-56971-020-1 $14.95
THE FREEDON NADD UPRISING
Veitch • Akins • Rodier
ISBN: 1-56971-307-3 $5.95
DARK LORDS OF THE SITH
Veitch • Anderson • Gossett
ISBN: 1-56971-095-3 $17.95
THE SITH WAR
Anderson • Carrasco, Jr.
ISBN: 1-56971-173-9 $17.95

STAR WARS
TALES OF THE JEDI
REDEMPTION

****REDEMPTION***
Anderson • Gossett • Pepoy • McDaniel
ISBN: 1-56971-535-1 $14.95

STAR WARS
JEDI vs SITH

****JEDI VS. SITH***
Macan • Bachs • Fernandez
ISBN: 1-56971-649-8 $15.95

PREQUEL ERA 1000-0 YEARS BEFORE STAR WARS: A NEW HOPE

***JEDI COUNCIL**
ACTS OF WAR
Stradley • Fabbri • Vecchia
ISBN: 1-56971-539-4 $12.95

STAR WARS
JEDI COUNCIL
ACTS OF WAR

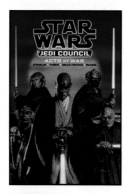

***DARTH MAUL**
Marz • Duursema • Magyar • Struzan
ISBN: 1-56971-542-4 $12.95

STAR WARS
DARTH MAUL
MARZ • DUURSEMA • MAGYAR • McCAIG

PRELUDE TO REBELLION
Strnad • Winn • Jones
ISBN: 1-56971-448-7 $14.95
OUTLANDER
Truman • Leonardi • Rio
ISBN: 1-56971-514-9 $14.95
***JEDI COUNCIL**
EMMISSARIES TO MALASTARE
Truman • Duursema • Others
ISBN: 1-56971-545-9 $15.95

STAR WARS
TWILIGHT

STAR WARS: TWILIGHT
Ostrander • Duursema • Magyar
ISBN: 1-56971-558-0 $12.95
EPISODE 1 —
THE PHANTOM MENACE
Gilroy • Damaggio • Williamson
ISBN: 1-56971-359-6 $12.95
EPISODE 1 —
THE PHANTOM MENACE ADVENTU
ISBN: 1-56971-443

MANGA EDITIONS
Translated into English
EPISODE 1 —
THE PHANTOM MENACE
George Lucas • Kia Asamiya
VOLUME 1
ISBN: 1-56971-483-5 $9.95
VOLUME 2
ISBN: 1-56971-484-3 $9.95

STAR WARS
JANGO FETT

***JANGO FETT**
Marz • Fowler
ISBN: 1-56971-623-4 $5.95

STAR WARS
ZAM WESELL

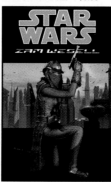

***ZAM WESELL**
Marz • Naifeh
ISBN: 1-56971-624-2 $5.95

STAR WARS

EPISODE 2 —
ATTACK OF THE CLONES
Gilroy • Duursema • Kryssing • McCaig
ISBN: 1-56971-609-9 $17.95
DROIDS
THE KALARBA ADVENTURES
Thorsland • Windham • Gibson
ISBN: 1-56971-224-7 $14.95

JABBA THE HUTT
THE ART OF THE DEAL
Woodring • Wetherell • Sheldon
ISBN: 1-56971-310-3 $9.95
***UNDERWORLD**
THE YAVIN VASSILIKA
Kennedy • Meglia
ISBN: 1-56971-618-8 $14.95
CLASSIC STAR WARS
HAN SOLO AT STARS' END
Goodwin • Alcala
ISBN: 1-56971-254-9 $6.95
BOBA FETT
ENEMY OF THE EMPIRE
Wagner • Gibson • Nadeau • Ezqu
ISBN: 1-56971-407-X $12.95

TRILOGY ERA 0-5 YEARS AFTER STAR WARS: A NEW HOPE

***A NEW HOPE* SPECIAL EDITION**
Jones • Barreto • Williamson
ISBN: 1-56971-213-1 $9.95
MANGA EDITIONS
Translated into English
A NEW HOPE
George Lucas • Hisao Tamaki
VOLUME 1
ISBN: 1-56971-362-6 $9.95
VOLUME 2
ISBN: 1-56971-363-4 $9.95
VOLUME 3
ISBN: 1-56971-364-2 $9.95
VOLUME 4
ISBN: 1-56971-365-0 $9.95
VADER'S QUEST
Macan • Gibbons
ISBN: 1-56971-415-0 $11.95

CLASSIC
STAR WARS
THE EARLY ADVENTURES

CLASSIC STAR WARS
THE EARLY ADVENTURES
Manning • Hoberg
ISBN: 1-56971-178-X $19.95
SPLINTER OF THE MIND'S EYE
Austin • Sprouse
ISBN: 1-56971-223-9 $14.95
CLASSIC STAR WARS
IN DEADLY PURSUIT
Goodwin • Williamson
ISBN: 1-56971-109-7 $16.95
THE EMPIRE STRIKES BACK SPECIAL EDITION
Goodwin • Williamson
ISBN: 1-56971-234-4 $9.95
MANGA EDITIONS
Translated into English
THE EMPIRE STRIKES BACK
George Lucas • Toshiki Kudo
VOLUME 1
ISBN: 1-56971-390-1 $9.95

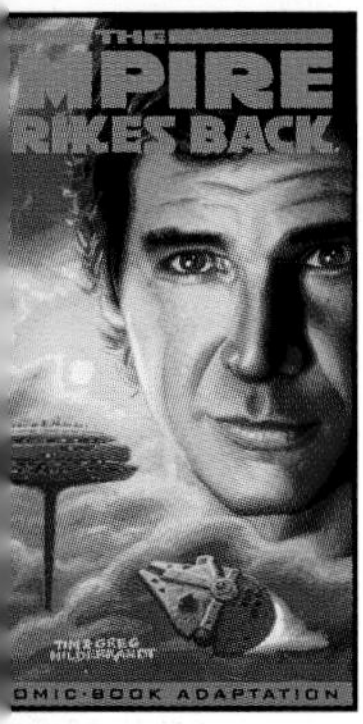
MPIRE
RIKES BACK
OMIC-BOOK ADAPTATION

IE 2
1-56971-391-X $9.95
IE 3
1-56971-392-8 $9.95
IE 4
1-56971-393-6 $9.95
SIC STAR WARS
EBEL STORM
in • Williamson
1-56971-106-2 $16.95
SIC STAR WARS
E TO HOTH
in • Williamson
1-56971-093-7 $16.95
OWS OF THE EMPIRE
OWS OF THE EMPIRE
r • Plunkett • Russell
1-56971-183-6 $17.95
RN OF THE JEDI
AL EDITION
in • Williamson
1-56971-235-2 $9.95
A EDITIONS
ted into English
RN OF THE JEDI
Lucas • Shin-ichi Hiromoto

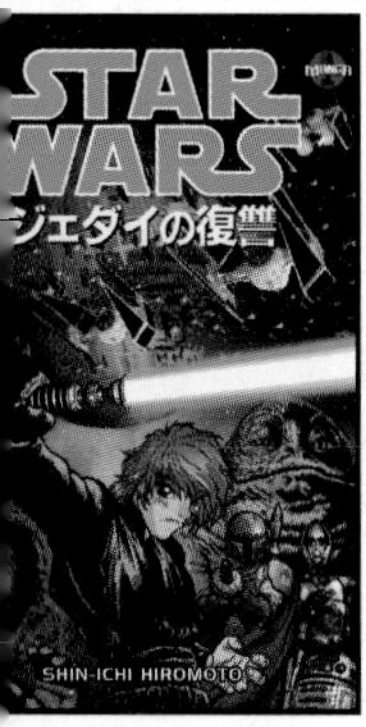
STAR
WARS
ジェダイの復讐
SHIN-ICHI HIROMOTO

IE 1
1-56971-394-4 $9.95
IE 2
1-56971-395-2 $9.95
IE 3
1-56971-396-0 $9.95
IE 4
1-56971-397-9 $9.95

SSIC SPIN-OFF ERA
5-25 YEARS
FTER STAR WARS:
A NEW HOPE

JADE
E EMPEROR'S HAND
Stackpole • Ezquerra
1-56971-401-0 $15.95

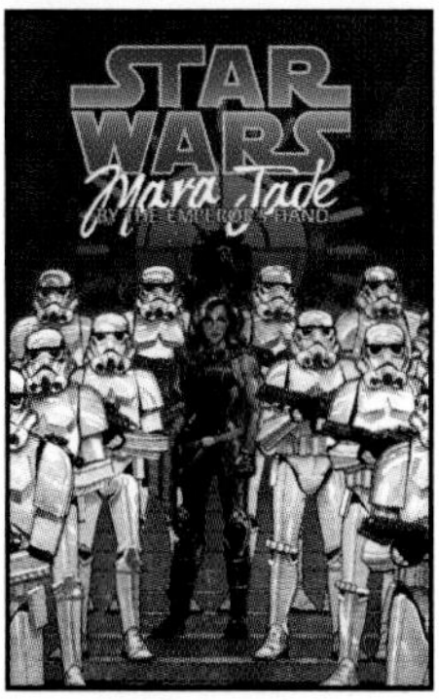
STAR
WARS
Mara Jade
BY THE EMPEROR'S HAND

SHADOWS OF THE EMPIRE
EVOLUTION
Perry • Randall • Simmons
ISBN: 1-56971-441-X $14.95
X-WING ROGUE SQUADRON
THE PHANTOM AFFAIR
Stackpole • Macan • Biukovic
ISBN: 1-56971-251-4 $12.95

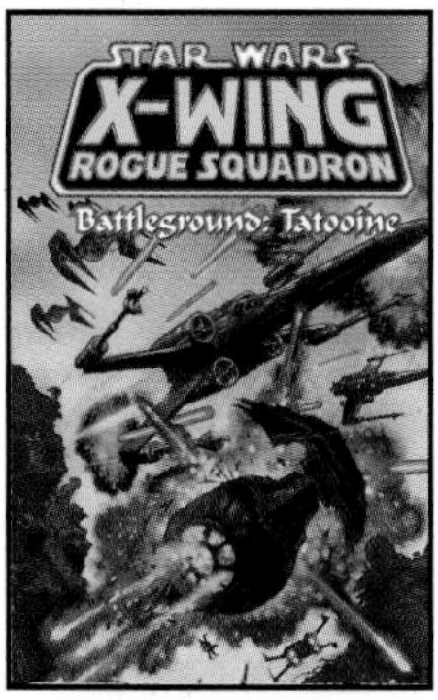
STAR WARS
X-WING
ROGUE SQUADRON
Battleground: Tatooine

BATTLEGROUND: TATOOINE
Stackpole • Strnad • Nadeau • Ensign
ISBN: 1-56971-276-X $12.95
THE WARRIOR PRINCESS
Stackpole • Tolson • Nadeau • Ensign
ISBN: 1-56971-330-8 $12.95

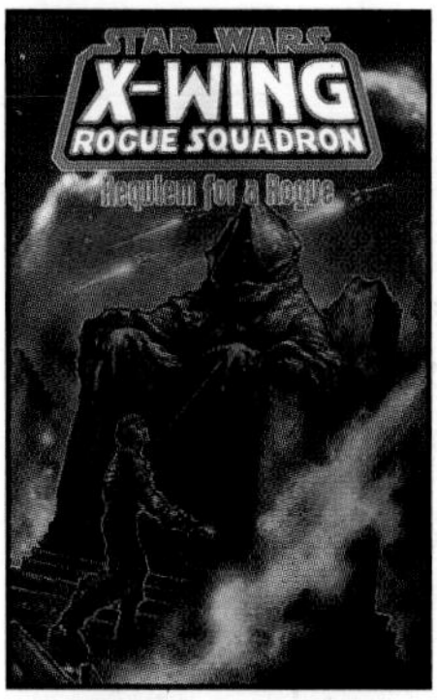
STAR WARS
X-WING
ROGUE SQUADRON
Requiem for a Rogue

REQUIEM FOR A ROGUE
Stackpole • Strnad • Barr • Erskine
ISBN: 1-56971-331-6 $12.95
IN THE EMPIRE'S SERVICE
Stackpole • Nadeau • Ensign
ISBN: 1-56971-383-9 $12.95
BLOOD AND HONOR
Stackpole • Crespo • Hall • Martin
ISBN: 1-56971-387-1 $12.95
MASQUERADE
Stackpole • Johnson • Martin
ISBN: 1-56971-487-8 $12.95

MANDATORY RETIREMENT
Stackpole • Crespo • Nadeau
ISBN: 1-56971-492-4 $12.95
THE THRAWN TRILOGY
HEIR TO THE EMPIRE
Baron • Vatine • Blanchard
ISBN: 1-56971-202-6 $19.95
DARK FORCE RISING
Baron • Dodson • Nowlan
ISBN: 1-56971-269-7 $17.95
THE LAST COMMAND
Baron • Biukovic • Shanower
ISBN: 1-56971-378-2 $17.95
DARK EMPIRE
DARK EMPIRE
Veitch • Kennedy
ISBN: 1-56971-073-2 $17.95
DARK EMPIRE II
Veitch • Kennedy
ISBN: 1-56971-119-4 $17.95
EMPIRE'S END
Veitch • Baikie
ISBN: 1-56971-306-5 $5.95

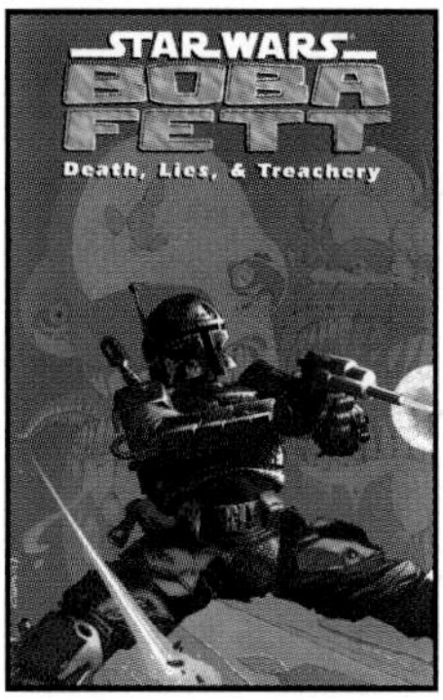
STAR WARS
BOBA FETT
Death, Lies, & Treachery

BOBA FETT
DEATH, LIES,
& TREACHERY
Wagner • Kennedy
ISBN: 1-56971-311-1 $12.95
CRIMSON EMPIRE
CRIMSON EMPIRE
Richardson • Stradley • Gulacy • Russell
ISBN: 1-56971-355-3 $17.95

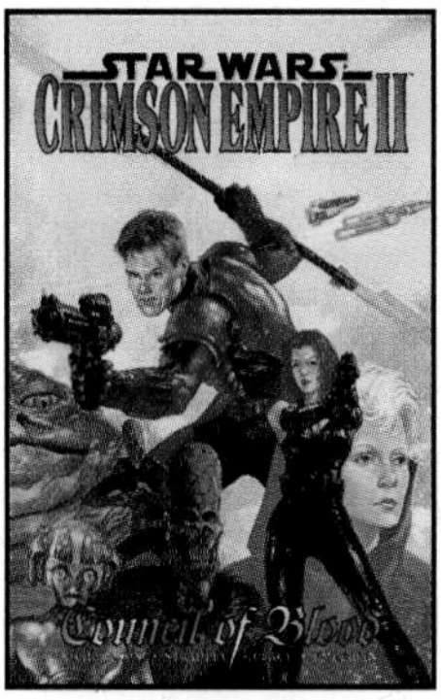
STAR WARS
CRIMSON EMPIRE II
Council of Blood

COUNCIL OF BLOOD
Richardson • Stradley • Gulacy • Emberlin
ISBN: 1-56971-410-X $17.95
JEDI ACADEMY
LEVIATHAN
Anderson • Carrasco • Heike
ISBN: 1-56971-456-8 $11.95

THE NEW JEDI ORDER ERA
25+ YEARS
AFTER STAR WARS:
A NEW HOPE

UNION
Stackpole • Teranishi • Chuckry
ISBN: 1-56971-464-9 $12.95

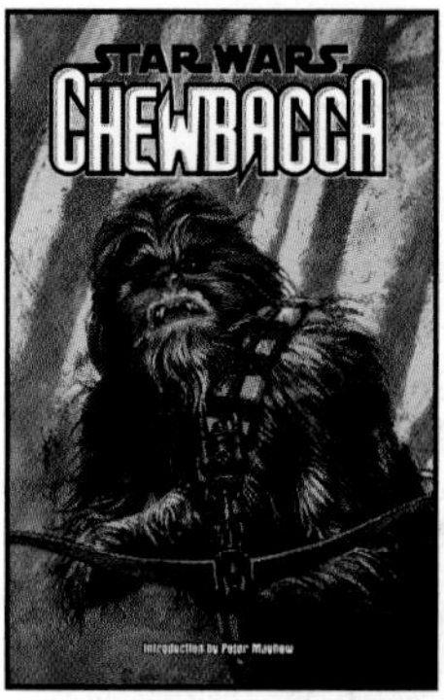
STAR WARS
CHEWBACCA

CHEWBACCA
Macan • Duursema • Others
ISBN: 1-56971-515-7 $12.95

INFINITIES — DOES NOT APPLY TO TIMELINE

***TALES VOLUME 1**
Marz • Plunkett • Duursema • Others
ISBN: 1-56971-619-6 $19.95
***INFINITIES — A NEW HOPE**
Warner • Johnson • Snyder • Rio • Nelson
ISBN: 1-56971-648-X $12.95

BATTLE OF THE BOUNTY HUNTERS
POP-UP COMIC BOOK
Windham • Moeller
ISBN: 1-56971-129-1 $17.95
DARK FORCES
Prose novellas, heavily illustrated
SOLDIER FOR THE EMPIRE
Dietz • Williams
hardcover edition
ISBN: 1-56971-155-0 $24.95
paperback edition
ISBN: 1-56971-348-0 $14.95
REBEL AGENT
Dietz • Tucker
hardcover edition
ISBN: 1-56971-156-9 $24.95
paperback edition
ISBN: 1-56971-400-2 $14.95
JEDI KNIGHT
Dietz • Dorman
hardcover edition
ISBN: 1-56971-157-7 $24.95
paperback edition
ISBN: 1-56971-433-9 $14.95

SPANS MULTIPLE ERAS

BOUNTY HUNTERS
Truman • Schultz • Stradley • Mangels
ISBN: 1-56971-467-3 $12.95

* *New*

•Prices and availability subject to change without notice

STAR WARS
TIMELINE OF TRADE PAPERBACKS FROM DARK HORSE

TALES OF THE SITH ERA 25,000-1000 YEARS BEFORE STAR WARS: A NEW HOPE

TALES OF THE JEDI
THE GOLDEN AGE OF THE SITH
Anderson • Carrasco, Jr. • Gossett
ISBN: 1-56971-229-8 $16.95
FALL OF THE SITH EMPIRE
Anderson • Heike • Carrasco, Jr.
ISBN: 1-56971-320-0 $14 .95
KNIGHTS OF THE OLD REPUBLIC
Veitch • Gossett
ISBN: 1-56971-020-1 $14.95
THE FREEDON NADD UPRISING
Veitch • Akins • Rodier
ISBN: 1-56971-307-3 $5.95
DARK LORDS OF THE SITH
Veitch • Anderson • Gossett
ISBN: 1-56971-095-3 $17.95
THE SITH WAR
Anderson • Carrasco, Jr.
ISBN: 1-56971-173-9 $17.95
****REDEMPTION***
Anderson • Gossett • Pepoy • McDaniel
ISBN: 1-56971-535-1 $14.95
****JEDI VS. SITH***
Macan • Bachs • Fernandez
ISBN: 1-56971-649-8 $15.95

PREQUEL ERA 1000-0 YEARS BEFORE STAR WARS: A NEW HOPE

***JEDI COUNCIL**
ACTS OF WAR
Stradley • Fabbri • Vecchia
ISBN: 1-56971-539-4 $12.95
***DARTH MAUL**
Marz • Duursema • Magyar • Struzan
ISBN: 1-56971-542-4 $12.95
PRELUDE TO REBELLION
Strnad • Winn • Jones
ISBN: 1-56971-448-7 $14.95
OUTLANDER
Truman • Leonardi • Rio
ISBN: 1-56971-514-9 $14.95
***JEDI COUNCIL**
EMMISSARIES TO MALASTARE
Truman • Duursema • Others
ISBN: 1-56971-545-9 $15.95
STAR WARS: TWILIGHT
Ostrander • Duursema • Magyar
ISBN: 1-56971-558-0 $12.95
EPISODE 1 —
THE PHANTOM MENACE
Gilroy • Damaggio • Williamson
ISBN: 1-56971-359-6 $12.95
EPISODE 1 —
THE PHANTOM MENACE ADVENTURES
ISBN: 1-56971-443-6 $12.95
MANGA EDITIONS
Translated into English
EPISODE 1 — *THE PHANTOM MENACE*
George Lucas • Kia Asamiya
VOLUME 1
ISBN: 1-56971-483-5 $9.95
VOLUME 2
ISBN: 1-56971-484-3 $9.95
***JANGO FETT**
Marz • Fowler
ISBN: 1-56971-623-4 $5.95
***ZAM WESELL**
Marz • Naifeh
ISBN: 1-56971-624-2 $5.95
EPISODE 2 —
ATTACK OF THE CLONES
Gilroy • Duursema • Kryssing • McCaig
ISBN: 1-56971-609-9 $17.95
DROIDS
THE KALARBA ADVENTURES
Thorsland • Windham • Gibson
ISBN: 1-56971-064-3 $17.95
REBELLION
Windham • Gibson
ISBN: 1-56971-224-7 $14.95
JABBA THE HUTT
THE ART OF THE DEAL
Woodring • Wetherell • Sheldon
ISBN: 1-56971-310-3 $9.95
***UNDERWORLD**
THE YAVIN VASSILIKA
Kennedy • Meglia
ISBN: 1-56971-618-8 $14.95
CLASSIC STAR WARS
HAN SOLO AT STARS' END
Goodwin • Alcala
ISBN: 1-56971-254-9 $6.95
BOBA FETT
ENEMY OF THE EMPIRE
Wagner • Gibson • Nadeau • Ezquerra
ISBN: 1-56971-407-X $12.95

TRILOGY ERA 0-5 YEARS AFTER STAR WARS: A NEW HOPE

A NEW HOPE SPECIAL EDITION
Jones • Barreto • Williamson
ISBN: 1-56971-213-1 $9.95
MANGA EDITIONS
Translated into English
A NEW HOPE
George Lucas • Hisao Tamaki
VOLUME 1
ISBN: 1-56971-362-6 $9.95
VOLUME 2
ISBN: 1-56971-363-4 $9.95
VOLUME 3
ISBN: 1-56971-364-2 $9.95
VOLUME 4
ISBN: 1-56971-365-0 $9.95
VADER'S QUEST
Macan • Gibbons
ISBN: 1-56971-415-0 $11.95
CLASSIC STAR WARS
THE EARLY ADVENTURES
Manning • Hoberg
ISBN: 1-56971-178-X $19.95
SPLINTER OF THE MIND'S EYE
Austin • Sprouse
ISBN: 1-56971-223-9 $14.95
CLASSIC STAR WARS
IN DEADLY PURSUIT
Goodwin • Williamson
ISBN: 1-56971-109-7 $16.95
THE EMPIRE STRIKES BACK
SPECIAL EDITION
Goodwin • Williamson
ISBN: 1-56971-234-4 $9.95
MANGA EDITIONS
Translated into English
THE EMPIRE STRIKES BACK
George Lucas • Toshiki Kudo
VOLUME 1
ISBN: 1-56971-390-1 $9.95
VOLUME 2
ISBN: 1-56971-391-X $9.95
VOLUME 3
ISBN: 1-56971-392-8 $9.95
VOLUME 4
ISBN: 1-56971-393-6 $9.95
CLASSIC STAR WARS
THE REBEL STORM
Goodwin • Williamson
ISBN: 1-56971-106-2 $16.95
CLASSIC STAR WARS
ESCAPE TO HOTH
Goodwin • Williamson
ISBN: 1-56971-093-7 $16.95
SHADOWS OF THE EMPIRE
SHADOWS OF THE EMPIRE
Wagner • Plunkett • Russell
ISBN: 1-56971-183-6 $17.95
***RETURN OF THE JEDI* SPECIAL EDITION**
Goodwin • Williamson
ISBN: 1-56971-235-2 $9.95
MANGA EDITIONS
Translated into English
RETURN OF THE JEDI
George Lucas • Shin-ichi Hiromoto
VOLUME 1
ISBN: 1-56971-394-4 $9.95
VOLUME 2
ISBN: 1-56971-395-2 $9.95
VOLUME 3
ISBN: 1-56971-396-0 $9.95
VOLUME 4
ISBN: 1-56971-397-9 $9.95

CLASSIC SPIN-OFF ERA 5-25 YEARS AFTER STAR WARS: A NEW HOPE

MARA JADE
BY THE EMPEROR'S HAND
Zahn • Stackpole • Ezquerra
ISBN: 1-56971-401-0 $15.95
SHADOWS OF THE EMPIRE
EVOLUTION
Perry • Randall • Simmons
ISBN: 1-56971-441-X $14.95
X-WING ROGUE SQUADRON
THE PHANTOM AFFAIR
Stackpole • Macan • Biukovic
ISBN: 1-56971-251-4 $12.95
BATTLEGROUND: TATOOINE
Stackpole • Strnad • Nadeau • Ensign
ISBN: 1-56971-276-X $12.95
THE WARRIOR PRINCESS
Stackpole • Tolson • Nadeau • Ensign
ISBN: 1-56971-330-8 $12.95
REQUIEM FOR A ROGUE
Stackpole • Strnad • Barr • Erskine
ISBN: 1-56971-331-6 $12.95
IN THE EMPIRE'S SERVICE
Stackpole • Nadeau • Ensign
ISBN: 1-56971-383-9 $12.95
BLOOD AND HONOR
Stackpole • Crespo • Hall • Martin
ISBN: 1-56971-387-1 $12.95
MASQUERADE
Stackpole • Johnson • Martin
ISBN: 1-56971-487-8 $12.95
MANDATORY RETIREMENT
Stackpole • Crespo • Nadeau
ISBN: 1-56971-492-4 $12.95
THE THRAWN TRILOGY
HEIR TO THE EMPIRE
Baron • Vatine • Blanchard
ISBN: 1-56971-202-6 $19.95
DARK FORCE RISING
Baron • Dodson • Nowlan
ISBN: 1-56971-269-7 $17.95
THE LAST COMMAND
Baron • Biukovic • Shanower
ISBN: 1-56971-378-2 $17.95
DARK EMPIRE
DARK EMPIRE
Veitch • Kennedy
ISBN: 1-56971-073-2 $17.95
DARK EMPIRE II
Veitch • Kennedy
ISBN: 1-56971-119-4 $17.95
EMPIRE'S END
Veitch • Baikie
ISBN: 1-56971-306-5 $5.95
BOBA FETT
DEATH, LIES, & TREACHERY
Wagner • Kennedy
ISBN: 1-56971-311-1 $12.95
CRIMSON EMPIRE
CRIMSON EMPIRE
Richardson • Stradley • Gulacy • Russell
ISBN: 1-56971-355-3 $17.95
COUNCIL OF BLOOD
Richardson • Stradley • Gulacy • Emberlin
ISBN: 1-56971-410-X $17.95
JEDI ACADEMY
LEVIATHAN
Anderson • Carrasco • Heike
ISBN: 1-56971-456-8 $11.95

THE NEW JEDI ORDER ERA 25+ YE AFTER STAR WARS: A NEW HOPE

UNION
Stackpole • Teranishi • Chuckry
ISBN: 1-56971-464-9 $12.95
CHEWBACCA
Macan • Duursema • Others
ISBN: 1-56971-515-7 $12.95

INFINITIES — DOES NOT APPLY TO TIMELINE

***TALES VOLUME 1**
Marz • Plunkett • Duursema • Others
ISBN: 1-56971-619-6 $19.95
***INFINITIES**
A NEW HOPE
Warner • Johnson • Snyder • Rio • Nelson
ISBN: 1-56971-648-X $12.95
BATTLE OF THE BOUNTY HUNTERS POP-UP COMIC BOOK
Windham • Moeller
ISBN: 1-56971-129-1 $17.95
DARK FORCES
Prose novellas, heavily illustrated
SOLDIER FOR THE EMPIRE
Dietz • Williams
hardcover edition
ISBN: 1-56971-155-0 $24.95
paperback edition
ISBN: 1-56971-348-0 $14.95
REBEL AGENT
Dietz • Tucker
hardcover edition
ISBN: 1-56971-156-9 $24.95
paperback edition
ISBN: 1-56971-400-2 $14.95
JEDI KNIGHT
Dietz • Dorman
hardcover edition
ISBN: 1-56971-157-7 $24.95
paperback edition
ISBN: 1-56971-433-9 $14.95

SPANS MULTIPLE ERAS

BOUNTY HUNTERS
Truman • Schultz • Stradley • Mangels
ISBN: 1-56971-467-3 $12.95

** New*
•Prices and availability subject to change without notic

Available from your local comics shop or bookstore!

To find a comics shop in your area, call 1-888-266-4226 • For more information or to order direct: •On the web: www.darkhorse.com •E-mail: mailorder@darkhorse.com
•Phone: 1-800-862-0052 or (503) 652-9701 • Mon.-Sat. 9 A.M. to 5 P.M. Pacific Time *Prices and availability subject to change without notice